HENRY JACKSON

O.M.

T0381612

HENRY JACKSON

(After the portrait in oils by Charles W. Furse 1889)

Henry Jackson, O.M.

Vice-Master of Trinity College
& Regius Professor of Greek
in the University of Cambridge

A Memoir

by

R. ST JOHN PARRY

Vice-Master of Trinity College

Cambridge
At the University Press
1926

CAMBRIDGE
UNIVERSITY PRESS

University Printing House, Cambridge CB2 8BS, United Kingdom

Published in the United States of America by Cambridge University Press, New York

Cambridge University Press is part of the University of Cambridge.

It furthers the University's mission by disseminating knowledge in the pursuit of education, learning and research at the highest international levels of excellence.

www.cambridge.org
Information on this title: www.cambridge.org/9781107630949

© Cambridge University Press 1926

First published 1926
First paperback edition 2013

A catalogue record for this publication is available from the British Library

ISBN 978-1-107-63094-9 Paperback

PREFACE

In preparing this memoir of Henry Jackson, I came to the conclusion at an early stage that the object of such a memoir should be rather to present a portrait than to attempt a full narrative of his life. His whole life was passed in the school and academic sphere; the events and movements with which he was concerned have been very fully recorded already, in histories of university reform and in other biographies, especially in the *Memoir of Henry Sidgwick*; and it seemed unnecessary to do over again what has been already well done. Moreover, the materials at my disposal, especially the correspondence, always the most significant part of biography, were copious, but left large gaps from the point of view of connected narrative. Considerations such as these have determined the form of this book. The first part consists of a memoir, brief but I hope sufficient to give the setting and mark the stages of Henry Jackson's life. In the second part, extracts from a large correspondence are classified to illustrate the variety of his interests, the temper and quality of his intellectual activities, and what may be described as the undress expression of his mind and character. In the third part, I have included two lectures and a sermon. The lectures seem to me to be valuable illustrations of his method of teaching— the first in his own special subject addressed to a university audience, the second on one of his hobbies addressed to a Sheffield Society. The sermon is, as far as I know, the only one he ever preached: it is at once a confession of faith, and an expression of his loyalties, personal and Collegiate, most characteristic of the man.

I hope in this way I may have been able to preserve, however imperfectly, the record of a character which made a perhaps unexampled impression upon contemporary Cambridge life, and to recall to his innumerable friends, old and young, some elements in a character which attracted their admiration and their love.

I am very conscious of the defects and inadequacy of this presentation. For such measure of faithfulness as may have been achieved, I am indebted in the first place to Mrs Jackson,

Col.-Comdt. H. C. Jackson, and other members of the family, who have freely placed at my disposal all the papers and letters which had been preserved, and have given me every assistance in their power. To many friends of Jackson's I am indebted for the loan of letters; and in particular to his oldest living friend Sir George Trevelyan, O.M., for the very interesting correspondence carried on during the War, and to Sir George Greenwood, for the many letters on Shakespeare and other literature, to Professor D'Arcy Thompson, Mr G. A. Hight and Mr Alfred Ollivant for the vivid illustrations which they have provided of the help he rendered so generously to other students. It will be noticed that a large proportion of the *Obiter Scripta* are extracts from letters to the late Professor J. A. Platt. He was perhaps his most regular correspondent for many years, a frequent visitor to him in Cambridge, and one of his most devoted and intimate friends. I am sorry that he has not lived to see this book. I have to thank Lady Mary von Hügel for her kindness in allowing me to include Baron Friedrich von Hügel's letter, and Mr J. A. Venn for the same privilege in the case of a letter of Dr Venn's. I am grateful to the Syndics of the Press for undertaking the publication, and to their Secretary and to the University Printer and his associates for the kindness, care and skill which they have devoted to its production.

R. St J. P.

TRINITY COLLEGE, CAMBRIDGE
November, 1925

CONTENTS

ILLUSTRATIONS

PART I
MEMOIR

HENRY JACKSON

PARENTAGE AND CHILDHOOD

HENRY JACKSON was born 12 March 1839, in St James'
Row, Sheffield. Both his father and grandfather were
surgeons in that town. Henry Jackson, sen., his grandfather, was a native of Wentbridge near Pontefract, and
married (1 January 1801) Olivia, daughter of Benjamin Sayle,
of the same place. He settled in practice in Sheffield in 1794,
having been articled to Mr William Lunn, surgeon, of
Sheffield, and completed his medical studies at St Thomas'
Hospital and Edinburgh. Only two children of this marriage
survived infancy—Olivia, who was born 27 December 1801 and
died 17 September 1870, and Henry, who was born 29 November
1806, and died 25 June 1866. Henry Jackson, sen., died
12 November 1836. His grandson, born after his death, writes
of him, from letters in his possession: 'I gather that my grandfather, though perhaps somewhat masterful, was sociable,
genial, and attractive: and a portrait, which is no doubt one of
the many pastels drawn by Chantrey in the first decade of the
nineteenth century, shows that he was an uncommonly handsome man.' His son, Henry Jackson, jun., father of our Henry
Jackson, followed his father's profession. The following
extract from a prefatory note written by his son (1914) for a
Descriptive Catalogue of 'The Jackson Collection' in the
Sheffield Public Reference Library, is of so much interest in
itself, and of such importance for realising the influences which
surrounded Henry Jackson's youth, that I make no apology for
inserting it in full.

My father, Henry Jackson, jun., surgeon, of Sheffield,
received his general education at the Rev. Peter Wright's school
in Sheffield, and, later, at Bingley Grammar School, of which
Richard Hartley, D.D., of Christ's College, Cambridge—'an
excellent classic, a hard-reading man, and of irreproachable
character' (Gunning's *Reminiscences of Cambridge*)—was then
head master. The second Henry's medical education began
with apprenticeship to his father. In 1828 he proceeded to
Dublin that he might study anatomy under James Macartney,

[3]

and surgery under James W. Cusack. As appears from his letters to my grandfather, my father made excellent use of the great opportunities which the hospitals of Dublin afforded; while occasional references to 'sack-em-ups' remind the modern reader that in those days the study of anatomy had a peculiarly grisly side. In 1830 my father left Dublin for London, where he attached himself to St Bartholomew's Hospital. In the same year he obtained his diplomas at the College of Surgeons and the Apothecaries' Hall. The letters in which he describes the two examinations are detailed, and, if a layman may have an opinion, very interesting[1].

On his way home, my father visited at Cambridge his old friends William Henry Brookfield—Tennyson's 'Brooks'—and John Henry Brown, then undergraduates at Trinity College.

Returning to Sheffield, he began practice with my grandfather, and on 10th September, 1832, was elected to the post of Surgeon to the Infirmary, which he held till a few days before his death. My grandfather died 12th November, 1836. On 27th June, 1838, my father married Frances, daughter of James Swettenham.

This is not the place for an estimate of my father's capacity and success as surgeon and medical practitioner. But I may briefly note certain personal characteristics. He was always observant, always ready to take responsibility, always quiet. He had a wonderful gift of sympathy. He was as discreet and reticent as a father confessor. He was the friend of his patients and the confidant of his colleagues. He called himself a Tory, but progress was his joy. He kept himself thoroughly posted up in medical literature, and was eager to avail himself of every new invention and discovery. At first he had doubts about anæsthetics, but they *very* quickly disappeared. When he died, antiseptic and aseptic methods had not yet established themselves: but I fancy that his use of a solution of nitrate of silver for scalds, burns, and bedsores, saved my life when in childhood I charged into a large saucepan of boiling water. Once, and once only, I went round the Infirmary with him: and, to my great surprise, I found that, in talking to his patients there, he dropped without an effort into the grammar and the vocabulary

[1] For extracts from my father's letters to my grandfather, see the *St Bartholomew's Hospital Journal* for October, November, December, 1904.

of old Sheffield. I had long known that he could read *Tom Treddlehoyle* as no one else of my acquaintance could do: but it had not occurred to me that he would use the second person singular as easily as if he had never known the conventional 'you' and 'your' of modern English. The Infirmary occupied much of his thoughts. I have waited for him there for hours when he had miscalculated the time which his work would require. He was devoted to his profession: and he was sorry when his brother-in-law, Wilson Overend, a brilliant surgeon, gave himself to municipal affairs. Nevertheless, he knew that a professional man should have a hobby or hobbies. He read widely in English literature; in particular, history, biography, and good fiction, were favourite subjects. He had an astonishing knack of discovering important books the moment that they appeared: for example, he knew Thackeray's *Second Funeral of Napoleon*, Oliver Wendell Holmes's *Autocrat of the Breakfast Table*, and J. F. McLennan's *Primitive Marriage*, before they were famous. He was a constant reader of *Notes and Queries*, and sent to it occasional contributions signed 'H.J.'[1]

Meanwhile, he was keenly interested in local antiquities. An accomplished horseman, he had gained in his youth, and always retained, a curiously exact knowledge of the topography of the district. He collected books printed at Sheffield. He noted additions to Hunter's *Hallamshire* in an interleaved copy. But it was not for him to do more than collect: he made no serious attempt to record his antiquarian knowledge.

The house in which my father was born, lived, and died, continued to be occupied by my brother Arthur and my mother until 1878, when the prospect of street improvements caused them to remove to a house in Wilkinson Street, now numbered 53. In 1883 the old house in St James' Row was pulled down, and the narrow paved walk was widened into a street.

Mrs Henry Jackson (1806–1899), daughter of James Swettenham, mother of our Henry Jackson, was a remarkable woman. 'If I am good for anything,' he writes to his brother Bernard in 1918, 'I owe it to father, mother and Cally.' 'I always feel that if I can teach at all I owe it to mother and Cally.' A long

[1] His old friend James Montgomery signed himself 'J.M.G.' I was myself 'H.J. (2)'; but I think that I was not alone in using this signature.

[5]

series of letters from school and college testifies to the close
bond which knit mother and son throughout. 'One of the
wisest people I have ever known' is another of his notes. On
her death at the age of 93 in 1899, a letter from Dr H. J.
Hunter of Sheffield thus describes her character:

So that sturdy model of Truth, Honesty and Friendship is
called away at last. She was by much the last of that generation
both in her own family and in those allied to her. She seemed
like a faithful rearguard holding on until the signal was given
for retirement....Never was a woman so little deceived by
appearances: she looked through the surface into the realities
of life more than anyone I knew.

To this may be added a note on it from Mr Bernard Jackson:

The broad clear outline (of this passage) gives so true a
picture of my mother that I can hardly venture any attempt to
fill in the details. But I cannot help feeling that it wants en-
largement in one direction:—it does not sufficiently represent
the happy, loving, sympathy which so admirably balanced the
integrity above depicted, and so completely removed from my
mother's character anything of the hardness and censorious-
ness which is frequently associated with uprightness. It was
this happy combination of qualities which made her the confidant and adviser of her sons through life. In considering my
mother's early influence on the career of a great scholar perhaps
something should be said of her own attainments in that
direction. Born just after the battle of Trafalgar her education
should not be judged by modern standards, and it may be at
once admitted that she would have had little chance of a
diploma at a modern university. But even in those distant days
the schools did sometimes turn out pupils well equipped for
the duties of life. Perhaps my mother was fortunate in this
respect: she escaped both the superficial proprieties of a
'finishing school' and the cut and dried chips of Miss Mang-
nall's *Questions*, and somehow acquired a full share of requisite
knowledge, and a genuine appreciation of things of interest, and
no delusion that she had finished her education. She could
hardly be called a great reader, but she had a keen interest in
literature and literary people. Scott's novels appealed strongly
to the vein of romance in her character; she was not indifferent

[6]

to the possibly overstrained pathos of Miss Sewell and Miss Yonge; she read with interest the 'Salem Chapel' series of Mrs Oliphant; and I well remember the keen appreciation with which she read the earlier novels of 'George Eliot.' She took little or no interest in politics, but followed closely certain ecclesiastical controversies of the time—the Oxford Movement, Tracts for the Times, Essays and Reviews, Bishop Colenso— besides more local subsidiary storms. She was a regular reader of *John Bull*—the Tory weekly with Church and literary tendencies in no way connected with the modern paper of that name: but the paper which most strongly appealed to her was the *Saturday Review* in its earliest days when under the control of Beresford Hope and his band of vigorous writers.

Mrs Bernard Jackson writes:

Mrs Jackson had a remarkably strong personality. She used to boast that she had been educated on Walter Scott's novels; her schoolmistress used to purchase them as they came out and her pupils read them with avidity. She had a strong dislike to untruthfulness or inaccuracy of any sort and an incident she told me herself well illustrates this trait in her character. A servant in her employment told her an untruth and she at once gave her notice, saying, 'I cannot have my children taught to tell lies and if they hear you they also may learn to be untruthful.'

I always thought that Mrs Jackson had wonderful self-control, for during twenty years of intimate friendship I do not remember seeing her lose her temper nor hearing her say a rash or unkind word and her judgment and advice were always sound and practical. She was simple to severity in her tastes and dress. She once remarked to a friend, 'that if she had had a daughter she should not have known how to dress her,' and her friend replied, much to her amusement, 'You need not have troubled, she would have found that out for herself.'

Mrs Jackson's two hobbies were genealogies and gardening. The former not from any snobbishness but from a keen interest in pedigrees, and she surprised Sir George Darwin who told her that she knew more about his ancestors than he did himself. And she often came across acquaintances whose relationships she could trace to others. She often mentioned

HENRY JACKSON

two servants in her employment called Wilkinson, who had a
pedigree of 500 years in the same farm, which was afterwards
purchased by Mr Bernard Waters of Sheffield.

Prebendary Jackson writes of 'Cally':

Her vigour was conspicuous in clearing off the many details
of daily work with a rapidity which astonished me as I grew
older. In those younger days she would delight us, when her
more active work was done and she sat down to the mending
of stockings and the like, with her tales of the village life at
Stainton where her cousinship included various parts of its
population. The tales revealed, of course, something of the
characteristics of the *dramatis personae*, but more still of the
elements of justice and wisdom of the homely and clever
narrator. Occasionally she would break into song; often there
was a pithy proverb, a sound aphorism, a phrase or simile
from rural Yorkshire. The atmosphere which she spread
around us—downright truth, loyalty, justice, duty, vigour—
enlivened by shrewd humour—must be accounted a powerful
supplement to the influence of similar characteristics in our
parents.

She had been a poor disciple in Sunday School when my
Mother had tried to teach her to read and write; but her greater
qualities had been discerned; and my Mother asked for her,
when just 15, as nurse to my brother Henry when he was a
month old. That was in 1839: and still in 1866 she was with us
—our great help in my Father's illness and death: still with my
Mother at Sheffield, King's Teignton, Brighton, she continued
her wonderful service till my Mother's death in 1899, and her
own death in 1904. She was buried at Stainton, the home of her
childhood. I have said nothing of her devoted love for us all—
Father, Mother, Brothers, Brothers' wives, and the next generation too—it was like the confident, unquestioning feeling which
belongs to the best kind of blood relationship—the love which
one neither states nor doubts.

SHEFFIELD COLLEGIATE SCHOOL

HENRY JACKSON was the eldest of four brothers. He first went
from St James' Row to school at the Collegiate School, Sheffield.
The Rev. W. S. Grignon was then head master. In a letter to

[8]

him written in 1892 Jackson says, 'My years under you at Sheffield were the most important of my school life. You taught me many good things, and above all to be on my guard against self-deception and "the unspoken lie," which according to Plato is more deadly than the "lying word."' He always retained the highest regard and affection for his first head master and that these sentiments were early reciprocated appears from the following extract from a letter of Mr Grignon to Mrs Jackson, on the occasion of some trouble in the school, in which he as monitor had to take a responsible part. 'I write at once to assure you most positively that he stands perfectly clear from fault in the whole transaction, having done his duty throughout it most properly and honourably....Henry's whole character and the proofs he has given of thorough truthfulness and honourable feeling leave not a doubt on my mind that he had acted in the matter just as he had represented to me. I can only repeat to you what I said not many days ago to one of the Sheffield clergy who asked me about the subject, "I would take Henry Jackson's word as readily as that of, I do not say any boy, but any man that I know."'

He began early to show promise that he would be a 'good and accurate scholar' and his record in the school for discipline and government shows his readiness to face responsibility with a strict sense of duty.

CHELTENHAM COLLEGE

In the autumn of 1855 he left the Collegiate School and went to Cheltenham College, where the head master was William Dobson, Fellow of Trinity, 3rd Classic in 1832 (Lushington, Shilleto, Dobson, Thompson), and was in the division taken by Holden, Fellow of Trinity, Senior Classic 1845, afterwards head master of Ipswich Grammar School.

From February 1856 his letters home are regular, generally to his mother, but often to his father, scarcely one without enquiry after 'brothers.' He receives regularly from his father

[9]

HENRY JACKSON

Notes and Queries and the *Saturday Review* and discusses them. In the first letter he refers to a 'theory on Shakespeare mentioned in the *Athenaeum*[1]—the notion started by a lady.' 'I made enquiries about the Library yesterday: and have got a catalogue. There are, I think, about 1500 volumes; and they are very well selected.' He sends regular reports on work and notes Holden's plan of reading large 'chunks' of the Classics rapidly, a book of Homer at one lesson.

John Morley and F. W. H. Myers were contemporary with him at Cheltenham, the former in the same class. Myers' poetry was already famous in the school. Classics and Mathematics made up the curriculum, the latter treated seriously as well as the former. He notes in one letter that he is reading Conic Sections by himself. He is sufficiently at home with French literature to send a motto from Boileau for an essay by his brother Arthur. But this seems to have been a matter of private reading. He takes a ticket for Thackeray's Lecture on the Georges, 'College fellows admitted half price.' (3 May 1857): 'I was very much pleased with the lecture, though at first a little disappointed, as the beginning, though good, was what might have been written by many men, and was not peculiarly in Thackeray's style. I liked him very much after the introduction. As you say, he looks very old.'

Hockey and football, cricket and fives, gave him exercise. He was interested as always in the rules of the game. He sent the Cheltenham rules of football to his brother Arthur at Sheffield—

---

[1] 'I am grieved to think that the *Athenaeum* has to change its ways. When *Esmond* came out in 1852, I, aged not quite thirteen, was already a regular reader of the *Athenaeum*, and when I was away from home, my father, to my great joy, sent me the issue of the month, i.e. the issue for the four weeks in a yellow paper cover. I remember to this day the passage which the reviewer extracted from *Esmond*. When I began to write for it, Hepworth Dixon was still editor....I liked writing for a paper which seemed to me to have a tradition of honesty; and I am personally grateful to it, for it gave me the opportunity of exercising myself in this sort of literature.' From a letter to V. H. Rendall, 22 December 1916.

at a time when Association Football was beginning to take shape. Fives he continued to play at Cambridge, as late as the middle of the 'nineties. He learnt the Eton game first at Cambridge.

Altogether a strenuous school time for mind and body. All the time he sent regular reports to his father on his work, and conducted an interchange of books and papers. He notes in later life that his father had a singular gift for 'spotting' important new books—McLennan's *Patriarchal Theory*, Holmes' *Autocrat of the Breakfast Table*, etc. (see above, p. 5).

TRINITY COLLEGE

HE was entered as a pensioner at Trinity on 29 February 1858 under Mr Mathison as tutor. He came into residence in October of the same year, and for his first term lodged at 2 Petty Cury, whence in January 1859 he moved into College, to an attic set, M, New Court, now attached as a bedroom to the upper set in the tower. From this time he had rooms in College continuously till his death, and kept every term by residence, with the exception of two terms spent at Rugby in 1863, and one term of illness at Bournemouth in the autumn of 1908. The rooms which he successively occupied are given below[1]. Whewell was Master at this time, and he lived through the Masterships of W. H. Thompson and H. M. Butler, and as Vice-Master received and installed Sir J. J. Thomson, the present Master, in 1918.

Some dates may be given here:

1858 (October), came into residence; 1860 (March), elected scholar; 1862, B.A.; 1864 (October), Fellow; 1865, M.A.; 1884, Litt.D.; 1866–75, Assistant Tutor; 1875–1906, Praelector in Ancient Philosophy; 1906–21, Regius Professor of Greek; 1914–19, Vice-Master.

[1] (1) Attic, M, New Court.
(2) Ground floor, I, Great Court.
(3) 2nd floor, G, Nevile's Court (next the Library).
(4) Attic on Kitchen Office Staircase⎱ Home at Croft Cottage.
(5) Attic on I, Great Court ⎰
(6) 1st floor, G, Nevile's Court; home at Cannes and Bournemouth.

HENRY JACKSON

To HIS MOTHER
2 Petty Cury, Cambridge
19 October 1858

My dear Mother,

I am now getting a little more settled, and have got my arrangements made, so I may as well tell you what I have to do every day—

A.M.	7	Chapel, or else at 6 P.M.
		Breakfast, etc., etc.
	9–10	Mathematical Lecture—Mathison.
	10–11	Classical Lecture—Cope.
	11– 2	Other reading.
P.M.	2– 4	Walking, etc.
	4– 6	Write letters, read newspapers, etc. at the Union.
		Dinner and then I have time for more reading and go to bed early.

Yesterday we went to lecture for the first time. Mathison told us to go to him if we wanted advice about private tutors, between 11 and 12. He told me that Burn did not take pupils this term, that Hammond had either given up pupils or was full, I am not sure which, and that the most likely men in the College were G. S. Sale (he says he is from Rugby) and R. C. Green whose name I see in the *John Bull* as having just got a fellowship. I at last determined on going to Green, who is to take me from 11 to 12 on Mondays, Wednesdays, and Fridays, besides which I shall have to do papers in his rooms two days a week.

When do you think of sending my things? Please send with them Wunder's Sophocles—Maclean's Juvenal (in the glass case) and a small interleaved Juvenal which is lying about.

Green is a cousin of Mammatt's. Last night Rex Wilson put my name down at the Union[1] and I paid my first subscription. I went there tonight before Hall. They have plenty of newspapers, magazines, and reviews, and a library. I see in the list of old Officers that W. H. Brookfield was twice president.

This morning Bagshawe and I went to the Trinity Library, but it was closing time, so we only put our names down in the book with place of birth, school, master, and Father's name.

---

[1] Then in Green Street.

[12]

I have not time to write more as I am going to Bull's (our old driver) to tea, and have some work to get ready for my coach.

Please give my love to father and brothers,

> and believe me,
> your affectionate son,
> Henry Jackson.

To HIS FATHER
27 November 1858

...This morning I got to Chapel when the gates were shut, so I shall have to go tonight I am sorry to say when the service is almost as crowded and disagreeable as on Sunday. Mr Grignon's friend Luard has written a pamphlet on University Reform. The motto is from the Psalms—'When the foundations are cast down, what shall the righteous do?'...

I have been to the University Library this afternoon, as it is wet, but I find that it closes at one o'clock on Saturday.

I have had a letter from Arthur[1]. He has had a fight with Corbet, and says he is more comfortable.

To HIS MOTHER
30 November 1858

I am told that Jebb of Charterhouse is a very great swell, and that Shilleto says he is likely to get the Craven first year, which hardly ever happens. He is reading with Shilleto, who is the crack coach. I believe all this as it agrees with what Robertson told me. There is also a Shrewsbury man at John's, Graves, who was declared by Kennedy fit to edit Thucydides.

These undergraduate years were those of a reading man who made much of the opportunities of many kinds which the society of College and University offered. He was as always pertinacious in maintaining friendships formed at home and at school. A marked difference, revealed in his letters, between Trinity as it was then and as it has become since, largely owing to himself, is that he seems to have had little intimacy with the Fellows, Junior or Senior. The only name he mentions as

---

[1] His brother at Cheltenham.

[13]

apparently on familiar terms is that of Mr H. M. Butler with whom he records a breakfast, and some composition work. It is clear that most of the teaching he received from private tutors, first R. C. Green and afterwards Shilleto. But he enjoyed to the full the society of a remarkable body of contemporaries, notably Jebb, Henry Sidgwick, G. O. Trevelyan, 'Pat' Currey and others. Breakfasts and an occasional wine party were the formal entertainments. But already he is forming the habit of late hours. J. M. Image, who came up in 1861, remembered that the walk in the Great Court running eastward from the Hall steps used, in his undergraduate days, to be called 'Jackson's walk,' because Jackson used to walk and laugh there at the dead of night with his friends—the laughter sometimes disturbing Image's slumbers.

He attends the Senate House meeting for the formation of the Cambridge University Rifle Corps (May 1859) when 'the Vice-Chancellor, Prof. Selwyn and Emery spoke: Emery justified the scheme from the Bible.' He goes to hear Spurgeon preach (July 1859). 'Spurgeon I was decidedly pleased with. After an exposition he made a prayer which was excellent, till he began to speak of his brother minister and press for his continuance among them, "grant that his ear may be nailed to the doorpost of the Sanctuary."...His English is very good: cut up into short sentences and hence much clearer than a sermon in long periods. Of course he aims at eccentricity.' He notes the appearance of a volume of Tennyson and 'a very poor review in the *Edinburgh*': and reports that he is working hard to get time for 'the great missionary meeting in the Senate House tomorrow' (31 October 1859): but no account of his is preserved of that meeting when Livingstone appealed to the University for 'darkest Africa.' In this year (1859–60) he is serving on the Union Library Committee. He describes a party at the Lodge which 'was relieved from being very dull by its absurdity. When we first went in the footman took us to Lady Affleck and she carried us off to have some coffee. I calculated there were between fifty and sixty visitors including

TRINITY COLLEGE

about nine ladies: four Trinity Fellows: twelve scholars: twenty-five Pensioners and Fellow Commoners, etc. and a few residents in Cambridge. Whewell talked to the Duke of St Albans and the other swells. We were in two splendid rooms hung round with old portraits: Newton, Bentley, Mrs Bentley, Pitt.' He attends an A.D.C. performance at the Hoop (28 May 1860). A few months later he records a nearly tragic happening: 'Shilleto nearly poisoned himself on Monday: just before going to bed he drank a glass of furniture varnish by mistake for his ale, and was so frightened that he telegraphed to his sister that he should not be surprised if he were dead tomorrow. He seems all right again today.'

CLASSICAL TRIPOS

IN February 1862 he took the Classical Tripos. Two notes from letters to his brother throw an interesting light on the Tripos atmosphere of those days:

Since the first paper I have not been particularly silly: but we have most of us been terribly pressed for time. The pace is extraordinary. Jebb appears to be doing very well: I watched him at work today: he reads over a piece and then seems to translate without referring to the original, and so of course can go at a pace much greater than people with ordinary memories.

When the list came out it was headed by Jebb, Graves, Jackson[1]. He writes on 30 March:

I have not heard much about the Tripos. Gunson told me I was very unlucky in not being second and seemed to think I ought to have got more if I had written my iambics out. He and Burn put me second in their papers. Three years ago men were bracketed for twenty marks, and the three cases in our first are thought so flagrant that I am told the question is to be brought before our Senate and finally decided....P.S. Shiletto placed us, Jebb, Jackson, Wilson, Graves, Carr, Burbidge. He knew nothing about Stone, Mosley (*sic*), Miller.

[1] The Chancellor's medals fell to J. R. Mozley and W. K. Wilson (*aeq.*).

[15]

HENRY JACKSON

None of the first three Classics had taken the Mathematical Tripos; in consequence they were not qualified to compete for the Chancellor's Classical Medals.

It is noticeable that Jackson's name does not appear in the lists of the winners of University Scholarships or Prizes. He refers to this fact in the following note written in his Commonplace Book in 1910:

From COMMONPLACE BOOK

6 *November* 1910

I have learnt to be glad that in my undergraduate time I was not one of the prize-getters. I think that those early successes teach a man to care too much for such things. In later life, they do less harm. Most certainly when they came to me, I hope that they were not mischievous. But I confess that I was pleased when I had honorary degrees from Aberdeen, Glasgow, Sheffield, Manchester and Berlin—and I gratefully acknowledge the kindness of friends who have dedicated books to me: Postgate, Tarver, Adam, Platt, Verrall, Susemihl, Goodwin, J. W. Clark, Archer-Hind, Shuckburgh, Hicks, D'Arcy Thompson[1]. They came to me, all, as surprises, and it pleased me much that these men should have cared to attach my name to their work. So I give myself the pleasure of confessing my gratitude. Five of them are dead. And when I note the things which have given me pleasure, I must not forget my election to be a foreign member of the Boston Academy, due to Goodwin, my appointment to be a fellow of Winchester, and the Order of Merit. Also degrees at St Andrews and Oxford. It had seemed to me a little strange that they had not given me a degree: for I have long known and loved Oxford and many Oxford men. And though the compliment was late, I liked it. I am very grateful to Stocks, the proctor, who proposed me, and to Sidney Irwin who prompted him. Also to the Arthur Sidgwicks who put me up.

A letter to Mrs A. J. Butler (4 October 1913) in reference to her husband's career at Cambridge illustrates the same point:

[1] See pp. 117 ff.

[16]

CLASSICAL TRIPOS

To MRS A. J. BUTLER
4 *October* 1913

I quite understand Arthur's 'want of ambition' at Cambridge, because I behaved myself in the same way. Finding that I was not one of the predestined prize-getters of the time, I let myself go. The Trinity fellowship was all important: but Tripos, etc. did not matter. Richard Shilleto said to me in the Lent Term of my third year, 'I thought that you would have got a University scholarship.' I said, 'I think that if you had said so a year ago, I should have got one.' These are confessions: I make them because I think that my own attitude to University successes will explain Arthur's. In later life I have sometimes thought that my carelessness was not altogether a misfortune, though at the time it hampered me. But I must not be egotistical.
...Perhaps I ought to have put upon Arthur the pressure which I certainly missed myself: but I think that I was very conscious that I was a 'coach' and that he was not one of my pupils; so that I should be meddlesome, if I volunteered advice. I had the same feeling when my own Horace took the same line which I had done myself. I could not interfere.

26 *April* 1917

I hope that what I wrote about his attitude to University competition is clear. I wrote for myself as well as for him. The freedom was such a joy that I could not slave as I did at school: and my undergraduate period was the idlest time of my life.

The indifference to prizes during his undergraduate time is surely characteristic of Jackson. His description of his undergraduate period as the idlest time of his life must be interpreted in relation to the relentless industry of his after years. He worked steadily for his Tripos and had no such confidence in his own powers as to allow for digressions into the side paths of University ambitions. There is, indeed, a note of regret in the last letters that he had not given special time in his last year to preparation for the Craven Examination. But otherwise there are no hints of desire for those distinctions.

As a B.A. he almost at once began to take pupils. In the Long Vacation of 1862 'I have got Lyttelton (afterwards Lord Cobham) reading with me. He seems clever enough in spite of his cricket, and ought to do well if he will but read.' In the Michaelmas Term of that year he had ten pupils. The practice of 'coaching' was still practically universal for Classics, as well as for Mathematics; and it was by taking pupils that Jackson became aware of his keen interest in teaching, and was ultimately led to adopt an academic career. A brief summary of the way in which this came to pass is given in the autobiographical note which follows:

From COMMONPLACE BOOK
18 *April* 1914

I have to confess that I myself drifted. I had no definite choice. When I was an undergraduate, I assumed that, like others, I should become a schoolmaster, and presumably take orders. Early in 1863 I had temporary work at Rugby, and decided that I did not care for it. At this time, *teste* George Howard, I said that I would *not* be a resident don, and I remember saying something of the sort to my Aunt Mary. But I began to incline to the don's life. Then in 1864 I quarrelled with Mathison. I applied for an inspectorship of schools, but had no hope. I debated whether to ask D. N. Barker to take me into the lead works, but did nothing. I applied to Barry for the Vice-Principalship of Cheltenham College, but he was taking an Oxford man. Meanwhile I was taking pupils hard, and in this way I much improved my scholarship. I learnt to teach, and gained in confidence. By the way, I debated whether I would try Australia: but a few words from my wise mother made me aware that, if my father died, I should be wanted at home. What a wise woman she was! In 1866 Thompson became Master, and my father died. At the end of the year Thompson got me made Assistant Tutor. Till February 1868 I continued to take pupils, having begun to lecture in 1867 in January. In those days the lecturing of Classical Lecturers was perfunctory. H. Sidgwick prepared his lecture at breakfast, and gave the rest of the day to Arabic. Myers, when his lecture was done, gave himself to mesmerism. I thought that I should give my time to physiology and began to learn the bones. But I soon saw that with my experience I could make a good thing of the Classical lectures, especially as I had Currey for my colleague. Before we were appointed lecturers the College had provided composition lecturers but not translation, except for questionists during the last month before the Classical Tripos. Currey and I had taken some of these questionists' papers. We were appointed composition lecturers. One had the second year, the other the third: one had three men, the other four. We made our men do the translation papers we had given to the question-ists. In the following October Term (1867) we invited freshmen to come, and we made translation papers a regular part of our business. We had nearly forty of the best men in College. In a word we superseded classical coaching. In this way I got immersed in Classical work. It is true that I once asked Wm. Overend whether I was too old to think of the bar. I had debated it in 1864, and decided that for want of money I must not think of it. Of course Wm. Overend was discouraging. And then Maggie came into my life. Meanwhile the agitations about Tests and University and College Reform and the con-sequences of the Tests agitation had largely occupied my thoughts. Till about 1875 I was fighting man rather than administrator. But from 1877–1882 I was in the thick of University Reform. In 1882 I was elected to the University Council, and from that time till my breakdown in 1908, with occasional intermissions, I was on the Council and much con-cerned with University business.

FELLOWSHIP EXAMINATION

In September 1862 he was for the first time a candidate for a fellowship, on an occasion made famous by *Horace at Athens*. He writes on 22 September, 'The papers have been very hard and I have done very badly. The favourites for the fellowships are Eve, Young, Trevelyan, Barker and Jebb.' Three of these appeared in the list of five fellows elected, F. W. Eve (11th Wrangler, 1860), G. Young (8th Senior Opt. and 2nd class Classical Tripos, 1860), and T. Barker (Senior Wrangler, 1862). But the other two were R. J. Crosthwaite (8th Wrangler, 1860) and R. C. Whiting (6th Classic, 1860). It will be observed that all the elected candidates, except the Senior Wrangler of 1862, were graduates of 1860 and therefore in their last opportunity

HENRY JACKSON

for election: and it is natural to suppose that this fact weighed decisively with the electors[1] (the Master and Seniors) in preferring their claims to those of men of such distinction as Jebb and Trevelyan. But Jackson gives a vivid description of the feelings of the disappointed candidates:

All Wednesday morning Jebb, Trevelyan and myself went about reviling the Seniors: Trevelyan vows he will not go in again: Jebb threatened to try and get a fellowship at a small College: indeed both of them thought the election more manifestly *unjust* than I did. After our indignation meeting the natural thing would have been a game at fives or rackets to get rid of the affair, but I had to shirk a game at rackets because H. said he should come at 2 o'clock and dine at Trinity. However he stopped at Ely and I spent my afternoon by myself with nothing to do

[1] Fellowship Elections, 1862–1864:

1862. Crosthwaite, R. J., 8th Wrangler, 1860.
Young, G., 8th Sen. Opt. 1860, 2nd Chancellor's Medal, 2nd class Classics, 1860.
Eve, F. W., 11th Wrangler, 1860, 2nd class Classics, 1860.
Whiting, R. C., 6th Classic, 1860.
Barker, T., Sen. Wrangler, 1862.

1863. Kitchener, F. E., 12th Wrangler, 1861.
Cobb, G. F., 11th Classic, 1861.
Jebb, R. C., Sen. Classic, 1862.

1864. Dale, T., 3rd Wrangler, 1862.
Jackson, H., 3rd Classic, 1862.
Wilson, W. K., Sen. Opt. and 4th Classic, 1862.
Leeke, E. T., 2nd Wrangler and 2nd class Classic, 1863.
Sidgwick, A., Sen. Opt. and 2nd Classic, 1863.

1865. Lobley, J. A. 8th Wrangler and 2nd class Classic, 1863.
Currey, W. E., 4th Classic, 1863.
Young, E. M., 7th Classic, 1863.
Turnbull, W. P., 2nd Wrangler and 2nd class Classic, 1864.
Moule, H. C. G., 2nd Classic, 1864.
Myers, F. W. H., 2nd Classic, 1864.

It is clear from this list that the policy of the electors attached considerable weight to seniority.

[20]

BRITISH ASSOCIATION

We may continue the quotation to illustrate the troubles of a host and impressions of the meeting of the British Association held that year at Cambridge:

To HIS MOTHER

3 October 1862

He (H.) turned up at night, and then Hambly in a flannel cap and Tinker Martin the Harrow man called. So I asked them all to tea after Willis' address. I went to the address with Snooke and Macfarlane and asked them all to tea. When we got back I found to my dismay that the bedmaker had picked up my note to her and never read it: and consequently I had to go to the kitchens to order fowls, to the butteries to fetch loaves, to Young's to borrow sugar, and in fact to seek everything I wanted. Finally at twelve o'clock Eve arrived wanting some tea. Knowing how I liked H. before you may guess what I think of his snobbism after enduring it for the last two days, particularly as I have felt quite done up and good for nothing. I went to hear Huxley's address yesterday, and then cut the whole thing, even Tyndall's lecture. Today I heard a fight between Huxley and Owen. Owen talked about the brain of a gorilla, and Huxley made the most spiteful attack on him I ever heard. Then came Rolleston and Flower on Huxley's side, a muff called Molesworth on Owen's: Humphry then tried to mediate: and then Owen replied very briefly. He thanked the audience for their attention and *Professor Rolleston* for the courtesy of his opposition: he told him he would find an account of the convolutions of the brain in a paper he wrote thirty years ago: and then he passed on to answer Huxley. He called his speech 'more frank than courteous, more courteous than candid.' I saw Owen to speak to at the Union this morning: I thought he recognized me at first, but then saw he did not. But he walked away with Trevelyan (who had met him at the Lodge) and I supposed asked him who I was: for he came back and made many enquiries after you and father. Fortunately for me H. has got an invitation to the great dinner in Trinity today and is going down tomorrow, so I live in daily expectation of getting rid of him. I hate to have to do with a man who says a thing by way of making conversation, and if you differ with him eats up what he had said from a mistaken idea of politeness. A man who says 'how nice' or 'indeed, indeed' to everything.

The fellowship election is a very serious thing for us: at present no one has been elected in Trevelyan's year, and only one in ours, so that there is a fair chance that (except Jebb and Dale) we may all have to stand over till the last time.

TEACHING

In the Michaelmas Term of the year 1862 he was fully occupied with pupils. 'I have got ten pupils.....It's rather fun making out as much as possible of each man in the first quarter of an hour's talk.' In the spring of next year (1863) he made his experiment in schoolmastering, by taking temporary work at Rugby on Dr Temple's invitation. Although the result was to convince him against taking up school work, it opened up a new line of interest in education which bore fruit later in his service on the Higher Schools Examination Board, and the close attention which he continued to the end to give to the question of school curricula and management, and to the interdependence of the Schools and the University. In the questions of Greek in the Little-go, of Entrance Scholarships and other such matters he was largely influenced by his experience at Rugby; just as his experience of private coaching led him to the development of College teaching in Classics, which ultimately influenced, it may be said without exaggeration, the whole development of teaching in that and other subjects in the University. In both cases we have good illustration both of the thoroughness with which he tackled and got the best out of each job as it came, and of the mental grip and tenacity with which he garnered and used his experiences.

The summer of 1864 was notable for the visit of the Prince and Princess of Wales to Cambridge. The following extract is characteristic:

The visit of the PRINCE *and* PRINCESS OF WALES
3 June 1864

I have cut the festivities as much as possible. I went to London on Wednesday, and did not return till Thursday evening, so that I completely avoided the racket of the Entrance into the Town. Last night everyone was at the Fitzwilliam (University) Ball (entrance, gentlemen 3 guineas, ladies 2 guineas). This morning at 10.45 I went to the Senate House and got a bad place. Proceedings began at 12. The cheering was terrific, especially for the Princess, Denmark, the King of Denmark, Stanley and Lord Palmerston. In the afternoon I went into the grounds of King's, opposite the tent where the swells sat to watch the boats pass. Tonight all Trinity and 600 other people are going to the great Trinity Ball. I gave up my ticket that Lee Warner of John's who has friends up might have one instead, so I shall have a very quiet evening. Everyone appears to have gone mad. One or two men have gone out of the way, and Henry Sidgwick walks about and utters little epigrams. So many dinners have been ordered that the cook has had to decline commission.

An echo of the AMERICAN CIVIL WAR
24 June 1864

The place is almost empty. I have been teaching people to play at fives who never played before....You will have seen the history of the fight between the Alabama and the Kearsarge. It is strange that an English gentleman should now be able to take his family out in a yacht to see an hour's fighting, and that at the end of the time one of the vessels should go down riddled through and through.

The fellowship examination of the year 1864 at last brought to Jackson the success for which he had been working. The autobiographical note given above (p. 18) shows that his ultimate aim in life was still quite unsettled: but it is obvious that the election to a fellowship gave him freedom of decision and time for deliberation. Only gradually did the decision for an Academic life take shape. One, and perhaps the most important, element of indecision was the fact that the appointments to the Staff lay in the first place with the Tutors and finally with the Seniors: and from neither quarter did Jackson expect much favour. Nor had he yet determined on the particular line of study which he afterwards made his own.

The following extract gives an interesting account of the

examination and admission. It is to be noted that the dissertation formed as yet no part of the tests for a fellowship:

To HIS MOTHER
29 *September* 1864

At present we do nothing but write papers all day and dine in
the evening. This morning we had a holiday, that is the Classical
men had....So Wilson and I went to the Tennis Court and had
a first lesson in that lazy game.

We began the Examination with a very good, hard, translation
paper, which would have suited me very well, if I had not been
driven mad by the clanging of a weathercock which must have
been out of order....The papers since then have mostly been
badly chosen: as might be expected.

10 *October* 1864

We were admitted this morning: the ceremony cannot be
called imposing: in fact I thought it decidedly laughable. First
of all we went to the Vice-Chancellor's in a body 'to sign the
book,' but till we got there, no one knew what was signified
by this mysterious operation: the present V.-C. showed us a
paragraph at the beginning of the book containing in fact a
declaration of conformity. So we did not go away thinking, as
Hammond professes to have done, that he had only signed the
V.-C.'s visiting book. We then had each a brief interview with
the Master who presented us with copies of the Statutes. Then
to Chapel, where we made a grossly illegal declaration that we
would never bring an action against the College whether as
Fellows or as ex-Fellows. We signed our names in a book
and were solemnly admitted by the Master as when we were
admitted to our Scholarships. I believe I am now entitled to
walk across the grass and to use College plate. What my other
privileges are, I don't know.

PRIVATE TUTOR—ASSISTANT TUTOR—PRAELECTOR

FOR two years after his election to his fellowship Jackson
continued to take pupils, but the appointment of William
Hepworth Thompson to the Mastership on Whewell's death in
1866 was the decisive turn in his career. One of the first acts
of the new Master was to appoint Jackson to the post of Assistant
Tutor, thus giving him a permanent place on the educational

[24]

staff of the College. It was again to Thompson that he owed nine years later his appointment as Praelector in Ancient Philosophy. This post qualified him for continuance in his fellowship after his marriage: it settled the permanent trend of his studies and teaching in the direction of Plato and Aristotle: and the fact that the lectures of a Praelector, by the rules of the College, are open to all members of the University, virtually established him as a Professor in that subject, though without professorial status in the University. In the same year the College provided a similar post in Moral and Political Philosophy for Henry Sidgwick. Michael Foster had been elected to a Praelectorship in Physiology in 1870. In both the latter subjects Professorships have since been established in the University, but Ancient Philosophy still waits for its due recognition.

An immediate result of his appointment as Assistant Tutor was a great advance in the organisation of the Classical teaching in the College. In co-operation with Henry Sidgwick, Richard Jebb and 'Pat' Currey, he extended to all Classical students the provision of individual teaching in translation and composition, which had hitherto been provided only for the fourth year men who were shortly taking their Tripos. It was in appearance a small reform: but in fact it was the first and decisive step in a fundamental change in the ideal of the position and duties of a College Lecturer, not in Classics only but in all branches of study. Hitherto the formal lecture had been regarded as his sole duty: individual teaching had been left to the private coaches, of whom Shilleto and Routh were in their respective subjects typical representatives. The difficulty of substituting a moderate amount of College teaching and guidance for the intensive culture of the private coach was due in large measure to the order of merit, by which at that time candidates in all Triposes were classified, and the excessive importance attached to the place gained in that order. The experiment initiated by Jackson and his colleagues depended upon securing the confidence of the candidates in the efficiency of the teaching for that end: and it was only by slow degrees that that confidence

[25]

was won even in Classics. The extension to other subjects was more gradual, and, indeed, cannot be said to have attained complete success, till the abolition of the order of merit, culminating in the disappearance of the fetish of the Senior Wrangler in 1910. But the tentative beginnings were made, as described in the autobiographical note above (p. 19). The new method had also its reaction on the schools, more particularly perhaps through the publication of *Translations and Compositions*—a selection of passages which had been set in Lecture Room by Jebb, Jackson and Currey, with the 'fair copies,' which they were accustomed to give after correction of the exercises of their pupils.

REFORMS

THE years immediately following Jackson's election to a fellowship were fruitful in beginnings. Movements were on foot for the reform of Triposes, including the Classical Tripos; for the admission of women to University education; for the abolition of tests; and for a general reform of University and College Statutes. Into all these movements Jackson threw himself with practical thoroughness and wide sympathies. He worked in close alliance with Henry Sidgwick, his senior in age by nine months, but in academical standing by three years and as a fellow by five years. Progress in all cases was slow. It has been recorded in all the detail that is necessary in the *Memoir of Henry Sidgwick* (Macmillan and Co., 1906), and the record need not be repeated. Moreover, for this period the remains of Jackson's correspondence are scanty. Fewer letters to his home, which have so far contributed the major part of our material, are preserved: and his friends being mostly among his colleagues in the College and University, there is little correspondence with them. But some notes on passing events may be given.

THE NEW MASTER

THE appointment of W. H. Thompson to the Mastership, on the death of Whewell in 1866, is thus referred to (13 March

1866): 'Our hopes and fears about the Mastership have been set at rest[1]. Thompson has been appointed and we are most of us very well satisfied, except those of course who have found him an awkward antagonist in argument. The betting column of *Sporting Life* of Saturday contained the following paragraph: "Trin. Coll. Cam. Betting at Doncaster. 2 to 1 on Vaughan, 10 to 1 against Thompson, 66 to 1 against Mathison. None others mentioned."' With time Jackson's appreciation of Thompson's mastership grew steadily higher: and in his Commemoration Sermon (1913) he paid a loyal and noble tribute to his work and character. The change came in the critical time of accumulating reforms, and the younger half of the Society felt that his headship promised a new atmosphere of 'freedom and independence.' This is not the place to enlarge on this theme, but there is no doubt that the active promoters of reform in the College during the next twenty years felt that they had in the Master, not indeed a vigorous leader, but, what was perhaps more important, a head of fine and sympathetic judgment, of scrupulous fairness, and of a courage which never shrank from responsibility.

To HIS MOTHER

25 *May* 1866

Our authorities have at last consented to dine at 6.15 on Monday next instead of holding the usual Whit *Sunday* feast at four o'clock. We shall therefore venture to ask our friends with a hope that the entertainment will be decently managed.

6 *December* 1866

Maurice delivered his inaugural lecture on Tuesday. It was better than I expected and could not have shocked the most orthodox. The *Pall Mall Gazette* states rather simply that his whole discourse was consistent with a belief in the inspiration of the Old and New Testaments.

---

[1] Cf. Henry Sidgwick (*Memoir*, p. 144): 'We are all somewhat relieved by the appointment, as we were afraid of a non-resident—at least of such non-residents as were talked of. Thompson will make a very good sort of Master, though not perhaps the best.'

HENRY JACKSON

21 *May* 1893

On Monday night and again last night I went to supper with the Myers' to meet George Eliot and her husband. The assembled multitude worshipped in a very amusing way, but I confess to being rather bored by the stiff way in which she wraps up platitudes in stilted language delivered in a peculiar, formal manner in a low voice.

MARRIAGE

IN 1875 took place his marriage with Margaret Thornton, second daughter of Canon Francis Vansittart Thornton, Vicar of Southhill w. Callington, Cornwall: in the same year, as already stated, he was appointed by the College Praelector in Ancient Philosophy, an office which enabled him under the then Statutes to continue to hold his fellowship. For the first fourteen years of their married life Mr and Mrs Jackson lived at Croft Cottage on the Barton Road, where five children, three daughters and two sons, were born. In this house, with its modest outlook on the road and two fine rooms at the back, they exercised a delightful hospitality to old and young alike. Jackson's rooms in College had already become a gathering place, open at all hours, but particularly at night, for all who wanted good talk and wise counsel: and the large study of Croft Cottage was now allied with Mrs Jackson's drawing room, where she delighted to gather parties of young people, for cheery evenings of round games and talk: dancing had not yet become the all-sufficient amusement of youth. Both hosts had a singular faculty for putting even the shyest guests at their ease; and with both the general hospitality led to numerous intimate friendships, to which many men and women owe much of the best in their lives. During this period Jackson occupied a garret in the Great Court for College purposes; it was a familiar sight to see him with his bag of books slung over his shoulder coming at a quick pace down the Grange Road, through the garden and by the avenue just in time for his eleven o'clock lecture. His double habitat was not always without inconvenience. He used to tell how late one night or in the early hours of the morning, making his way

MARRIAGE

home in a fog, he fell into the side ditch opposite his house, arousing the grave suspicions of an opportune policeman who helped him out. But this happy time was not to last. Towards the end of the 'eighties Mrs Jackson's health failed and in 1889 the home was removed to Cannes; in January 1890 Jackson returned to College and took the rooms in G, Nevile's Court, which he occupied for the rest of his life.

CANNES

At Cannes their first home was at the Villa Mauvarre, of which he gives a description in the following letter to his brother, Mr Bernard Jackson:

29 June 1889

I have neglected you shamefully of late: so I take the opportunity of this quiet place to get into better ways again. Not that there is anything to write. You would think our establishment a very odd one. Just on the edge of the town, on the rising ground to the East, is the Hôtel Montfleuri. A quarter of a mile further up the hill, quite out of the town, stands this villa. It was built for a pension, and has many more rooms than we can use. We have a French housemaid with whom Alice[1] had made acquaintance at the Grande Bretagne, an excellent servant, who can turn her hand to anything. The cook comes for part of each day. The garden is like the garden of Dr Watts' sluggard: all overgrown with weeds and bushes run wild, and besides, full of all sorts of trees—cactus (I think), eucalyptus, cypress, orange. It joins to a bit of wood, through which a path leads to the high road, half a mile away. From my study I see the roof of our hotel, and then the sea, and the Esterel—the hilly promontory to the West. From a place under the trees lower down, we see more roofs, more sea, and more Esterel. From the west bedroom on the upper floor we command the town. I have not been out of the grounds except once since I came. It is very hot and I live accordingly. The flies are disgusting: the ants hideous: the mosquitoes teasing. It is a question whether it is better to keep the shutters closed, in which case both I and the flies are somnolent, or to have them open in which case they busy them-

[1] Their servant.

[29]

selves about me. All this tends to indolence. I have written some letters, thank goodness, and I have done some lecture work. Also I have read part of a German book about Plato. Also I have scribbled some stuff about totemism. Also I have read two or three plays of Molière, and E. Yates' *Memoirs*, and *The Passenger from Scotland Yard*, and Payn's *Memoirs*, and some French stories. But it is not easy to do things steadily in this climate—which by the way, not very much to my surprize, upset my stomach a day or two ago. Our doctor has gone home to England: so our sense of desolation is complete. His last patients started this morning. (There is another mosquito! I don't like to think that I am going to sleep tonight without mosquito curtains.)

30 June 1889

When I went to bed last night the flies were buzzing in the bed curtains like a swarm of bees, and I have been food for mosquitoes. Nevertheless I have slept very well. In the middle of the night we had a tremendous thunderstorm which sent all the household on their travels. The downpour was terrific, and the air is the better for it this morning.

The next letter (to Mr Bernard Jackson, 9 January 1890) may be read as a companion to the above, describing his new rooms in College:

Villa Mauvarre
9 January 1890

We propose (i.e. Hal[1] and I) to start on the 14th and go through to Dover, so as to reach Cambridge on the 16th. Term will then have begun. If, as I hope, I get the large rooms in my old staircase in Nevile's Court, the removal of my properties will occupy my spare time. At present I am feeling very curious about these rooms, which I know very well, but have never studied from a selfish point of view. I fear that I shall never be able to 'live up to' the magnificent cielings [*sic*]. The great question is whether my large bookcase will find a place in the inner room. Ever since I have known Cambridge these rooms have been occupied by mathematicians, so that their capacity for library purposes has not been tested, the walls having been used only for pictures and Japanese crockery.

[1] His eldest son.

[30]

BOURNEMOUTH

THE domestic settlement thus begun was destined to become
permanent. Mrs Jackson's health, which necessitated the
removal to Cannes in 1889, never allowed a return to Cambridge. In 1895 it was decided to move to Bournemouth, and
at Bournemouth the home remained till Jackson's death.
Jackson's own arrangements were dictated by this. He spent
the term in Cambridge, established in his rooms in Nevile's
Court; and as soon as term, with its many occupations, was
fully over, he went to Cannes or Bournemouth, with books and
papers, and spent the vacation there. This regular change of
headquarters was varied only once in the thirty years, when in
1908 a severe illness kept him at Bournemouth for the Michaelmas Term. He enjoyed his vacations at Cannes greatly, and
was especially fond of the Villa Mauvarre, their first house.
Bournemouth, on the other hand, never gained his affection.
But the quiet and rest of the vacations spent there were undoubtedly invaluable in repairing the strain of the term's work,
which became increasingly exhausting as the years went on;
the more so, as in 1899 he developed a complaint which required at times a rigorous dieting, and was never completely
cured.

THE NEW MASTER

IN 1886 the Master, to whom Jackson owed so much, died, and
was succeeded a few months later by Dr H. Montagu Butler.
Three years later R. C. Jebb was elected to the Professorship
of Greek in succession to Dr Kennedy. Jackson was a candidate
and delivered a Praelection on the political causes of the
accusation brought against Socrates. In this year a large number
of friends subscribed for his portrait. Charles W. Furse was chosen
to paint the portrait which now hangs in the College Hall.
The subscription list was large enough to allow of a second
portrait by the same artist, which was presented to Mrs Jackson.

Little else occurred to disturb the regular course of College
life beyond the recurrence in 1894 of the periodical deliberation

on the extension of the College buildings. Jackson took a leading part on this occasion.

He held very strongly the opinion that it was the duty of the College to provide a large increase in the accommodation available for undergraduates in College, and that for this purpose the Paddocks site should be utilised. A considerable minority consistently opposed the scheme; and in the course of the deliberations the Master, who began by an almost eager advocacy of the proposal, saw reason to change his mind, and after prolonged deliberation the proposal was dropped. A fund for College Extension was established, and the proposal was re-vived after the war; but in spite of a general willingness to proceed, the great expense of building blocked the way and the latest large addition to the College buildings is still the Whewell's Courts, the magnificent benefaction of Dr Whewell.

In University business he took his full share and his influence was great. He sat on the Council of the Senate from 1882 to 1906, with slight intermission, and was for many years an active member of the Library and Press Syndicates, of the General Board, the Classical Board, the Joint Board for Higher Schools Examinations, and several occasional Syndicates. He took a keen interest in the development of the study of Modern Languages both in the schools and in the University. As a good French scholar and widely read in French literature, his aid was frequently claimed in the revision of school editions. He served the Board of Modern and Medieval Languages from its institution for many years.

SOCIAL LIFE

No account of Jackson's place in the College would be nearly complete which did not emphasise the unique position which he occupied in its social life. His rooms in Nevile's Court were a centre of unceasing hospitality. The oak was never sported except when he was out. His habit of sitting up very late made him accessible at all hours of the evening and far on into the early hours of the morning, and there were few evenings throughout those more than thirty years when he was alone. It was his regular practice to give a general invitation to the table in Combination Room to adjourn to his rooms to smoke: and at the larger parties and feasts he would walk round the tables inviting the hosts to bring their guests. In fact Jackson's smoking parties on such occasions became a regular College institution, at which old members of the College on their visits, and members of other Colleges, could always count on meeting their friends and making new acquaintances or improving those already made.

The most characteristic of these meetings took place after dinner on the Commemoration Day in December. It is the practice of the College to entertain on this occasion a large number of guests including the scholars, prizemen and some other junior members: and from very early days in the tenure of his fellowship Jackson made a practice of inviting all to his smoking party after the dinner in hall was concluded. At one time when he occupied only a small set of rooms in College he used to borrow the set in Nevile's Court which he afterwards occupied himself; but as the numbers attending the celebration increased, the venue was moved to two of the large lecture rooms in the Great Court, thrown into one and furnished for the occasion with card tables, smoking apparatus and a piano. Here Jackson, a cigar box in hand, met his guests, old and young, and by midnight the cloud of smoke and the din of talk culminated. Speeches from distinguished visitors and songs with popular choruses, especially the more famous school songs, succeeded one another in rapid succession: and the new day was well advanced before the last card players had finished their games and Jackson returned to his rooms.

It would be difficult to over-estimate the value and influence of this constant and catholic hospitality in the life of the College and of the University. It gave opportunities of easy and familiar intercourse to men of all ages, and of all opinions; and conduced to maintaining a standard of personal friendship and loyalty amid the inevitable controversies of academic life. Moreover, in Jackson's rooms there was always the heartiest welcome for the younger members of the Society: the 'least donnish of dons' never lost his frank and brotherly interest in young men, and many generations of undergraduates found themselves at home there. It is not too much to say that Jackson's character and personal example were the strongest influence in establishing that friendly understanding between youth and age which has increasingly characterised his College.

UNIVERSITY REFORM

Three movements of reform, in which he was especially interested, deserve more particular mention.

1. The Tests Act.

WHEN Jackson became a fellow, he found himself at once in the thick of reforming activity in the College. The most stirring question at issue was the removal of tests imposed upon fellows at their admission. Lempriere Hammond, Coutts Trotter and Henry Sidgwick were the College leaders in this movement, strongly backed by the veteran Adam Sedgwick; and Jackson threw himself eagerly into the fray. The constitution of the College at that time made all change slow. The government was entirely in the hands of the Master and eight Senior Fellows; with the provision that resolutions might be proposed, after due notice by any five Fellows, at the General Annual Meeting. But no such proposition could be voted upon at the meeting at which it was first brought forward; and no resolution carried at such a meeting was binding on the College unless it was re-affirmed by a majority of two-thirds of those present at the next succeeding meeting. Under this leisurely progress it was not till December 1870 that the College accepted by the requisite majority a resolution[1] 'That the Master and Seniors take such steps as may be necessary in order to repeal all religious restrictions on the election and conditions of tenure

[1] See *Henry Sidgwick, a Memoir*, p. 173.

[34]

of fellowships at present contained in the Statutes.' Even after this, efforts at obstruction were continued, but the question was finally settled by the Tests Act, 1871. To this matter he refers in the following letters to his mother:

To HIS MOTHER
22 November 1869

We have been making arrangements for a political meeting at St John's Lodge about the abolition of tests; and as Hammond [Lempriere] has gone down and Sidgwick [Henry] resigned his fellowship I had to do what was necessary in preparing motions for the December College Meeting.

A further vista is opened up in a later letter:

29 May 1870

We are still up to the ears in politics and very much afraid that the Lords will throw out the Tests Bill. One of my parliamentary friends tells me that he thinks the Government may go out on the Education Bill, which will be a sad blow to us. I was hoping that the Tests Bill might be passed without further delay, and that we might then be able to take steps towards getting a Royal University Commission. We must have one soon to revise College Statutes and to settle the relations between the Colleges and the University. It is impossible to go on tinkering the College Statutes bit by bit. Whenever it comes we shall rather astonish the Conservatives with our suggestions— unless we determine to show our hands in advance.

In fact from 1867 onwards the College was working steadily at the reform of its Statutes; so that by the time the desired Royal Commission was appointed in 1877, considerable progress had been made in preparing new Statutes. As early as 1873 (February) Henry Sidgwick writes:

Reformers believe that we are on the eve of considerable changes in the way of completer organisation of the Colleges into a really academic body. We are partly waiting on Providence and Gladstone, but meanwhile we shall make some attempt to manage our own affairs. In Trinity we have passed (as far as the consent of the Fellows goes) a large scheme of reform and are now waiting the sanction of the Privy Council.

That sanction was refused, to the great indignation of the reformers, on the ground that a commission would shortly be issued. But, in spite of still further delay, the work had not been wasted. The Statutes, which had been thus prepared, provided the ground on which the College met the Commissioners of 1877 and were the basis of the new Statutes made by them and still governing the College. The change thus effected was considerable. The government of the College was put effectively into the hands of the Fellows. A new executive was created in a College Council largely elective. All restrictions on marriage were removed; and the tenure of fellowships beyond six years was made dependent on service to the College or the University. In the University perhaps the most important change was the taxation of the Colleges for University purposes, and the partial organisation of studies under the General Board and the Special Boards of Studies. Not all that was hoped for from this constitution has yet been achieved: but the great development of studies in the University in the last forty years may, in great measure, be credited to the new constitution, and to the additional funds put at the disposal of the University.

In all this movement Jackson took, from the beginning, an active and often, and in an increasing degree, a leading part. He regarded the claims of the College and the University for all kinds of administrative service as a charge upon his time inferior in importance only to the teaching duties of his office. With all his enormous capacity for work, it was inevitable that there must be some sacrifice, and the sacrifice which Jackson chose was that of literary output. To this is due the fact that the chief record of his studies lies in occasional papers. No *magnum opus* preserves his name and reputation for posterity.

2. The Higher Education of Women.

It was in these years that the movement for the higher education of women at Cambridge had its origin and took its shape. He was present at a meeting in London, with Kingsley in the chair, which decided to form a joint board of members of Oxford and Cambridge Universities to establish an examination for 'Governesses.' The result at Cambridge was the establishment of an 'Examination for Women,' later called the *Higher Local Examination*, first held in June 1869. This was rapidly followed by the setting up of a Committee for organising lectures in Cambridge for women (1869), the opening of a hostel for women students in Regent Street, with Miss Clough in charge (October 1871), and the opening of 'Newnham Hall' (the Old Hall, Newnham College) in October 1875. Meantime a Committee, of which Miss Emily Davies was the moving spirit, established the hostel at Hitchin, which ultimately became Girton College at Cambridge. The story of the development of these institutions, and the opening to their students of the Tripos examinations, first by the voluntary kindness of examiners and afterwards officially by the University, need not be told here. In the successive steps thus taken, and in the movement for giving degrees and full membership to women, Jackson took an active part. He never wavered in his opinion that the right ultimate settlement was to admit women to full membership: and he had to the last hoped to see this brought about in his own lifetime.

3. Classical Studies.

The Classical Tripos, since its establishment in 1824, had tested the quality of candidates solely by their performance on papers in unseen translation and composition. The reform now initiated aimed at including a test of knowledge of classical history, philosophy, and philology. The teaching on the philosophical subjects fell to Jackson: and from about 1870 to the end he concentrated his efforts on this branch of classical study. The position was made definite by his appointment to a Praelectorship in Ancient Philosophy in 1875, and from that time onwards he lectured almost exclusively on Greek Philosophy from Thales to Aristotle. In the early years of the undivided Tripos (1872–1882) he lectured regularly on the set books of Plato and Aristotle, and these lectures were attended by the great majority of the classical students of the University. After 1882, when the special subjects were for the most part relegated to the second part of the Tripos, and were taken only by a small proportion of those who had passed the first part, the numbers attending his lectures became small. But the large classes revived again at a later period when a general knowledge of the history of Greek Philosophy was once more required of all candidates for the Tripos.

THE TEACHER

AN attempt may be made here to give some account of Jackson's methods as a teacher.

He always lectured on a text. A dialogue of Plato or a book of Aristotle's *Metaphysics* formed the most frequent subjects. A close and vigorous translation, with brief but decisive explanations of idiom and phrase, formed the basis on which he laid a penetrating examination of the author's meaning, leading to the more general exposition of the subject-matter in parts and as a whole. There was something peculiarly attractive and stimulating in this method: he exhibited by it his own mind at work upon the problems in hand. It appears that he never wrote out in full such lectures; the text of his author was annotated beforehand in the margins and between the lines, and each lecture was prepared with minute labour, however often the same text might have been lectured upon before. He seemed to come to each difficulty fresh and with an open mind, to offer his solution, and to show how he reached it. The consequence was that the minds of his audience were on the stretch throughout; and, for those who could follow, it was a most exhilarating and stimulating experience, a constant challenge to thought. This was partly due to the strength and vigour of his own thought and expression, partly to the strong impression which he conveyed, that his author was to be taken seriously, *au pied de la lettre*, unless and until he was proved to be unworthy of such treatment. The primary aim was to develop the meaning of the author, as he meant it, not as it could be interpreted or applied under modern conditions and relations. It would be unfair to say that he ignored or made light of this secondary aim: but, as introducing young thinkers to ancient philosophy, he held that the essential thing was to bring them into direct touch and, if possible, intimacy with the writers themselves and their ways of thinking; giving them thus the discipline of themselves passing through that examination and statement of fundamental problems, by which Greek philosophy laid, as he held, the foundations of all later thinking.

It followed from this that his lectures were an excellent training in scholarly method for the majority of men, even for those who did not further pursue the study of philosophy. For the few who went further, it may be said of him, as it has been said of Henry Sidgwick, that, while he formed no school, and indeed rather challenged and stimulated opposition, he impressed upon them a standard of thoroughness and sincerity in statement, and a scrupulous loyalty in judgment, which permanently and strongly influenced the character of their own thinking and studies.

Good examples of his exposition are preserved in the two Praelections which he delivered when he was a candidate for the Professorship of Greek in 1889 and 1906. But they do not preserve, as of course they could not, those more important characteristics of his teaching, when it took the form of keen discussion with a small class or with individual students.

The following note by one of his pupils gives a vivid impression of his manner and quality as a lecturer and teacher:

Few teachers in any age can have been more admirable than Jackson was during those years, and few of those who heard him will forget that experience. Two large lecture rooms were thrown into one, to hold an audience of seventy or eighty students. Punctually at eleven o'clock Jackson walked quickly into the room carrying a large satchel, took his books out of it and placed them on the desk before him, set his back against the niche on the west side which divided the two rooms, and began his exposition of Plato or Aristotle. He never began where he had left off but devoted the first ten minutes to a rehearsal of his previous lecture. He was never in a hurry, as each of his courses lasted through the three terms of the academic year; yet he was never discursive or irrelevant, never obscure, never dull or mechanical. It was obvious that he attached great importance to his subject, that he had taken infinite pains to prepare his discourse, and that he himself enjoyed the exercise of his powers. There was much to be learned from his exposition; and the mere sight of that sturdy figure, the mere sound of that emphatic voice, made a wonderful impression on the minds of young men. It was said of Dugald Stewart that he breathed the love of virtue into whole generations; it may as truly be said that every man who attended Jackson's lectures could learn from him to prize intellectual honesty and to spare no pains in the pursuit of truth.

I append here an estimate of Jackson as a teacher and scholar which has been kindly supplied by his old friend Mr R. D. Hicks:

In the nineteenth century the chair of Greek in Cambridge was held by scholars eminent in their day and generation. From Porson and Monk to Jebb they have left behind them permanent memorials of their achievements and live in their writings. With Henry Jackson the case is different. His fame rests mainly upon his lectures and his pupils: it is inadequately represented by his writings. But so great was that fame, it seems hardly possible to enhance it, even if his lectures could now take permanent shape. Not that he left little in writing: on the contrary, he was a regular contributor for more than forty years to the *Journal of Philology*. There are also his Praelections, an edition by him of a single book of Aristotle's *Ethics*, a selection of texts to illustrate the history of Greek philosophy, besides encyclopaedia articles on the Sophists, Plato, Aristotle and other thinkers. But no great work of his own ever appeared. Circumstances had decided that he should always remain much too busy with endless lectures to write more. His devotion to his subject arose from many causes. There was the precedent of Hepworth Thompson whom he greatly admired. There was the fashion of the time as set by Grote and Jowett whose works were eagerly discussed and widely criticised. Then there was the responsibility of novel academic tasks. For when the University of Cambridge decided that it was time to reform the Classical

Tripos, one of the new subjects introduced was Greek philosophy, and this became Jackson's special province. By the
regulations of 1872 all the subjects prescribed were expected
from all the candidates. Classes in ancient philosophy soon
became very large. The effect of fresh changes in the Classical
Tripos in 1881 was greatly to diminish the large classes which
had for twelve years attended Jackson's lectures. But the rem-
nant continued to include the pick of the classical students. At
a later date some knowledge of ancient philosophy was made a
subject (though not a compulsory subject) of the first part of
the Classical Tripos. But widely as the regulations might differ,
were the class large or small, he always had some of the best
students, those whom he would have preferred to all others.
Plato and Aristotle every year with occasional divergence to
Plutarch or Lucretius or even Cicero provided a never-ending
series of discourses from a repertory so various that to a single
student it was always new. None of these numerous courses
was ever repeated in exactly the same form. Besides the
Republic and half a dozen other Platonic dialogues, his repertory
included the *Nicomachean Ethics*, the *Metaphysics*, the *De Anima*,
and other works of Aristotle. His course of lectures on the
history of Greek philosophy was at one time advertised as preparing for publication but though so often, almost annually,
repeated and never without revision it, too, failed to appear,
or appeared in the tantalising form of a meagre summary. It
is much to be regretted that he never executed an early plan of
publishing the fragments of the Pre-Socratics, or at any rate of
Parmenides and Empedocles. Of his most characteristic work
little has survived beyond such meagre fare as magazine articles
afford. His most permanent memorial will always be his pupils
and his pupils' writings. He lives in most of the editions of
Plato and Aristotle which Cambridge scholars have brought out
for the last forty years. He can be traced in more or less
elaborate detail in Archer-Hind, Seymer Thompson, Gaye,
Adam and others. He was above all things a Platonist. On the
much-controverted question, In what order were the dialogues
of Plato written? he had early reached a definite conclusion.
This he set forth in the longest series of his published papers
(*Plato's later theory of ideas*)[1] between 1881–6. His main contention that on various parts of his mature doctrine the *Republic*

[1] In the *Journal of Philology*.

[41]

was not Plato's final word, is now universally accepted and regarded as well nigh axiomatic. That other dialogues contain more advanced doctrine is not now seriously challenged. But there still remains the problem, How is the change from one statement of Platonic doctrine to another to be explained? Jackson's solution, from which he never varied, is clearly expressed in the articles in the *Journal of Philology* already referred to. His hopes of obtaining the support of other eminent Platonists were early frustrated. Zeller for Germans and Jowett among English Platonists duly expressed their respectful but emphatic dissent. Nor is the Platonic riddle any nearer solution to-day. The latest historian of Greek philosophy among us, Prof. Burnet, has since propounded a fresh solution which no more satisfied Jackson than Jackson's own thesis had satisfied Jowett thirty years before. Whatever be the ultimate conclusion of the controversy, the hypothesis of some such development of Platonic philosophy, as he strenuously contended for in the *Journal of Philology*, seems likely to win more and more support. But of even greater value was the detailed exposition of Plato's six later dialogues. It is hardly too much to say that his papers form the first complete presentation at all adequate to its importance which this phase of Platonism received.

Perhaps some clue to the nature of his lectures is given by the familiar title of the 'Cambridge Socrates' which in days now far distant was applied to him. On one occasion, when the lecture was upon Socrates, an undergraduate was so busily absorbed in comparing the portrait of Socrates with the lecturer himself that he listened breathlessly without taking down a single note. Of the Aristotle lectures those on the *Politics* were especially appreciated by many who found the *Metaphysics* and *De Anima* too dry. It is the more to be regretted that subsequent changes in the curriculum forced him to leave that work to others. It was a subject to which he was specially qualified to do justice. For himself however there is no doubt that the more difficult the task the greater its attraction. Moreover he had the rare faculty of inspiring the class with his own enthusiasm, his own unsparing devotion of strength and time to problems always arduous and possibly insoluble. Once when light seemed at last to dawn upon a puzzle which had for long defied his attempts, he remarked that a time would come when all such problems, like Alpine peaks, would be conquered. No one could be more generous or more judicious in passing judgment, no one more enthusiastic in appreciation of a pupil's good work.

His interest in learning was wide-spread and by no means confined to the subject which he had made his own. In various branches of inquiry he was eagerly, not to say passionately, absorbed. This was particularly the case with folk-lore or the comparative study of primitive customs. He followed with enthusiasm the investigations of McLennan, Robertson Smith, Tylor and Sir James Frazer. When lost works of Bacchylides, Herondas and Aristotle were brought from Egypt and published in 1891, he took the liveliest interest in them and contributed his quota to the mass of conjectures proposed. In the main however his own activities centred upon the old-world task of correcting faulty texts. On Clement of Alexandria he was never tired of working. Textual criticism of the *Eudemian Ethics* afforded even more congenial occupation. The care with which he pruned and purged this unexciting treatise was characteristic. When a work on some passages in the seventh book was completed, he dedicated it to Franz Susemihl, whose industry, courage and sagacity he fully appreciated. But of all the German scholars of his time he had perhaps the greatest admiration for Jakob Bernays and with other admirers regretted that Bernays left his commentary on Lucretius unfinished. In his own critical notes the influence of Cobet and Madvig is plainly to be traced. He was not often carried away by brilliant conjectures. He preferred the strictly reasoned suggestion which leans on hypothesis, cogent if not peremptory.

Nor were his conjectures confined to classical authors. He had proposed emendations of the text of Miss Austen, some of which are approved in the Clarendon Press edition of 1923, an honour not lavishly bestowed by its learned editor.

Perhaps the feelings of younger students cannot be better represented than by the following extract from the late R. K. Gaye's preface to his essay on the *Platonic Conception of Immortality* (Camb. Univ. Press 1904):

I cannot conclude without reference to what is really my greatest debt, though it can be ascribed to no written source. I am sure that all who have studied under Dr Jackson will agree with me in acknowledging the immense help they have received from his oral instruction, not only in the Lecture Room, but still more in those informal conversations in which they have attempted to play the part of Theaetetus. I could not venture to estimate the extent to which in this essay I have been consciously or unconsciously inspired by hints and suggestions which have come to me in this manner: but my indebtedness and, I hope, my gratitude are not the less because I am unable to acknowledge in detail my obligations to one who carries out so faithfully Plato's injunction to teachers—δεῖ δὲ εἰς δύναμιν μηδὲν παραλείπειν αὐτῷ, πάντα δὲ λόγον ἀφερμηνεύειν, ἵνα οὗτος τοῖς ἄλλοις μηνυτής τε ἅμα καὶ τροφεὺς γένηται[1].

HELP TO OTHER STUDENTS

IT is impossible to estimate the amount of time and labour which Jackson devoted to the task of assisting other students in their work: but it is safe to say that it took a very considerable proportion of his working hours. Some idea may be gathered from the many references to his assistance which appear in the prefaces of learned works, and the number of such works dedicated to him. An appeal of such a kind, whether on particular points, or for the laborious business of reading proofs, he generally found it impossible to refuse, and to all such appeals, when accepted, he gave his best. To give but a few instances.—A mass of correspondence was continually passing between him and Mr Archer-Hind, not only when the latter was engaged on his editions of the *Phaedo* (1883) and *Timaeus* (1886), but also for his incomparable little volume of *Translations into Greek* (1905). The last-named contains the beautiful dedication:

VETERI AMICO
HENRICO JACKSON
COLL. SS. TRIN. SOCIO
φιλοσόφῳ φιλοκάλῳ φιλοφίλῳ

and the last paragraph of the preface runs thus: 'My last and deepest debt is due to my friend Henry Jackson for his extreme kindness in reading through the proof-sheets and offering much

[1] Plato, *Laws*, 809 B.

[44]

invaluable criticism—a labour which none but a very busy man
would have found time to accomplish.'

The proofs of Adam's large work on the *Republic* passed
through his hands and received the most scrupulous attention.
The following letter is characteristic, in answer to the author's
thanks:

To JAMES ADAM

Aldourie, Bournemouth

1 *August* 1902

My dear Adam,

Very many thanks for your letter and especially for the
kind sentences at the end of it. My own feeling is that I have
done you little service if any. For you had covered the whole
ground of your commentary, and I only a small part of it.

I have often been ashamed of the rough and ready form
of my remarks: but it was easier to write in that way, and I have
always trusted you not to misunderstand curtness. My endeavour has been, at all costs, to put my ἀπορίαι into the most
distinct shape possible: but I have constantly recognised that
on further consideration I might come round to your view. That
the book will have a great and permanent value, I am convinced.
Sincere congratulations.

Yours ever,

Henry Jackson.

At about the same time he was reading the proofs of the
edition of the scholia on Aristophanes for Mr John William
White (Cambridge, Mass.) and annotating them laboriously:
though he expressed himself as greatly disappointed at their
comparative lack of interest. These are only examples of many
instances of the large assistance he was always ready to give to
friends in their special work. But his correspondence shows in
addition the frequent appeals made to him, especially perhaps
as Regius Professor of Greek, for advice on special points from
students in all quarters of the world. This subject may be illustrated by a selection of letters:

HENRY JACKSON

To H. RACKHAM, of Christ's College
23 October 1901

I gather from your letter that you want some modern reading in *Ethics*. Correct me if you used 'moral science' in the looser (Cambridge) sense.

My notion is that you should read Sidgwick's *Outlines of the History of Ethics*, and then choose for yourself authors to study. But if you will write to me again, I will consult one or other of the men here who have special experience.

I think that in ancient philosophy the *politics* and the *laws* are good choices, and that in the *laws* you might find some problem to attack. The beginning of the *politics* touches upon certain questions in regard to primitive society which I have always thought very interesting....

Many thanks for your kind sentence about our pleasant year of working together.

22 November 1891

I told Sidgwick that I had advised you to begin with his sketch of Ethics, and starting from it, to take up what interested you. He approved this advice, and said what would interest *him* would be Hobbes—Adam Smith—Hume—Kant. (I wonder at the inclusion of Adam Smith.)

He says that the moralists in the Tripos pay special attention to the English ethical writers of the present day, and he specifies besides his own *Methods of Ethics* (which should, I think, come first), Martineau's *Types of Ethical Theory*, Mill's *Utilitarianism*, Spencer's *Data of Ethics and Justice*, Green's *Prolegomena to Ethics*, and perhaps Leslie Stephen's *Science of Ethics*.

For myself I wonder that modern moralists do not pay more attention to (*a*) the history of the development of moral ideas, (*b*) the criticism of current moral ideas. The only book which, so far as I know, attempts to deal with these matters systematically is Whewell's *Elements of Morality* (the 4th edition was published in 1864). Whewell can be bought cheap second-hand. ,

I should have thought that Sidgwick would care about these things: but he seemed rather surprised at the suggestion that they were included in Ethics. If you were to take to the study of the early part of (*a*) you would get into the (to me) fascinating

[46]

study of anthropology. In a word, Sidgwick endorses my view that you should begin with his sketch of the theory of ethics, and then take (*a*) any of the authors who, as described in his sketch, interest you, (*b*) his *Methods*. He would advise you after that to take Martineau, etc. You will find Bain's cram book (*Mental and Moral Science*) useful.

To a GIRTON CLASSICAL STUDENT
12 *June* 1906

I enclose a testimonial. Please send me a line to say it has reached you. I have not made a copy of it, so please keep it for future use.

I am heartily glad that you have liked the year's work. It seems to me that Greek philosophy is a very good subject for the right people, and that the time spent on it is not wasted. The Greeks raise the great questions, and they make us think about them for ourselves. If I have been able at all to help you, I am glad: but the teacher is only a fellow student who has already faced the difficulties, both for himself and in others, so that he has some notion which are real, which are imaginary.

I have never supposed that you did not take trouble. If I may criticize and suggest, I think that you ought to have more belief in yourself; and that, when you begin to teach, you ought, in order that you may hit the mean, to cultivate a little wholesome rashness. Remember that in teaching a certain rapidity is valuable. The teacher must run some risks. I believe that you read slowly. Reading slowly, and reading quickly, are distinct arts, both of them valuable. Don't try to quicken your slow reading, but cultivate quick reading also, (1) in Greek and Latin by re-reading quickly what you have read slowly, (2) in English by skimming books. There was a time when I fell a victim to slow reading, so that I morbidly read every reference and, if I omitted any, seemed to myself to have told a lie. This disease must be defied.

Forgive me for this sermon, especially if, as may be, it is not to the point.

The *Memorabilia* is a good book to read rapidly and currently.

In reply to a pleasant letter sending him a work on Law— sent in for the Doctor's degree:

[47]

HENRY JACKSON

14 *December* 1902

I am very grateful to you for sending me your dissertation. I congratulate you on your new dignity. As you have guessed, I know nothing of your subject; and though I have long intended to learn a little Dutch, I shall not begin upon a learned law book. So I propose to try to find some legal friend to whom your treatise will be interesting, and to give it to him. My experience is that making out things is always interesting, but that writing down in book form what one has discovered is *hateful*. I am not easily satisfied: so I write, and rewrite, and rewrite again, until what really is new seems to me to be quite old and dull. Nevertheless I have never repented that I chose the student's life, and I often regret that in our times the student has to do so much practical work. Do not misunderstand me. Affairs of a practical sort are interesting to me: but they interfere too much with my proper work as a student.

I have no doubt that you will find the practice of law very interesting: and I sincerely wish you success in it.

From MR C. C. CLARK
of Yale and Johns Hopkins—visiting European Universities
Oxford, 18 *October* 1902

Dear Dr Jackson

It gives me great pleasure to send you the quotation from Goethe. Let me copy here one other sentence from *Wilhelm Meister*. 'It is inconceivable how much a man of true culture can accomplish for himself and others, if, without attempting to rule, he can be the guardian over many.' Surely it will not be immodest to say I have taken this thought for my ideal. And as I work to make it real you will stand before me, encouraging and stimulating. Again I thank you for what you have given me this week; I shall pass from your mind and to you the events of the week will be

'...Little nameless, unremembered acts
Of kindness and of love.'

To me they form one of the most important periods of my life.

Sincerely yours,
C. C. Clark.

HELP TO OTHER STUDENTS

To MR C. C. CLARK
Trinity College, Cambridge
20 *October* 1902

Best thanks for your letter and for the quotation. It is very kind of you to think that you have got some help towards your work in the future by observing the ways of one who has been teaching for nearly forty years. It is not often that University men think about such things: so your interest has interested and encouraged me.

I have sometimes thought of trying to formulate my notions about Academic teaching. But I don't believe in minute rules and stereotyped devices: and general principles—such as 'don't be the slave of any one method,' 'try to be various,' 'always criticize yourself,' 'always prepare your lectures, that you may be fresh and definite, and then you can afford to digress without preparation now and then'—don't carry a man very far. I enclose a letter of introduction to Mr Percy Matheson, one of the 'tutors' of New College. [N.B. at Cambridge only those who are also administrators are called 'tutors': at Oxford nearly all teachers are so called.] I should like some time to hear of your doings, if you can afford the time to tell me of them.

From MR G. A. HIGHT *to the Editor*
2 Bardwell Road, Oxford
22 *March* 1924

Hicks tells me that you are preparing a memoir of the late Henry Jackson, and would like to see the letters which he wrote to me between the years 1901 and 1918[1]. I have about fourteen of them. They are mostly about questions of Greek philosophy, in reply to some of my difficulties which I had submitted to him. The only interest which they could have for the general reader would be for the light which they throw upon the extraordinary humility and courtesy and helpfulness of the writer. To appreciate them you must know that I came to him as a complete stranger in 1901, aged 50, but as altogether a beginner in Greek philosophy, and you will see with what patience and at what pains he set himself to explain my little difficulties. I owe much to him; indeed, without his help and encouragement I could scarcely have had the perseverance to go on with these studies.

[1] See below, pp. 131 f., 155 ff., 163, 205.

P

[49]

4

HENRY JACKSON

PROFESSOR D'ARCY W. THOMPSON

THE following impression of Henry Jackson has been contributed by Prof. D'Arcy Wentworth Thompson:

It was only some seven and twenty years ago, I find, that Henry Jackson wrote me the first of many letters; I thought it had been longer ago. His friendship was so valuable, his letters so welcome to me, I had wellnigh forgotten that before ever they began I had passed the middle of the way. We men of the Science Tripos spent years in Trinity never hearing a word from Jackson of the older wisdom, never coming under his great influence at all; and though what we got from Michael Foster, and for all too short a while from Balfour[1], was a great thing, yet we might have been all the better naturalists had we heard of Aristotle from Jackson and of Lucretius from Munro.

For the most part I put Jackson's letters carefully away; sometimes I did not. Some of those which are lost I still remember and regret; but I have more than a hundred now before me. It is no easy task to write of them, for they are mostly about my own affairs and to talk of them is to talk of myself; but I know that this book will be little used by strangers, and will be read as it should be by old friends. A few letters of his or a few extracts from them may at least help, with other memories, to show how constant was his friendship, how infinite his kindness towards a younger man; how gentle and charitable was his criticism, how boundless his desire to help, even after age, sickness and adversity had come upon him. Here, without more ado, are some of my letters.

Though, as I say, I have lost some of Jackson's earlier letters, I still have the first he ever wrote me. In 1898 I spent a day or two in Trinity, for the very first time (I think) since I had left College; and Jackson bade me to his rooms. On coming home I sent him a little paper I had written, in which I sought (much as Svoronos, the Greek numismatist, was doing) to show an astronomic meaning in the symbolism of certain Greek coins—a theory, by the way, which I hold to still. I got the following reply:

[1] Francis Balfour.

FROM D'ARCY THOMPSON

5 *September* 1898

My dear Thompson,

I am very grateful to you for sending me your paper 'On Bird and Beast in Ancient Symbolism.' I have read it with great interest, and shall very soon read it again side by side with what you have written on the same subject in your *Glossary of Greek Birds*. Most certainly you seem to me to make out a *prima facie* case. I wish that I knew enough of numismatics to test it. Two questions occur to me from my standpoint of ignorance: (1) Can you explain in any case or cases why the zodiacal reference is preferred? (2) Are you wise in rejecting, absolutely, Ridgeway's explanation of certain symbols?

I add a word or two of explanation. If you were to examine the seals used by people in England in the present century, you would find that the symbols had very various origins. Many people have heraldic devices: Rd. Owen had a representation of a vertebra, I think, the exact meaning of which I forget: I found among my father's seals a head of Socrates, and use it because I respect that G.O.M.: and so on. Similarly I am prepared to allow that the devices on Greek coins may be explained, some on Ridgeway's system, some on yours, others on others. But I think that, on the principle which leads you to conjecture that the gate at Mycenae is 'in some manner oriented to the midsummer sun,' you should show that there is some reason why the people of a particular place put upon their coins a particular astronomical fact. You don't mean, do you, that what they meant was, 'See, we know this fact of astronomy'?

But I am writing without knowing the whole of your case. I will look up the rest of it as soon as I return to Cambridge.

It was a real pleasure to me to make your acquaintance the other day. I have long wanted to meet you: for in a dim way I knew that you were prepared to join hands with people who are not zoologists.

With best thanks, I am, Yours very truly,

Henry Jackson.

About that time I was working in odd moments at Aristotle's *Historia Animalium*, and I began to write often to Jackson, sending him my suggested emendations on the admittedly faulty text. Some of my conjectures may have been better than others, some were certainly worse; but Jackson took them all seriously, and never failed to reply helpfully. For instance, Aristotle speaks of the female Tunny as possessing a fin (πτερύγιον) which the male lacks—a statement not confirmed by natural history; I suggested that we should read ταρίχιον, that is to say, some sort of pickle, to wit, the roe or 'caviar' of the fish. To this Jackson replied:

29 October 1899

...Here are certain doubts which on reflection trouble me about your emendation: (*a*) it is odd that the physical characteristics of the female of a species (roe) should be described by a term of cookery (pickle) which unquestionably applies to more than the said physical characteristics; (*b*) why should A. mention, as a specialty of the female tunny, what must, I presume, be true of other female kinds? Can you dispose of these difficulties? They seem to me rather serious.

A month later he came round, more or less, to my opinion:

28 November 1899

...Your last letter was very much to the point. I have mislaid the reference, so that I have to trust to my memory; but my difficulty was (I think) that A. (according to you) writes as though roe existed only in this particular fish. If that of this fish only was put to practical use, my objection (so far as I remember) falls to the ground. I had foreseen your answer....

Another of my emendations, which Jackson commends as 'very ingenious' but with the important reservation 'as the critics say,' I have clean forgotten. A third was an obviously unsuccessful attempt to emend a difficult passage in the Ninth Book, where Aristotle describes the bees making one kind of cell at a time, ἐφεξῆς ἓν εἶδος εἰργασμένον δι᾿ ἀντλίας—as the text has it. To this Jackson replied in the letter of which the last extract is part:

I am not at present prepared to accept your emendation, for several reasons: (*a*) ἀντλία is the bottom of the hold, where the bilge was, not the top where the rowing benches were fixed; (*b*) for ἐρεσσόμενοι, you must write ἐρέττοντες; (*c*) διά seems to me the wrong preposition; (*d*) you have to reconstruct on a large scale. On the other hand, I am inclined to suggest that δι' ἀνταίας (sc. ὁδοῦ) might conceivably mean 'straight forward,' i.e. without interruption.

Jackson's suggestion of δι' ἀνταίας is all but identical with Piccolos's emendation διανταίως: but the adverbial form does not occur elsewhere, and Jackson's seems to me the better of the two. About the same time there came from him the following postcard, which I give for the sake of its last sentence:

I was reading yesterday *Hist. Anim.* III. 7. 57, with your proposal to read ἄνω δὲ τῆς ῥάχεως ᾗ περαίνει: but I have not got A[ubert] and W[immer] here, and until I can look again at their treatment of the difficulty, I had better keep my solution to myself. I don't see how the πλευραί can be said to be ἄνω τῆς ῥάχεως.

Some day I should like to preach to you or to some one about the theory of emendation.

For the next four or five years I can find no letters, though I know that I had many. Here is one acknowledging (I suppose) a copy of my *Glossary of Greek Birds*, which I had not sent him when it appeared, nearly ten years before:

27 *September* 1904

I am very grateful to you for your very kind letter and for the book which accompanied it. I am sure that, to use a phrase of Dew Smith's, I shall *read in it*, though, probably, I shall not read it consecutively. It comes to me very opportunely: for an American friend of mine is editing the scholia of the *Birds* of Aristophanes, and he sends me the proofs. I am sorry to say that the scholiasts on Aristophanes appear to me to be incompetent asses.

Once upon a time I came into possession of two or three little Tanagra figures, little votive figurines to hang upon the vines for luck; and one of these I gave to Jackson, asking him to let it lie upon his mantelpiece—on that untidy mantelpiece of his, among the other odds and ends. Jackson was delighted with it, and wrote me his thanks twice over, in two characteristic letters:

HENRY JACKSON

24 February 1907

On Friday I received from you a figurine, presumably Tanagraean. It is perfectly beautiful, and might have been designed to disprove Verrall's audacious statement, that the Greeks knew nothing of mythological beings having wings. You do not say what its destination is to be. Are you sending it to one of the Museums? If so, to which?

Please tell me what you know about it—what it is. It is delightfully quaint, graceful, and artistic.

11 March 1907

I ought long before this to have written my grateful thanks for the Tanagraean. I have looked at it again and again, as a proof of Greek genius. From this point of view it is more remarkable than the Venus of the Louvre. When you look at the Venus, you think of the genius of the man: when you look at this humorous, graceful, little work, you think of the race. I am sincerely grateful, and I am only sorry that I dare not leave it on my mantelpiece, at the mercy of careless bedmakers.

In 1908 I happened to come up for ballot at a certain club, Jackson being my seconder. As the time approached he wrote me letter after letter, and busied himself about the matter as though the fate of worlds depended on it; it was perhaps not wholly without cause, for I lived remote and my friends were none too many. On the day of election he actually came up to town from Cambridge, on purpose to attend the ballot and win me votes from his friends. He wrote next day:

Everything went well. There were good names on your card: and I found a good many people who knew of you, and some who knew of your father. The result,..., was thoroughly satisfactory: for there are *always* 3 or 4 black balls.

I tried to send you a wire. But your votes were not counted till 6.15: at 6.15 I dined: at 6.30 I left the club: and when there was delay at the telegraph office, I was obliged to hurry to catch my train at 6.55. So I posted a card to you on my arrival.

I was able to give some help to my friend Sir Henry Trotter's candidate..., and I think that Trotter gave some help to you. I say this in case you should chance to meet him.

One of these letters contained a curious *obiter dictum* on

[54]

Thomas Taylor, the Platonist, of whom I had happened to speak in a letter of mine:

Thomas Taylor was a man of huge industry and considerable learning. You will find that he sometimes makes very acute remarks: but you must never take him on trust. He must have been a real enthusiast, and he found an enthusiastic patron who financed his publications. I think that he must have been a little crazy: but his reading was really wide.

It is a fairer and more charitable judgment than Taylor has often received.

In 1910 my translation of Aristotle's *Historia Animalium* appeared, and I sent a copy to Jackson to whom I had dedicated the book[1]. He was hugely delighted, soon afterwards, when I told him that some of my friends found difficulty in construing the said dedication. Here is his letter to me:

21 October 1910

I thank you with all my heart for your book and for the dedication. I think you know that I always rejoice when the new learning does not despise the old. The old is antiquarian, but it is a part of the new, and my notion is that we should all of us work at a bit of the field, and leave the combination to take care of itself. I rejoice to think that there are a few naturalists who do not despise the old evidence. You are one: Thiselton Dyer is another. I shall read your book with great interest, though I have not the knowledge which would qualify me to appreciate. I am heartily glad that they have relaxed their rules about commentary.

Some months afterwards he wrote:

I know that you have been for years at work upon these things, and I heartily approve. The man who takes his subject seriously can always manage the linguistics: and the fact that Aristotle is writing informally makes Aristotelian linguistics as such easy.

Here is one of Jackson's own Aristotelian emendations. The rest of the letter refers to a discussion of certain passages in Greek which deal with the question of 'maternal impressions,' or the power of influencing the unborn child through the mind of the mother.

[1] See pp. 117 ff.

[55]

HENRY JACKSON

I ought long before this to have thanked you for your excellent answer to Heape's question. It seems to me completely to cover the ground. I am ashamed of my ignorance of the reference to Empedocles: but the fact is that the extant fragments of the poems have interested me so much that I have not given proper attention to traditions of doctrine.

By the way, a paper of Arthur Platt's led me to look at hist. anim. iv. 8, 533^b 15–20. Read, for ἐκ τοσούτου τόπου, ἐκτὸς τοῦ τόπου, 'outside that space.' In other words, strike out the ου which I have underlined.

ὅπως must mean 'in order that': it cannot mean 'so that'; also note that τοῦ τόπου refers to the preceding clause. This seems to me a certainty: but Arthur Platt demurs: why, I do not understand.

The next letter is one which, were it not so interesting, modesty would bid me withhold:

I do not know whether I have ever thanked you for your Herbert Spencer Lecture. If I have not done so, I have been very ungrateful. But, in any case, I want to tell you that I have today read it again. It seems to me an excellent piece of work, and it is admirable from the literary point of view. I have long wanted such a statement as this about Aristotle's zoological observations. Also, I think your pronouncement about Herbert Spencer skilful and judicious.

From my point of view, Aristotle, with his modified Platonism, came to the conclusion that there are natural kinds or *infimae species* of animals and vegetables, clearly marked off from one another; and that what we can know of them is their respective resemblances and differences. Hence he regarded classificatory Zoology and Botany as sciences in the full sense of the term, whilst he considered Mineralogy inexact for want of natural fixities to determine the grouping. All this he got from Plato, who however was theorist only. I imagine that Speusippus also, in his '῞Ομοια,' was working on similar lines. Forgive me for joining on what you say about the zoology to my own theory of the philosophical development.

By the way, Bywater and I are determined to bring out the

FROM D'ARCY THOMPSON

Journal of Philology twice a year, at regular intervals, and we want to widen the scope of our articles. Possibly you may have papers or notes for us on zoological matters. We are hoping for articles on the botany of the ancients from Thiselton Dyer. Possibly you may have something for our October number.

With regard to your p. 30, the difference between Plato and Aristotle is not so great as at first sight appears. Aristotle resolves the particular member of a natural kind into (1) *potentiality* (δύναμις) and (2) a specific *form* (εἶδος, μορφή) received proximately from a previous member of the same species, (3) in accordance with *nature's design*. Plato resolves the particular member of the natural kind into (1) *space* (χώρα), and (2) the *reflexion*, of (3) a *transcendental form* (εἶδος, ἰδέα), which εἶδος or ἰδέα transmits the reflexion directly. Note the correspondence. The difference is that Plato declines to call anything *real* which is in time and space, whilst Aristotle declines to call anything *actual* which is not in time and space. They both regard natural kinds as the proper study of the man of science: but Plato contemplates the field from the point of view of eternal reality, Aristotle from that of temporal actuality. Forgive me!

Lecturing one day to children at the Royal Institution, I happened to tell them some story of beasts or fishes out of Aristotle's *Natural History*; and an old clergyman, doubtless an Oxonian, who had sat attentively on a front bench, asked me afterwards whether that were 'the same Aristotle who wrote the *Ethics*'! I thought the story worth passing on to Jackson, who replied on a postcard, as follows:

20 January 1919

Thanks for your story of the old Oxonian, bred on the *Ethics* and knowing no more of the G.O.M. But they gained greatly by their study of the *Ethics*. It is an aperient book, if you will excuse the epithet. When I was an undergraduate, I read only half of it: but it made me wonder whether I ought to have gone to Oxford to be taught it.

One Sunday night in 1919, Jackson talked to us in his rooms about the passage in the *Eudemian Ethics* where Aristotle speaks of Blind Man's Buff, or 'Hoodman Blind' as Jackson preferred to call it: 'If a man were to kill the "hoodman blind" that he might not catch him, it would be absurd to say that he did it under compulsion: to make compulsion, there must be the threat of some greater evil.'

Not, alas, before I had left the room, but in the watches of the night, it occurred to me that a passage in the *republic* contained a not less cogent reference to the game. It is an essential part of the game, as children know and as Phrynichus and Pollux tell us, that the blindfold player, on catching his victim, must say whom he has caught. Now Plato tells us that the common herd, like Hoodman Blind, gropes blindly after the course of things ($\psi\eta\lambda\alpha\phi\hat{\omega}\nu\tau\epsilon\varsigma$ οἱ πολλοὶ ὥσπερ ἐν σκότει), and when they find, or think they have found them, give them the wrong names (ἀλλοτρίῳ ὀνόματι προσχρώμενοι). I think, I still think, that the allusion to the game is obvious, but Jackson was not to be convinced; his criticism was a trifle less gentle than it was wont to be:

15 *January* 1919

I am heartily glad that you liked your time here. This morning your second letter arrived, with its enclosure. It raises several points.

(1) 'Susemihl is all wrong in regard to this passage,' i.e. that in the *Phaedo*. Where does S. say anything about it? Please do not overlook this question.

(2) For 25^a 14, read 1225^a 14. You have taken a contracted reference from S.'s index.

(3) Your reference to the Cyclops and Jacob seems to me quite irrelevant: for they were really blind and were not playing at being so.

(4) I cannot feel *sure* that in the *Phaedo* Plato definitely thinks of the game. If there had been no such game, the passage would still have been quite natural and intelligible: as in Jacob's case.

(5) Can you run down the natural χαλκῆ μυῖα? I have not looked for it. I am very grateful to you for your reference to this name for the game.

Jackson had a curious regard for that graceless scamp Casanova (as he also had for Jean Jacques Rousseau). Many another

[58]

scholar has had the same; I remember, for one, how Davis, the editor of the *Eumenides*, knew him by heart, and I rather think that Casanova was the only modern whom that learned but eccentric Irish scholar had any real liking for. The rogue's shameless self-revelation of his most scandalous life has its inscrutable fascination. Jackson was fond of talking of Casanova, and mentioned him in his letters now and then. Here is an example:

26 March 1918

This is a supplement to our talk the other night. If you have not read the last volume of Casanova, you have missed the finale of (perhaps) the most amazing of his amazing episodes.

For Lucrezia and her sister Angela, see vol. i, ch. ix. For Lucrezia and *their* (his and her) daughter Leonilda, see vol. v, ch. x. For Leonilda and her maid, see vol. viii, ch. v. For *their* (his and her) son, see vol. viii, ch. viii. It is the most shameless thing in literature.

4 July 1918

The chapter to which I recommend your attention is in book viii, ch. 5, 'Mes amours avec Calliméne — —, mon heureux voyage a Salerne, mon retour a Naples, mon départ de cette ville et mon arrivée a Rome.' 'Lucrezia et Leonilde' ought to be added. Then come three chapters, and a lacuna of two.

At the Athenaeum in a dark corner of one of the libraries, in a sort of gallery, there is a German book about the people mentioned by Casanova. Probably it is mentioned in the Catalogue under *Casanova*.

My other source for *Barry Lyndon* is Foote's book about Lady Strathmore.

I have never read Bérard: but I once met him, and found him very interesting. He is an amateur scholar, but that sort of man is to me delightful.

Jackson's interest in *Edwin Drood* is well known. I had ventured on a suggestion (doubtful at the best) that Datchery was no other than Mr Grewgious. Here is what Jackson said:

3 April 1919

I have owed you letters for long enough. I began to be in arrears early in the term in respect of your letters to the *Literary Supplement*, etc., and then there was a pleasant birthday letter.

But the man of 80 is apt to be behindhand with his correspondence, and thanks to scholarship examination and heavy family
business I am very badly in arrears.

But *Edwin Drood* will not be gainsaid. There is one argument which seems to me to dispose at once of Bazzard, Grewgious and Helena. It was not till the Staple Inn conference, the
morning after Rosa's arrival in town, that the allies knew of
the proposed persecution or could plan counter-operations. But
Datchery is already at work counter-operating at Cloisterham.
Therefore he is not any one of the Staple Inn allies.

Recognizing this, I had propounded the hypothesis that
Dickens had written the Datchery chapter out of its order: but
the proofs down to the end of the fifth number show that
Dickens had *elaborately* corrected them, and had *not* altered the
order. *Therefore* I abandon Datchery = Helena, and I cannot
accept Datchery = Grewgious.

Look again at my chapters on this part of the subject.

7 *April* 1919

Many thanks for your careful letter. I fear that discussion
cannot give any decisive result: because, in dealing with fiction,
we cannot know where exactitude ends and vagueness or error
begins.

It is of course conceivable that Grewgious is already counter-
plotting and yet does not confess it to his allies.

Also I acknowledge that the words 'at about this time' are
vague. But I find it difficult either to *identify* the humour of
Grewgious with that of Datchery, or to imagine Grewgious
playing Datchery's *part*.

And then there comes the subjectivity of the author and the
subjectivities of the interpreters.

The elaborate correction of the proofs down to the end of
Part V makes me think that the appearance of Datchery in
ch. xviii is not an oversight or an accident. But I have not printed
what I have to say on this subject.

I am sorry to hear that you have been in the wars in more
ways than one. You have however more than twenty years the
advantage of me: so I congratulate you and wish you good
things. Try to keep at a distance my various disabilities.

The next and last letter was, I believe, the last he wrote me.
I had told him of a little discovery I had hit upon, that the

FROM D'ARCY THOMPSON

Blackboard was the invention of Prof. Pillans of Edinburgh, and was first used by him when he was a master in the Edinburgh High School, just about a hundred years ago.

(Dictated; no date)

Best thanks for your letter. What you write always interests me, even if I have to cut my answers short.

I am still out of sorts and have not been able to do justice to 'Circus.' I am sorry that I have had to neglect it.

I shall like to hear about the Blackboard. The Greeks used a *white* board, but for the moment I forget what my proof is—probably you will remember.

I am very sorry to hear of the Influenza. I am myself suffering from stomach troubles, which make of me a very worm, and incapacitate me for work.

I must look up D'Artagnan when I can raise the energy, but Dumas and accuracy do not live in the same world.

I wish that instead of distributing honours and hurrying up the Armistice they had attended to business. As it is, we seem to do nothing except make ourselves acquainted with new muddles, and I myself do not even achieve this humble end.

I hope to write again soon.

So I have opened and may close my little packet of Henry Jackson's letters, of which I have omitted many and chosen but a few. I can hardly hope that they may show to others all that they have meant to me, during the long years when they kept me in touch with a great place and with its greatest man. They may at least help to confirm the wonderful thing a brother-don of Trinity has said of Jackson, that 'he had that amazing simplicity and generosity, the authentic mark of a truly great man, which gives credit to others for the same capacity and knowledge as himself.'

I know that these letters of mine are but a tiny part of the vast correspondence which Jackson maintained, always with the same patience and generosity; and that privileges such as he extended to me were given to innumerable friends, among wellnigh all sorts and conditions of men. I do not know whether Arthur Platt's correspondence with Jackson is to see the light, but I hope it will; it might be a memorial, not only of Jackson, but of the old friend and most kindly scholar whom untimely fate has just taken from us. I know well, and Jackson told me so himself, that of all the men of my generation Arthur Platt had the warmest place of all in the great heart of our Master and Friend.   D'A. W. T.

ALFRED OLLIVANT

In March 1903 Mr John Murray wrote to Jackson to enlist his interest in Mr Alfred Ollivant, for whom he had just published the novel with the title *Danny*. Jackson at once replied and began a correspondence with Mr Ollivant extending over some six or seven years. The following letter from Mr Ollivant to Col. H. C. Jackson explains the circumstances, and a few of Jackson's letters are added:

From MR ALFRED OLLIVANT *to* COL. JACKSON
15 *April* 1922

. . . . .

My connection with your father arose thus. John Murray began to publish for me about 1903. I was at the time feeling the lack of a University education and wanting guidance in my reading. John Murray put me on to Henry Jackson and G. W. Prothero. Both these men showed themselves extraordinarily kind to an unknown young man. And the advice they gave me was characteristically different. G. W. P. drew out for me a syllabus which your father told me was practically the same as that suggested to undergraduates reading for the final History school at Cambridge. Your father was all for desultory reading on large and general lines. His was the advice I took. And for some years he wrote to me regularly. His kindness was quite extraordinary. I was an invalid at the time; and once when I was in London for an operation that busy man found time to come and see me; that was the only time we ever met. And I remember now the straight-from-the-shoulder shake of the hand and the way he came forward to my bed the palm of his hand and fingers flat and extended as though he meant to get as good a hold and grasp as much of you as he could. It was the rugged integrity of his personality that impressed me most. I remember he asked me then and later to go and stay with him at Trinity. This I

ALFRED OLLIVANT

was never able to do—to my chagrin; as I had heard that in
his rooms there was to be heard about the best conversation
of the time. For some years he wrote to me regularly, then the
correspondence gradually dropped—my failure, not his.

The last time I heard was in 1917 after a lapse of several years
when he wrote me a kind note about *The Brown Mare*.

His general advice to me in the matter of reading was to feed
my *imagination* and not worry about *knowledge*: Macaulay,
Carlyle, Froude among the historians: these were the men he
wanted me to go for. There was never a less donnish don (see
his remarks on Marcus Aurelius!)—hence his appeal to me.
And I remember my delight to find that he delighted in the
books of that day that were appealing to the plain man—Henry
Seton Merriman, A. E. W. Mason, etc.

To A. OLLIVANT
22 *March* 1903

Having now come home, I write my promised letter.

In effect, Murray asks me to give you advice. Now in general
I shrink from such a thing, and it is obvious that in this instance
I am wholly disqualified. So you must let me say what I
suppose the situation to be. If my conjecture is at all near the
mark, what I suggest may possibly be worth considering as
suggestion, you must not regard it as *advice*. If my conjecture
is beside the mark, please say so.

Danny is in my book box, which has not yet arrived. I
have as yet read very little of it: but I have seen enough to
realize that you can write, and that you can make fiction. My
supposition is that, desiring to exercise your gift of story
telling, you feel that, in consequence of your long illness, you
have not seen, read, and done, enough to have the material for
further imaginative production, and that you are afraid of
getting into a way of evolving every thing out of your inner
consciousness. I conjecture also that you have not had other
employments for your day, and that, in consequence, you have
spent upon imaginative production a great deal of your time
and your thought. Consequently you think—at least, so I
suppose—that you ought to study men and things, in order
that your imagination may have material to work upon, and you
do not see how best to do this.

Is this at all near the mark? If it is, (1) You must not expect
to spend *all* your time in literary production. Macaulay wrote

[63]

two pages a day. Trollope—who worked like a machine—
usually wrote for exactly three hours a day. John Stuart Mill
thought that his hours at the India Office left him all the time
which he could profitably spend in philosophical writing. The
old scholars filled up their days with mechanical work, such as
index-making.

(2) As you gain in health, you will be able to see more of men
and things. Meanwhile, I suspect that it would be a gain to you
to have, in addition to continuous fiction, literary work of a less
severe order. Have you ever thought of doing—simultaneously
with continuous fiction—shorter stories, literary criticisms, miscellaneous articles? Such things are mischievous, if they prevent
a man who has other business to do, from attempting something more solid: but I can conceive that a man who gives his
whole time to literature gains by having such things in hand by
the side of a larger work. I think that they would be a relief, and
that they would help him to store up material for larger works.

Now that I have written this, I begin to wonder whether
you will think it trite or futile, whether perhaps I may have
completely mistaken the situation. If so, you will forgive me,
I am sure.

I may add, that I read a good many novels, and regard writers
of fiction as public benefactors.

Please write, and please write soon: for I shall be anxious
until I hear from you.

7 January 1905

A few nights ago I made up my mind to write to you: but my
correspondence has been heavy. So before I had time to write
your letter of Jan. 1st reached me. There were certain old
friends to be written to, and I am very busy with an agitation
for the abolition of the tyranny of Greek in universities and
schools. I am sure that for some men Greek is an excellent
instrument of education; but I am equally sure that for others
it is a very bad one. So I am eager to abolish our existing regulation, which requires Greek from all except natives of Asia.
The question has come up again. If we are beaten this time,
I can hardly hope to live to see the reform carried. So I am doing
all I can to forward the movement.

I am grieved to hear that you have had 'a troublous time.'
But let me congratulate you on your reading. It seems to me

exactly right; and I shall think all the better of it, if you have chosen for yourself, and have not acted under regular guidance. Marcus Aurelius was a horrid prig, but his priggishness is a warning, and his earnestness does us good. Browne, Browning, Lamb, and even Pater, are good for the literary man. Anatole France knows at any rate how to write. Raleigh is one of the most attractive of men. I can quite understand that he may draw you to Oxford.

Now about the devices for helping the memory. I have never learnt any of them: but, within due limits, I believe in them. I have no doubt that one of the systems would make it easier for us to remember isolated facts: but I don't believe that any method would produce much effect upon the capacity of remembering. I have myself a bad memory for words: I cannot learn by heart. Also I forget the details of ordinary life very easily. On the other hand I generally know where to find facts which I want, and, to speak the truth, I don't value feats of memory very much except when they represent an intimate knowledge of a subject. But I certainly think that it is worth while to assist the memory, and I have often regretted that I never had a course of training.

I don't believe that your Rugby friend won his successes in virtue of the mnemonic training of which you speak—but plainly he meant to get on, and got on accordingly. Who was he?

I have never for one moment set down memory-training as quackery. I believe in it profoundly, within limits; and I have no doubt that the habit of fixing things artificially would have a certain good general effect upon the memory.

A brother of mine told me that by one of the methods he always remembered the number of a cab, the number of his room at a hotel, and things of that sort, which I always forget immediately.

What suggests quackery is that the teachers bind their pupils not to teach others. I can hardly blame them for thus protecting themselves, so this does not prejudice me.

I wrote thus far last night. I began again to-night (8 January).

I cannot remember whether Anatole France's *Le crime* is a pamphlet which I read a year ago, but I think that it must be. It was certainly very good. He is capable of great things: but sometimes I fancy that he thinks it sufficient to turn out beautiful French, whether he has anything to say or not. Have you read any Rostand? *Cyrano de Bergerac* seems to me an excellent play, and his *Discours de Réception* at the Academy is marvellous prose.

You say that you have 'written somewhat.' I have no wish to be troublesome, but I should like to know what you have been writing. Anyhow I am glad that the troubles of these last months have not prevented you from using the pen.

14 January 1905

Best thanks for your letter. You say that you have been addressing me wrongly. How so? I wonder. I believe that the quite correct address is

Henry Jackson, Litt.D.

But no one ever addressed me so. At one time certain friends of mine used to omit *all* superfluities, and I was quite content.

We shall win about Greek sooner or later: but I don't feel so confident that I shall live to take part in the shouting either about this or about women's degrees.

I quite understand what you say about the overwhelming absorption of work. I expect that you ought to refrain absolutely from writing at night. I wonder whether you are living alone or with friends, and how you spend your evening, whether you play whist or bridge.

By all means send me anything you like: but I must warn you that I return to College on Monday, and that I am looking forward to a horribly busy term, so you must not be shocked, if I don't immediately answer. My lectures will be heavy: the Greek question will take time: I am concerned in the business of our Free Trade Association: I shall be to the front at a very controversial College meeting: and besides all this business I have several things that I want to get written out. My experience is that thinking about things is delightful, but that writing out the results *for the printer* is the very devil. That is the real mischief of the University education: we become fastidious of expression. But I must not get upon the subject of methods of literary work, which is, as perhaps I have told you, a hobby of mine.

When you next write, tell me how you are getting on physically.

13 August 1907

I am heartily glad that you have read and liked the life of H. S.[1]

[1] Henry Sidgwick.

[66]

I don't think that it was his classical education which limited him. It was of the essence of his *thinking* that it should spend itself in the elaboration of details, and of his *acting* that it should be determined by minor considerations, sometimes this way, sometimes that.

The phrase commonly used of him that 'he sat on the fence,' always seemed to me wrong. On the contrary, he was sometimes on one side of it, sometimes on the other. And for the time being, he was quite cocksure. He often said, 'I have changed my mind': 'I have passed through that phase.'

I agree that fundamentals cannot be *proved*. On the other hand, I don't like 'the evidence of the *heart*': for that suggests that the wish for proof can be regarded as proof. Rather I would say that I cannot make a theory of the finite, imperfect, universe, without postulating a mind, not limited, as ours is, by dependence on a body. As for detailed statements about God, I regard them as aids to the religious imagination—stop-gaps to fill lacunae in our knowledge. 'Now to insist upon it that everything is precisely as I have described, is unworthy of a man of sense: that however this or something like this is true of our souls and their dwellingplaces, seeing that it is evident that the soul is a thing immortal—this does seem to me to be worthy of one, and that it is worth while for him to run any risk in this belief: for noble is the hazard, and it is well to encourage oneself by such incantations, for so one may call them, as these, for which reason in fact I have been ever so long spinning out my fable.' So E. M. Cope translates Plato's *Phaedo*, p. 3, at the beginning. Plato's 'fable' or 'myth' is exactly 'faith': a working hypothesis, which makes it possible to colligate facts, but which is always provisional, subject to revision.

H. S. changed his mind so often and so much about these things that the book may be thought to imply more definiteness of position than there really was. His very last words to me on the day before the operation indicated a belief in prayer.

There is no doubt of one thing, that H. S. found an inordinate pleasure in exact statement. For example, he had once stoutly resisted a certain policy, and when he was beaten, asked to be allowed to formulate his opponent's circular. I wonder what else you have been reading, and what you have been writing.

HENRY JACKSON

ON religious questions Jackson was habitually reticent. I doubt if he ever opened such questions after he had attained to positive convictions, unless it was within his family circle. But on the other hand it is clear from the following letters, especially those addressed to two old friends, that he was very ready to declare his position when the subject was opened by others. I suspect that this case was much more frequent than the material put into my hands would suggest; and that there were not a few young men who sought and received advice from him on their most intimate difficulties. For a great part of his life he received the Communion in the College Chapel, and in the last years, when his infirmities prevented him from attending Chapel, in his own rooms. But it is best to let him speak for himself.

To W. *and* E. JACKSON *on their* CONFIRMATION
Trinity College, Cambridge
12 *February* 1893

My dear Twins,

I write a few lines to you which you will receive, I hope, before Thursday. I am thinking of you a great deal, and I want to say to you very earnestly—may God bless you now when you are to be confirmed. Try always to do what is right, and ask God to help you in trying. Do this and God will help you, and life with all its troubles will teach you to trust in Him more and more.

It is no new thing for you to know our Saviour's love for you, but you will, I am sure, realize it the more when you take upon yourselves the promises made for you by others, and when you go to the Altar at the Holy Communion.

May God help and keep you always, my dear little women.

Your loving

Father.

To A FRIEND
16 *November* 1902

You say that 'this summer I had somewhat of an upset in theology' but you do not explain. I too have scruples about writing about these things, for I think that everyone must think

[68]

for himself. But it seems to me that these difficulties arise because men, naturally, seek for definite assurance: and that as definite assurance is not obtainable, they must learn not to expect it. Of one thing I am sure, that God is good, and I don't ask for assurance which is not given.

I am ashamed to think that I have never thanked you for your letter of August 3 on serious questions interesting to anyone who thinks. You must not suppose that my silence meant indifference. On the contrary, I was sincerely grateful to you for telling me something of your phases of faith. With much of what you say I heartily agree. There is very much in popular theology which I cannot for a moment accept; and I recognize that if, as I believe, there is a God, He has not intended us to know much about Him. But the fact is that I cannot conceive a Universe without a God: and it seems to me that men may fairly use such imagery as enables them to think of Him. So it does not trouble me much that David's way of imagining God is not my way. I am quite sure that, if there is a God, He is good. Indeed by God I mean good. I regard Christianity as an attempt to express the unknown principle of good; and as such I thankfully accept it. I am therefore in my way a Christian, glad to believe in a good God and to see in Christianity the expression of this belief. Popular talk about Hell and the Devil seems to me wholly unchristian. I am ashamed of sending this shabby answer to your full and excellent letter: but I am very busy just now, and must not try to write at length. Perhaps what I have written will indicate to you, who have read so much about these things, the way in which, after several years of complete agnosticism, I came again to see in Christianity a *belief* which filled a gap in my philosophy of life.

...It was good of you to write to me at length about matters theological. I do not think that you and I differ very much in our statement of facts. In a sense we are both *agnostics*: but it seems to me you go a little beyond pure agnosticism, and say, to use the Oxford verse, 'What *I* know not, is not knowledge.' On the other hand, there is after all so much in this world that is good, that I cannot think that everything is rotten; and when

HENRY JACKSON

I see the misery of some lives, I cannot but think that they have other opportunities. Many years ago I was maintaining that 'this is the worst of all possible worlds' at a Cambridge Essay Society. Old Lord Houghton, Monckton Milnes, said 'But is there not a great deal that is good in human nature?' I thought that it was a good answer, and unless this is a thoroughly bad world, I cannot help thinking that we may hope for what is good, rather than expect what is bad. Now so far as I can see, this is the difference between you and me. You will see that I do not take up the cudgels on behalf of ordinary presentations of Christianity. I see no obligation to do so. But I think that most men who have had to face trouble of a serious sort find it difficult to dispense with the assumption that there is a God who is good, and that they find some comfort in the assumption. When you tell me that you find it a relief to get rid of some things which some people have said, I quite sympathise, but I do not see that the more complete is the negation, the more complete is the relief. On the contrary, just as I resent the doctrine of eternal damnation, so I resent the doctrine of temporary damnation in this world, falling upon some, very unfairly, if there is nothing but this world, and if life here teaches nothing.

But to use your own phrase, 'I must not try to teach you theology.' So far as I can see, theological belief is not a meritorious thing, which is to receive a reward, but a conviction which helps some people, who want the help, in this world. If others find that they can get along without it, I infer that they are fortunate, but I can quite understand their position. But if they go on to argue that, because they are satisfied with this world, there is nothing else, they seem to me to desert the agnostic position. Forgive me for trying to put my notions about these things. I should not feel quite honest, if, when you invite me, I did not try to say what I think.

To F. BRANDT (*following a passage on Austen Leigh—*
see p. 132—from Bournemouth)

31 *July* 1906

I write chiefly that I may thank you for the concluding paragraphs of your letter. When you say, 'I can believe all that I believe it is necessary for one to believe,' I feel sure that you see things much as I do. In early days I wanted 'Know-

[70]

ledge,' and, as I could not have it, I despaired. But, reading books on the other side, I came to the conclusion that anyone who thinks must have a *theory* to complete the gaps in his knowledge: and that this theory, if it supposes that the universe is good and not bad, is religion. Further, it seemed to me that human nature, with all its imperfections, was a proof that the universe is good, and that there is an absolutely good intelligence. How much dogma is necessary in order to make this conviction operative, I did not care to ask. Faith or belief is a tentative supplement where knowledge fails and I am content to say with Plato, τὸ μὲν οὖν ταῦτα διϊσχυρίσασθαι οὕτως ἔχειν ὡς ἐγὼ διελήλυθα, οὐ πρέπει νοῦν ἔχοντι ἀνδρί· ὅτι μέντοι ἢ ταῦτ᾽ ἐστὶν ἢ τοιαῦτ᾽ ἄττα περὶ τὰς ψυχὰς ἡμῶν καὶ τὰς οἰκήσεις, ἐπείπερ ἀθάνατόν γε ἡ ψυχὴ φαίνεται οὖσα, τοῦτο καὶ πρέπειν μοι δοκεῖ καὶ ἄξιον κινδυνεῦσαι οἰομένῳ οὕτως ἔχειν· καλὸς γὰρ ὁ κίνδυνος· καὶ χρὴ τὰ τοιαῦτα ὥσπερ ἐπᾴδειν ἑαυτῷ, διὸ δὴ ἔγωγε καὶ πάλαι μηκύνω τὸν λόγον[1]. So thinking I can set aside difficulties which had troubled me much; such as (1) I can find no comfort in a system of religion which does not recognize other systems: (2) in view of our ignorance of anything outside this life, I cannot regard religion as a qualification for another existence, except indirectly, in so far as it enables us to make the best of this life, and to prepare us for another; (3) no historical evidence is sufficient to convince me of the truth of statements, which I should unhesitatingly reject if they were made at the present day. If religion is not knowledge, but what I find necessary to fill the gaps in my theory of the universe, I may fairly hold that there is a good God, I may fairly hope that there is for us another existence; I may fairly go to the good God with my anxieties and lay before him my troubles; I may fairly be thankful for the help which faith gives me in this life without for one moment seeing in that faith anything meritorious or in the want of it anything more than temporary misfortune. God is good, and if he has not revealed himself as clearly as we should have wished, I am content to wait and to trust. When I read your letter I thanked God that you had found what I regard as the greatest of all helps in the life which we are living. Forgive me, if I have written too much about this.

[1] See p. 67.

HENRY JACKSON

MRS JACKSON'S *note to the letter to* F. BRANDT

Of this I feel sure the light did not come through reasoning and intellect but through that wonderful childlike spirit which asked for light and accepted it when it was shown to him.

THE GREEK PROFESSORSHIP

THE death of Sir Richard Jebb in December 1905 made a vacancy in the Regius Professorship of Greek; and Jackson, after much searchings of heart, determined to be a candidate. His chief misgiving seems to have been due to his age: he was now close on 66; but he rightly decided that the question thus raised should be left to the electors. The other candidates were Dr A. W. Verrall, Sir William Ridgeway, Dr James Adam, and Dr Walter Headlam. It may well be doubted whether the University had ever had a choice among so many highly qualified scholars. It is remarkable that Jackson survived all but one, though all were junior and two far junior to himself. The Praelections, which were delivered in accordance with the Statute, on 25, 26, 27 January 1906, in the Senate House, were afterwards published in a single volume by the University Press.

The following letter written to a friend on this occasion gives his summary of his studies:

23 January 1906

There is, I am told, a notion amongst some members of the Senate that I have 'published nothing.' It is easy to see that this notion has arisen because I have written mainly for experts and published mainly in technical periodicals. Many years ago (1) I planned an edition of Plato's *Philebus*, and made collations and collections for it, and (2) I planned a history of Greek Philosophy: neither has appeared. The explanation is that in my preparations for these books I came to conclusions, especially about the significance and the development of Plato's philosophy, which differed widely from those in vogue in Germany and elsewhere. This being so, I deliberately abandoned the book about the history of Greek Philosophy, which I could not complete without spending time on mere compilation, I deferred the edition of the *Philebus*, and I proceeded to work out my heresies. Seeing that it would take me many years to complete the exposition of my theory in all its parts and to trace its consequences upon the interpretation of the writings of Aristotle, I adopted the plan of publishing my results in instalments in the *Journal of Philology*, hoping some day to collect them in a volume. At present I have published eight such instalments, amounting to 282 pages. The praelection which I am to read on Thursday contains the outline of a ninth part, and there are others which I contemplate. Meantime I have printed other Platonica. I have published an edition (pp. 157) of the fifth book of the *Nicomachean Ethics*, and a pamphlet (pp. 52) on passages of the *Eudemian Ethics*, addressed to Professor Susemihl on occasion of his jubilee. I have published papers on the *ethics*, the *politics*, and the *metaphysics*.

I have written on the history of Greek Philosophy in the *Journal of Philology*, in the *Encyclopaedia Britannica*, and in the *Companion to Greek Studies*. I mention these last works, because my contributions to them contain in outline a considerable amount of new· work which I have not yet set out *in extenso*.

I have written also about Clement of Alexandria and other Greek writers.

I calculate roughly that I have printed about 330 octavo pages about Plato, 240 about Aristotle, 150 about the history of Greek Philosophy, and 30 about other writers.

I do not include in this estimate contributions to the *Classical Review* about Herondas, etc., nor some forty contributions to the *Proceedings of the Cambridge Philological Society*, nor reviews of Classical books, of which at one time I wrote many, nor anything printed mainly for the use of junior students.

Jackson expounded Plato's *Cratylus*: and the exposition is a typical example of his method alike of study and of teaching. The exposition of the dialogue leads up to a full though concise statement of his view of Plato's position as a writer, teacher, and philosopher, of the order of the dialogues, and of the progressive development of his philosophy. It is a masterpiece of clear statement to a general audience of what might well have been considered a problem for specialists: and in this particular a characteristic specimen of his method as a teacher. But besides all this it contains his *apologia* for his life both as a student and as a teacher. It is worth while, in illustration, to quote the last two paragraphs of the Praelection:

In answer to the other question, 'If there is doubt about the interpretation of Plato's writings, is it worth while to spend time and trouble upon them?' I can speak only for myself. Most certainly I do not repent time and trouble given to the study of Plato. For he speaks to me in more ways than one. I am a student of Greek literature: and in my opinion, of all who have used that wonderful instrument of many strings, the prose of Athens in the three hundreds, I know of none who can take precedence of him. Again, from early years it has been my business to teach, I like teaching, I have no desire to cease to teach: and as a teacher, I recognize in the *republic*, as Jean-Jacques Rousseau did, 'the finest treatise on Education ever written.' Then again, wholly apart from philosophy strictly so called, Plato was interested in questions which from his time to our own were in abeyance, and have come up again within our own memories, questions about the consequences of over-population, about the effect of the healing art upon the race, about the use and abuse of athletics, about social privileges and limitations, about the severities of war, and the like; and in dealing with them he seems to me, always original, always judicious, always suggestive. Finally, though to most men of my time metaphysical truth is an aspiration rather than an end, Plato in his later years propounded a scheme to explain the unity of our manifold cosmos, which seems to me even now to deserve consideration. In a word, if Socrates is the master of those who teach, and Aristotle the master of those who know, Plato is the master of those who think.

Mr Vice-Chancellor and Members of the Senate, my task is done. I am aware that to many of my hearers, my theme may have seemed uninteresting and, possibly, unimportant: and I beg leave to make my apologies. My excuse is that for many years the study of the development of Greek thought has been my professional hobby; and that I have thought it proper, on this occasion, to bring before the Senate results obtained, but not yet published, in the subject which, both in teaching and in writing, I have tried to make in an especial sense my own. For myself, my faith is that no inquiry is uninteresting, or unimportant, or in any way unworthy, provided that it is pursued methodically and with a view to the discovery of truth.

The election was received in all quarters as a due recognition of a lifetime spent in the service of Greek learning and of the students of Greek literature and philosophy. The feelings and hopes of large numbers of such students may be gathered from the selection of letters subjoined. In particular, Baron Friedrich von Hügel's letter expressed what was a general hope that Jackson might now find leisure to put together, in a more complete form than he had yet done, the results of his studies in Greek philosophy and in particular of Plato. But it was too late. And yet, perhaps, that does not put the case accurately. It is illuminating to note how in the paragraphs above quoted he speaks of teaching as his business, and of the study of the development of Greek thought as his professional hobby. I believe that these phrases express his true mind on the subject. Circumstances and character alike led him from the beginning to place first the duty of putting his great abilities and un- relenting industry at the service of others: he considered that this was the first and most urgent service he could render to the pursuit of truth. Subordinate to this primary duty was the perfection and publication of the results of his own studies. The consequence was that he never had sufficient leisure for this latter business: and that his work in great measure is to be found in occasional publications, and in the larger works of other men. It may be questioned whether, if he had become Professor of Greek seventeen years earlier, when he was a candidate and Jebb was elected, the result would have been different.

The following letters illustrate these conditions. The quota- tion from *The Guardian* was copied by him into his Common- place Book.

From 'THE GUARDIAN'

7 February 1906

Our Cambridge correspondent writes: *The Guardian* of last week contained the announcement of Dr Henry Jackson's

[75]

election to the Regius Professorship of Greek, and a list of his Academic distinctions and his literary productions. But that list, though a long one, is no measure of the regard in which he is held by Cambridge men, whether in or out of residence. His name is written in the hearts of many generations of pupils and fellow workers, and it is no exaggeration to say that most of his erudition has found its way into other men's books. His special province is ancient philosophy, but he has few equals and no superior here in any branch of Greek Scholarship[1].

To BERNARD JACKSON
29 *May* 1906

In 1889 I wrote about the political causes of the accusation brought against Socrates, a subject which was historical rather than philosophical. This year I decided to take a strictly philosophical subject, to give in outline some new results, and to try to make clear to laymen the sort of problem which I was attacking. This was ambitious: but I was pleased to find that men like John Peile[2], who are not technical students of Greek Philosophy, considered my discourse to be clear and intelligible. On both occasions I said to myself that 'I must try to show that I can expound a thesis methodically.'

To C. E. SAYLE
22 *February* 1906

Very many thanks for your very kind letter, and the congratulations which it brought me. This sort of success is not to me an unmixed pleasure: but the letters of friends, and the greeting which I had from the undergraduates of St John's on Jan. 30, are things which I shall be grateful for all my life.

To DR V. H. STANTON
30 *January* 1906

I cannot sufficiently thank you for your exceedingly kind letter. I was sincerely grateful for it. For, all through, I have recognized that my candidature might fairly be criticized on the score of my age, if not for other reasons. In the earlier stage, I said to myself that the Electors must judge of such things, and that I was not responsible. Now, when the Electors have decided

[1] Contributed by Dr H. F. Stewart, Fellow of Trinity College.
[2] Master of Christ's College.

to trust me, the approval of old friends like yourself becomes especially valuable as it will help me to face the work of the post. I am not one of those who see only the pleasant side of a successful competition.

I could not say this to you at Bateson's. So I write now.

To PROFESSOR BYWATER
8 *May* 1906

I have never written my thanks for your very kind letter of Jany 30. But I think that you have understood that I valued exceedingly your congratulations and good wishes. Do you note a sign of the times? There is an inclination to run down scholarship in the supposed interest of humanism. I am sure that you agree with me in thinking that the 'humanism' which opposes itself to scholarship is dangerous.

To PROFESSOR GILDERSLEEVE
27 *February* 1906

I am sincerely grateful to you for the very kind letter which reached me this morning. At Trinity I have been for many years my own master, free to teach in my own way. Now, when I come under the University, I cannot help feeling a little shy, a little conscious that I am no longer at home. Kind letters, such as yours, will help me to face the change. Our statutes and ordinances do not say how many lectures the professors are to give. But I have no intention of regarding my election as a member of the House of Commons regards a peerage. I shall not give quite as many courses as I have given hitherto: but I shall try to do something for junior honour men, for senior honour men, and something for those who are no longer candidates for examinations. And I think that this programme will give me substantial work to do.

To PROFESSOR SEWARD
14 *February* 1906

I have never thanked you for your very kind letter of congratulation written more than a fortnight ago. I am afraid that you wish me a *very* long life when you wish that I may see our cause[1] succeed. But we must hope. Do you know Clough's 'Say not the struggle nought availeth'? I often thought of the poem

[1] The abolition of compulsory Greek in the Previous Examination.

during the reign of Toryism, and most certainly in the Election we have seen 'come flowing in the main[1].'

. . . . . .

When I see you I will tell you how the recent fight affects some people's notions of the Greek professor's duties: I am told that they are to expound to people who are *not* students of Greek the excellence of Greek culture. But please consider this *confidential.* On the other hand another friend of mine congratulated me on believing enough in my subject to hate compulsory Greek. You may be quite sure that I shall not take to popular lecturing. I would not, if I could, and I could not, if I would.

To F. W. MAITLAND
11 *March* 1906

I thank you for your congratulations. I fancy that I wrote to you just before the elections and told you how I regarded the issue. Since then I have been very busy, as my lectures this term have been heavy, and I have had a good deal of miscellaneous business to do. In the intervals, I have thought a good deal about the use to be made of the professorship, and I have framed my scheme for the next Academic year: one Part I course (Hist. Gr. Philosophy): two Part II courses (*Theaetetus* and *Timaeus*) and one course irrespective of Tripos (fragments of Eleatics). I have had a strange diversity of advice: (1) address yourself, about Greek culture, to people who know *no* Greek, (2) give *no* lectures to men who are reading for a Tripos, (3) do just what you are doing, (4) no one expects anything from a professor.

COAT OF ARMS
To C. E. SAYLE
21 *January* 1913

I am very grateful to you for taking so much trouble for me.

I think that you a little misunderstand me. 1°. I should avoid anything which would suggest the arms of any Jackson family: for to the best of my belief I have no Jackson relations. 2°. In like manner, I should avoid anything which suggested the arms of the City of Sheffield. When I mentioned arrowheads, I did it on the spur of the moment: and if they are on the Sheffield coat, they probably were suggested by it. 3°. If I pick and choose, having regard to the uses made of armorial

[1] The General Election, 1906.

[78]

bearings at the present time, I should choose charges which can easily be represented in·black and white and on silver.

I had said to myself that I should prefer something such as Argent, on a bend sable, three escallops of the first. But I have no strong feeling about the particular tinctures. When I talked of arrowheads, I had forgotten that I thought of *escallops* as having (since pilgrimages went out) no particular associations. For, as a *novus homo*, I want to keep clear of associations.

Note. Heraldry was one of the hobbies with which Jackson amused himself: and as the letter shows he took great pains about his Professorial coat. The coat is shown on the Memorial Brass in Trinity College Chapel, reproduced on the Plate facing p. 116.

A few of the many letters of congratulation, which he received, may be quoted.

From A. W. VERRALL (*a candidate*)
29 January 1906

Please accept my very hearty and sincere congratulations. Of all your friends, few can be more thoroughly pleased and contented than I am.

From PROFESSOR JOHN E. B. MAYOR
n. d.

I congratulate the University on its recognition of your great services to ancient learning for so many years. Many, outside your College walls, are very grateful for encouragement and instruction received from you, when they most needed help.

I think both Adam and Headlam would have done credit to Cambridge. I am glad that the electors recognised your claims as paramount. The others can wait.

From the REV. F. B. WESTCOTT
21 February 1906

My congratulations are late, I fear, but they are none the less sincere, on your election to the Greek Professorship. The vast majority of Cambridge Classical men must have felt it was only your right to be chosen to sit in Erasmus' seat. Well do I remember the most living instruction you gave me in the winter term of 1880, and I have often said since it was the best teaching I ever had in my life.

HENRY JACKSON

From BARON FRIEDRICH VON HÜGEL
30 *January* 1906

My dear Jackson,

This morning's *Standard* brought me a very *very* great pleasure, indeed a true delight, in the announcement of your having gained the Regius Professorship of Greek. Of course, directly upon Sir Richard Jebb's death—for which I was so sincerely sorry—I realised that you would be at the very head of the possible, probable successors. And I have been thinking about the matter, and heartily wishing you to get the Chair, ever since. And though I resisted a frequently recurring impulse to write and tell you of my keen interest, I will not now deprive myself of the pleasure which lies in saying out how happy one is in the success of one's friend.

I know well that, this time also, the competitors—the others—were well qualified men: if you had not existed, I think I should have wished for either Archer-Hind or Adam, as giving us a Greek *Philosophy* authority: for Drs Butcher and Sandys seemed to me too much like Sir Richard in their strong points: and variety is very important.—But then, with you going, there could be no thought of anyone else: since you had the philosophy still more fully than those two juniors, and you have, besides, so much else.

I feel as happy at your getting the post, as if it had been achieved by me for you, in return for those hours we read together, up in that roof-chamber at Cannes, facing that glorious mountain-range! For I have, of course, never forgotten that time; and whenever I do a further bit of Aristotle, your help wakes up again anew, particularly useful and stimulating.

I cannot help telling you—tho' neither of the points are, I know, at all recondite or likely to remain unurged by others—what I now much hope will happen, and what I hope will *not*.

What I don't want to happen is that the Professorship should, as a matter of fact, turn out to be the occasion of such further confirmation, perhaps even extension, of your simply endless kindnesses and attentions to others, as to block the way, on and on, to your productivity *as Author*. And what I want is that this *Authorship* may now grow again soon, and on a large scale, and for long. We still are without the great Plato-articles worked into a book; and without the short history of Greek Philosophy: indeed, without many another such thing, which

[80]

you alone could give us as we want it, and which, I do hope and trust, the new post will be the occasion for your taking in hand, even if it means the serious curtailing of your social, individual helpfulness towards others.

You will, I know, forgive these remarks: I make them because —when again will you have so definitely fresh a start for your arrangements? And indeed we must not let our little chance go by, of helping you to determine upon now becoming a more prolific author.

With renewed earnest good wishes and congratulations,

Yours ever sincerely

Fr. von Hügel.

MORE ADMINISTRATIVE WORK

It is almost a tragic comment on Baron von Hügel's letter that soon after the election to the Professorship of Greek, he was persuaded to accept two important pieces of public work. He writes, 29 May 1906, to his brother Bernard: 'Don't be shocked: I have undertaken to serve on an important commission which will be named in a few days. I don't like meddling with such things: but I am assured that we may hope to finish our job by next January. I thought it my duty to accept.' The important commission was the Royal Commission on the Irish University; and the 'job' was not finished till 1911: it involved not only the establishment of the Irish University, but also the revision of the Statutes of Trinity College, Dublin. He threw himself into the business with characteristic energy: but it meant a great demand on his time and strength, with frequent journeys to Dublin and much correspondence. About the same time he was placed by Mr Asquith on the Treasury Committee for University Grants, which again made much larger demands upon his time and thought than he had been led to anticipate.

DUBLIN

To PROFESSOR J. A. PLATT

Dublin, 2 *November* 1910

I came here tonight nearly an hour late after a rough passage: and I expect to return tomorrow night, reaching Cambridge on Friday morning. It is a laborious way of syndicating. But before long the job will I suppose come to an end. In a way, I shall be sorry: for I like my glimpses of the Irish metropolis. They are so naively metropolitan; and, as I am an ingrained provincial, their simple-minded metropolitanism interests me. *Suave mari magno*—I look on and rejoice that I am free from metropolitan anxieties; that at Cambridge I can wear a soft hat, or no hat at all, whereas, when I came here in 1906, I shocked the proprieties by wearing a soft hat, and was excused only because my critics had known me to commit the same enormity in London. In fact, I was let off with a caution, on the plea that 'I was lost to all sense of decency.' Do you know Whewell, M.C., to one of the Marshalls, his nephew by marriage? 'Sir, do you mean to insult me? or are you lost to all sense of decency?' Marshall was wise enough to take his seat upon the latter alternative.

ILLNESS

IT can hardly be doubted that the strain caused by these engagements was the main reason for a serious illness which overtook him in the autumn of 1908. In August of that year at Bournemouth he had an attack of erysipelas in the face, resulting in the loss of the sight of one eye, and keeping him away from Cambridge till the middle of January 1909. He amused himself during his recovery by tackling the problem of *Edwin Drood*. With other enthusiasts he visited Rochester in 1909 to satisfy himself on the local conditions, and published at the University Press in 1911 the very characteristic monograph on the subject, in which he advocates the identification of Datchery with Helena—a solution of one of the elements in the problem which he afterwards abandoned, though he wrote no more upon the subject.

To R. ST J. PARRY
Bournemouth
12 *December* 1908

You will wonder how I am getting on at the Eye home. They make me very comfortable here—food good, attendance good, Matron obliging. I go out every morning in a donkey-chair along the sea-front. They seem to have expected me to feel very much humiliated, but I am as bold as brass. The bandage round

my head advertises my quality—as an invalid, so I don't
imagine that anyone accuses me of laziness. They tell me that
the eye is doing very well and that the ulcer on it has made
some progress. I am now taking oxygen, as I am told footballers
do at the interval. I have had one experience of it and so far
I don't think it as good as champagne. The idea is that the eye
wants vitality. This notion will provide me with an illustration
the next time I lecture on the beginning of the 2nd book of
Aristotle's *de anima*....I shall think of you all on Monday
night. Commemoration always goes well, so I need not wish it
success. I wonder which of the College guests will be the
orators of the night.

PUBLIC RECOGNITION

DURING these years recognition of his services to Scholarship
and to the State came from many quarters. In 1908 he received
from the King the Order of Merit. The Universities of Oxford,
Aberdeen, Glasgow, Manchester, Sheffield, and St Andrews
conferred honorary degrees upon him; he was elected Fellow of
the British Academy.

On the Order of Merit he writes to his old friend, Dr F.
Melland (29 June 1908):

I have to thank Mr Asquith for suggesting me for a very great
honour, which I am to receive from the King, on July 21, the
Order of Merit: I know that you, my oldest friend, will congratulate me.

And to A. J. Butler (15 July 1908):

Best thanks for your congratulations received this morning.
I am no doubt guiltless of volumes, but I am responsible for a
considerable number of pages notwithstanding. Yes, I have to
visit the King in [knee] breeches and a sword, with my doctor's
scarlet over all. My portrait is to be done by Strang. Some
impudent paragraph writer in the *W.M.G.* records that I am
in the habit of entertaining the boats' crews, and that I wear blue
spectacles when the smoke becomes thick. Also that I once laid
in 2 dozen of whiskey after consultation with Coe, apparently
that I might shock some one who chanced to be present. But
the apocryphal anecdote is not very clearly told. Of course the
paragraphs were reprinted in one of the Sheffield newspapers.

HENRY JACKSON

I cannot imagine how the blue spectacles come in. As for the two dozen—Coe and I may have speculated in early days. But I have long known that the difficulty is to have a sufficient supply of long clays.

The 'impudent paragraph writer' was evidently writing at second or third hand about Jackson's smoking party after a Commemoration Feast. 'Coe' is Edward Coe, who was at one time Jackson's gyp, afterwards Head Porter (1895–1924).

A further demand upon his time was made by his interest in school education, and in the new Universities. He represented Cambridge in the government of Sheffield University College, afterwards Sheffield University, and of Nottingham University College: and for many years as Governor of his own school, Cheltenham College, and of Winchester College (1905–1918). The connection with Winchester gave him peculiar pleasure. The Governors held there the old status of Fellows; and he delighted to think of himself as a Wykehamist, with all the greater interest, because his second son Horace was educated there, and after taking his degree from Trinity, went back as a Master.

WINCHESTER

To F. MELLAND
23 *April* 1905

I am very grateful to you for your congratulations on my appointment to the Governing Body of Winchester. The title of Fellow is what people call an empty honour: but it is an honour which I value very much; for during my boy Horace's time there I have learnt to be very much interested in Winchester, and I heartily like my colleagues.

To A. O. PRITCHARD
23 *March* 1918

It was a sorrow to me to resign my seat on the G.B.[1]: but I am gouty and rheumatic, and I realized that these disabilities were making me irregular in attendance, and would make me more so. So I cut myself adrift. And I have a further disability. I am rather deaf, and miss the asides of a discussion. So I

[1] The Governing Body of Winchester College.

[84]

reconcile myself, as best I may, to private life. But I still like to think myself something of a Wykehamist; and I am eternally grateful to Winchester and New College for the welcome and the kindness which they have given me during a dozen years.

LOSS OF FRIENDS

IN these years Jackson paid the penalty of advancing age in the loss of many old friends. W. E. Currey ('Pat' Currey), perhaps the most intimate of them, died in September 1908, just before his own severe illness; and in 1910 W. Everett, R. D. Archer-Hind, J. Peile, J. W. Clark and many others. Of A. J. Butler he wrote later to Mrs Butler:

To MRS BUTLER
19 *December* 1912

I was very glad to receive your letter: for I had been wishing for news of you. I think that the Commemoration feast specially reminded me: for Arthur seldom missed it, and I used to arrange with the Junior Bursar that he and his guest were to be my neighbours. I find myself constantly regretting that there is no one left who shares my pleasant memories of the late sixties. It was in some ways a very good time of my life.

To BERNARD JACKSON
29 *October* 1917

I am told that Quiller Couch's *Memoir of A. J. Butler* is about to appear. I have seen part of it, and I think that 'Q.' has done it remarkably well. If you should see it, read A. J. B.'s pronouncement about Dante and Petrarch as representatives of asceticism and aestheticism. The antithesis always occupied A. J. B.'s thoughts, and this lecture written at the close of his life is a sort of *apologia pro vita sua*. I am very glad that they are going to print it with the life. I miss A. J. B. very much: for he was the last survivor of the Trinity people with whom I lived in the late sixties, Swainson, Currey, Crawleys, W. P. and C., etc. It is true that Fred. Pollock, 'the dear old sport,' remains. But he is still a ghost.

Another letter to Mrs Butler (2 March 1912) notes another loss which he felt severely:

We have had bad trouble at home. You may perhaps remember

HENRY JACKSON

that the twins, when they were quite young, had a nurse called
Alice Preston. She remained with us, and was the trusted friend
of all. About a fortnight ago she had influenza and then pneu-
monia, and last Saturday she became suddenly worse and died.
It is a very great blow to Maggie and to all of us. Meanwhile
I have been an invalid myself, and my doctor was sufficiently
alarmed to telegraph for a twin. Edith came and looked after
me for a month: but I was soon able to take my 'small' lecture
in my rooms, and I am now fairly well.

In fact his own health was increasingly precarious and infirmities grew upon him; he had another very serious breakdown in July 1914: but he recovered sufficiently to undertake
the office of Vice-Master, to which he was elected on the death
of Mr Aldis Wright, 19 May 1914, and which he held throughout the war, till June 1919.

UNIVERSITY REFORMS 1906–1914

THE question of University Reforms became active again soon
after 1906. The compulsory requirement of Greek in the
Little-go, and the position in the University of the Staff and
Students of the two women's Colleges were problems still
unsettled. But new questions were arising: the organisation of
studies, and the relation of Colleges and University as teaching
bodies; the further provision for poor students, raised by Bishop
Gore in the House of Lords; the difficulties of University
finance; and reform of the Constitution of the University. There
was a good deal of activity among a small body of reformers in
the University during the five years before the war; but no
material progress was made beyond the elucidation of the
various subjects and, to some extent, the formulation of policies.
In the discussions which were thus carried on Jackson took no
active part, though he was always ready with counsel and advice.
But the failure to convince a majority of the Senate on the
women's question in 1894 and on the Greek question in 1904 ff.,
had convinced him that the necessary condition of any settlement of these or other grave matters was a large measure of

[86]

UNIVERSITY REFORM

constitutional reform. This view found its ultimate justification in the appointment of the Royal Commission on Oxford and Cambridge in November 1919. The following letters explain his attitude:

To R. ST J. PARRY
4 August 1909

I like to hear about University and College Reform, and to say my say about them: perhaps all the more because I recognize that, having had a good deal to do with the reforms of 1882, it is expedient that I should take a back seat in 1909. You will tell me if at any time I can be useful. If I seem backward, it is only because I know that the interference of 'the old gang' is apt to do harm: and what I desire is *to see things done*: so I shall not meddle unless I am sure I shall not do harm. I should do harm if I were to preach aloud that what is wanted is constitutional reform on simple lines, because it would be said that this is the policy of the people who have not got beyond the reforms of 1882. But we have not had constitutional reform since 1858–9: and if we can get it now, it will be absurd to deal with other things under the unreformed constitution.

To LORD EDMOND FITZMAURICE
22 July 1907

I wrote to you in haste this afternoon about the suggested University Commission: but I felt all the time that the things about which I wrote would hardly concern Bishop Gore. So I have been trying to think of some point of view from which he could approach the subject.

Is it that he is dissatisfied with the local Universities in the large towns, and wants enlarged provision at the old universities for the sons of the uneducated? Not long ago, this notion was propounded by some ignoramus. If so, let us distinguish between (*a*) those who are able, and up to a Cambridge second class in honours, and (*b*), those who have only ordinary abilities. Now of the former class—those who are up to a Cambridge second class in honours—we have already a *great many* at Cambridge. With the help of Scholarships, Exhibitions, Sizarships, savings and other assistance of different sorts, they come to us and do well. When I was Chairman of our Sizarship Committee, which arranges for the prolongation of emoluments for

[87]

a fourth year, I was surprised to find how many of our under-graduates come from humble homes; and I suspect that at other Colleges, where the competition is less severe, there must be many more. But it may be said, and probably will be said, if there are at Cambridge so many of this sort, must there not be many more who would come, if there were more emoluments available? I doubt it. If there were many such, I think that the local universities would be better supplied with able honour men than I suppose them to be. In a word, my belief is that an able man, who is fit for a Cambridge honour course, i.e., able to take a second class in a tripos, usually gets his opportunity. I come now to (*b*), those who have only ordinary capacity. I see no reason whatever for making a special endeavour to bring such persons to the old universities. I have *no* sympathy with the view expressed by an old friend of ours that all pass men should be excluded from the University. But I have no desire at all to see special efforts made to bring such people in. And let me point out that we shall be stultifying ourselves if, when we have brought University education to the great towns, we proceed to draw off to the old Universities the clientèle of the new ones.

The truth is that the old Universities should continue to work the higher studies, and in particular those, such as the higher Mathematics, Classics, History, which are not utili-tarian: there will still be work left for the local universities to do. But we must not imagine that there are at the local Universities a number of young people burning for access to the higher studies of Oxford and Cambridge. It is not so.

If you want facts about the new Universities, they are to be found in a Report prepared by *Sir T. Raleigh and Dr Alex. Hill for an Advisory Committee* of the Treasury 'on grants to University Colleges,' published some time this year, perhaps 3 or 4 months ago.

In brief, (1) I think that advanced studies, more especially in academic subjects, should continue to be in an especial sense the function of the old universities: (2) I do not believe that those who are especially fitted for advanced studies in academic subjects are at present precluded from going to the old univer-sities: (3) I deprecate the attempt to make special provision at the old universities for students who are not especially fitted for such advanced studies.

UNIVERSITY REFORM

I think that people are apt to forget how much is done by Scholarships, etc., to open the old universities. I suspect that at least two-thirds of those who take honours hold College emoluments, and of these very many hold emoluments derived from other sources as well.

Of course I am only guessing at the possible purport of the Bishop's resolution. If you know what he means by it, please let me know.

To THE SAME

Bournemouth

25 *July* 1907

Best thanks for your letter. I read the *Morning Post* report of the debate with very great interest. I am still at a loss to understand what Bishop Gore's standpoint is : is it dislike (which he dares not express) of the new Universities? He is quite wrong in his notion that the Colleges are wealthy, and he forgets that so far as teaching is concerned, the demands made by the Colleges upon the lecturers are *very much* greater than the demands made by the University upon the professors, so that money spent on College teaching does far more educational good than the same sum spent by the University. It would be an excellent thing to provide additional funds for the University, but *not*, if those funds are to be taken from the Colleges, which are now making excellent use of them. You will remember that just thirty-nine years ago Trinity extended its classical teaching, and killed 'coaching' for all but third class men. Our example was followed in the other Colleges, and in the other subjects: and, as all the more important College lectures are open (for a *small* fee) to all the Colleges, the teaching provided by the *Colleges* is good all round. Nothing must be done which would injure this system, and drive people back to the old system of perfunctory, formal, lectures supplemented by universal coaching.

The truth is that the prize fellowship system is dying a natural death, and should be allowed to die. We want a statutable revision of the constitution of the senate: but we don't know exactly what the new system should be. The relations of the old Universities to the new cannot be settled by statute, *pace* that solemn platitudinarian Percival, especially as the new Universities have not ascertained very exactly what they

[89]

ought to do and can do, and are only gradually finding out their limitations.

I don't like preaching delay. But I believe that the present moment would be exactly the wrong time for making new statutes, and I note that the people who are raising the outcry are for the most part journalists and others who do not know the question from the inside.

Next term I shall try to get the question about the constitutional powers of the Senate informally discussed. If we could devise a scheme for limiting them, and one for the purging of the electoral roll, we should have got something definite to be altered by Act of Parliament. Prize fellowships are being dealt with by the Colleges. The abolition of final triposes and of Compulsory Greek ought to come from within, when once the powers of the Senate have been curtailed and the Electoral Roll has been purged.

I believe that the best legislation of all would be an *Act of Parliament* which dealt with these two questions, and left the University with its revised constitution to do the rest.

But you will not bless me for writing all this now. I only want you to know that I have schemes for reform, though I do not believe in Bishop Gore's method.

If the government is at any time thinking of taking up any of these matters, please give me an opportunity of talking to you.

So far as Oxford is concerned, it is a grievous thing that Henry Pelham of Trinity is dead. He was out and out their best academic statesman. I don't see who there is to take his place: but I will make a point of talking to one or two of their influential men.

I thought Crewe's speech very judicious, and I guessed that you were silent only because the matter dropped.

To THE SAME
11 *December* 1912

...I have myself dropped out of administration both in the University and in the College: but of course I am still in the thick of the work of my department, and of discussions about University reform. These discussions remind me of old times when I used to write and talk to you about such things. I have been trying to persuade people that we ought to ask for a commission, to reform our constitution and *to do nothing else*;

[90]

because, with our present rotten constitution we have no means of testing the opinion of the academic residents, whilst detailed reform requires that a commission should work hand in hand with the academic residents. Or perhaps a commission might be instructed to begin by reforming the constitution and not to go to work upon details until the constitutional reforms had been carried out. But I should prefer to have constitutional reform first, and, after we had got constitutional reform, a new commission to deal with details in conjunction with the university as newly constituted.

But I cannot get people to see the importance of the constitutional reform. They are all of them eager for a commission to deal with this or that detail. Now the misfortune is (1) that the details discussed are not very important and do not hang together, (2) that there is not much consensus about them, and (3) that, under the existing constitution, we are not in a position to discuss the said details effectively.

You will see that habit is strong with me and that I begin pouring out to you as I used to do in 1875–1877.

In 1906 I was on a Commission (Royal) to make proposals for the reform of Trinity College, Dublin: it was then plain to me that, though a Commission might usefully point out matters to be taken up and indicate principles, the details ought to be devised by the home people and submitted by them for criticism to the outsiders. I believe, that our recommendations largely influenced the T.C.D. people in the proposals for reform which they made from within, and which a King's letter authorized.

THE WAR 1914–18

IN June 1914 Jackson had a very severe illness, which at one time seemed likely to be fatal. But the great vigour of his constitution brought him through and by the middle of July he had recovered so far as to resume his ordinary occupations. At the same time the level of health and activity was definitely lowered. He writes on 14 July to J. M. Image: 'You will have heard that I have had quite a serious breakdown which leaves my near future in uncertainty.' It is not too much to say that during the next seven years there was a perpetual struggle with growing infirmities, and the struggle was aggravated by the growing oppression of anxiety which the Great War brought upon all, and perhaps on none more severely than on those of the older generation who could contribute little, as their share of its burden, but patience and a cheerful courage. He felt, as the following extracts will show, very bitterly the inaction to which he was condemned, and set himself with a determination, which his ever-growing infirmities made little short of heroic, to carry on his routine duties of teaching and correspondence, and to support in every way the efforts of the College to make itself useful. His domestic anxieties were great: his eldest son was in the regular army and in the thick of the fighting from the beginning. His younger son left his post at Winchester College, when he could be spared, and for the last two years served at the front in the K.R.R.C. His youngest daughter was with the hospitals in France.

For the first two months of the war the cloisters of Nevile's Court with a number of the vacant rooms were used as a hospital: and his daily walk to Hall took him through a double row of beds, on which were laid men who had been wounded in the retreat from Mons. The numbers of the College and the University dropped at once to a third and of these the great majority were engaged in qualifying for commissions. From January 1915 onwards the town presented the appearance of a large military camp, a succession of divisions being stationed there for their last period of training before going to one of the fronts. In March 1916 it became the headquarters of three battalions of Officer Cadets training for Commissions: and so it remained till the end of the War. The fifth battalion was quartered in Trinity.

Jackson was elected Vice-Master on William Aldis Wright's death in June 1914, and it fell to him to welcome the officers of the successive battalions which were attached to the College, as guests of the high table. He continued to keep open hospitality in his rooms every night after dinner, and none were more welcome than these new friends, however short their stay in Cambridge might be.

THE WAR

Meantime the academic routine was carried on with ever decreasing numbers of teachers and students. Jackson's classes in Greek Philosophy for the Tripos diminished very rapidly but never quite disappeared: though latterly they could be and were taken in his own rooms. He persevered in teaching, for some time under great difficulties, till within a year of his death: he never willingly acquiesced in acknowledging these difficulties. The dialogue of Plato or the book of Aristotle, on which he was lecturing, was generally open on the great round table. He cherished the hope in these years of revising and collecting into one book his various papers: and in particular greatly desired to 'say his say' on the *Parmenides*, which, he once said, 'I really believe I understand now.' But the power of continuous application was failing, and the project, which he alone could carry out, was never seriously begun, though an invitation from the University Press that he should publish with them such a collection gave him great pleasure.

The only notable event in the College life of these years was the death of Dr Butler, Master since 1886, in January 1918, and the installation of the present Master in March of the same year. The Vice-Master, at the head of the Fellows, takes the leading part in the reception and installation of the new Master. Jackson's account of the proceedings, and a draft of his speech in Hall on proposing the health of the Master, are given below, from his Commonplace Book.

The following letters and extracts give the best picture that can now be given of his life during this period:

To R. ST J. PARRY

Bournemouth
4 *August* 1914

I do not see how England can honourably or honestly stand down. Our honesty and honour are the most important of our vital interests.'

8 *August* 1914

The Belgians have done wonderfully well. I hope that by this time our own force is across the Channel; that is to say the first

HENRY JACKSON

division of it. Hal is at the War Office, fretting that he is not the first to cross the Channel. Horace is doing civilian's work at the Winchester Barracks.

I had not thought that the north Germans, though I knew them to be cads, were such pigs. Did you see the manifesto from......and Co.? They telegraphed to me, and I wired a decisive *No*.

To THE SAME

Bournemouth

16 *August* 1914

An emergency meeting is called at Girton to consider a letter from the Officer Commanding the First Eastern General Hospital. I think of *the Princess*.

Everything suggests that Cambridge is to be a principal hospital centre, and not for a short time only. In that case, shall we be able to accommodate even a diminished number of undergraduates? and will it be desirable to accommodate them? The question is not one which can be answered at present: but the manifestos of the two V.C.s seem to me unduly optimistic, or rather that of the Cambridge V.C.

Have you any views about the housing of evicted inhabitants of Nevile's Court? If the undergraduates are told not to come up, there will be rooms for the exiles. But if the undergraduates come here, evictions will make trouble for the evicted. I have been debating whether to come to Cambridge soon, in order to select books which I shall urgently want: but I rather think I shall not do so. I brought here some of the notes which I shall most urgently want next term for the lecture room....

Hal hopes to come down tomorrow for a few hours. I expect that he will soon be on the other side of the Channel. I think that the attention of the Hospital authorities should be called to one small detail. When we lunch under the library the echo makes the noise of voices, plates, knives, etc. appalling. I cannot think that invalids will be able to bear it.

To THE SAME

19 *August* 1914

Hal came down on Monday, leaving Waterloo at 10.15 and arriving about 5.15. He returned at 8.45. He, then, did not know when he would leave. We had a letter this morning to say that last night at dinner he had a wire telling him to start at

[94]

5 a.m. this morning. So I suppose that he is now 7 p.m. in France. (No: they will arrive in the night.) Address is 'attached Royal Flying Corps, Expeditionary Force' but I am not sure that even this simple fact is public. I am glad that they are insisting on secrecy. E. M. Oakley says that firing has been heard at Dover.

To THE SAME

30 *August* 1914

Things march quickly, and this afternoon we have a very alarming *Daily Mail* report. I am glad that the Prussians are exhibiting themselves in their true character as cads of the worst. The destruction of Louvain is unpardonable. I had always had the feeling that the Prussians were 'bounders,' but I had said to myself that they could not help it. It now appears that they are proud of it, and the Emperor is the very worst of them. I am glad to hear that we are not relying upon the sweating cloister as a permanent hospital. I am glad too that they do not propose to combine in the same buildings University work and hospital work.

To SIR G. O. TREVELYAN, O.M.

Cambridge

18 *October* 1914

I am indeed a wretch. I ought long before this to have written my grateful thanks: for I found the book[1] here when I returned to College on October 1. I deferred writing because I then hoped to read the volume forthwith: but then came the flurry of term and the worry of private business: and this accursed war is always with us, dominating our thoughts and depressing our spirits. I have now begun my lectures to a class sadly reduced in numbers, and I hope to read and to enjoy your volume.

We have a new Cambridge, with 1700 men *in statu pupillari* instead of 3600. In Septr Nevile's Court and the Trinity backs were turned into a temporary hospital, with an operating theatre in one cloister, and beds in the other and in tents. There is now a permanent hospital on the King's and Clare cricket ground. Medical Colonels and Majors and Captains dine in hall in khaki. James Robertson's son Dennis was admitted a fellow dressed in khaki, and wearing a sword. I think that 8 members

[1] The second volume of *George the Third and Charles Fox*.

[95]

of the Trinity staff are away on military duty—at the War Office, training, teaching musketry, improving aeroplanes, etc.

Some of us have our private anxieties. My Hal is one of Smith Dorrien's flying observers. (One day a bullet penetrated the seat of his machine, cut his overcoat, and was stopped by the steel rib of his belt. So he escaped with a bruise.)

To me the depravation of Germany—its gospel of iniquity and selfishness—is appalling. For, though I never thought the Prussians gentlemen, I had a profound respect for their industry and efficiency, and I attributed to them domestic virtues. As it is, their good qualities subserve what is evil, and their domestic virtues fall into the background and cease to affect their conduct away from home.

I envy you your study of the letters to Atticus. I know little or nothing about them. But I know that good judges of literature say about them things which I sh^d say about Horace Walpole. We classical specialists have to stick to our professional subjects, and so do not get from the great literatures the enjoyment which you—like Macaulay—have done.

The anxiety about the War is especially near to us here. Sir John French once said to us very emphatically—'*When* they invade us, Cambridge will be the first place occupied, on account of the railways.' I think that we are all going about our business cheerfully and hoping for the best. But it is sad to think that, whilst we have been trusting to luck and talking of disarmament, the Germans have been elaborately preparing for war and have learnt to think that Germany is above morality; and ought to dominate the world. The horrible thing is that this view is shared by scholars whom we know, and, so far as science and learning are concerned, respect.

The younger generation is doing excellently at the front, keeping up their spirits and making the best of things. A night or two ago I saw a letter from a young Arbuthnot, who left Trinity a year ago: he wrote that the front was like a first-rate club, as you met all your friends there; and he went on to name a host of young Trinity men.

Meanwhile, the older generation is passing away. But, so far as I am concerned, though my intimates of the late sixties are, nearly all of them, dead, there are still a good many of my intimates of the early sixties.

I expect that you will think this a very gloomy letter, and so

it is. But we cannot *talk* gloomily: so your letter tempts me to
pour out to you.

I think that the country is behaving magnificently *now*: but
why have we been so stupid and so supine in the past? Eight
years ago an official in the treasury told me flatly that, if I
advocated expenditure on the army and navy, I was not a liberal.
I do not consider neglect of 'national insurance' a plank of
liberalism. When I was an undergraduate, I thought that
literature was everything, and that politics might be left to those
who did not care for literature. Army and navy did not enter
into my thoughts, except in connection with past history. It is
strange that I could have been so blind. But I think that very
many of our contemporaries were equally obtuse. I think that
we were dominated by two leading ideas: (1) that Europe was
tired of great wars, and would never again venture upon one,
(2) that the sea was a sufficient protection to England, and that
we were not justified in meddling in European politics. Also,
so far as I was myself concerned, I had an insufficient notion
of the duties of a citizen, and thought that a mere reading man
might stick to his books and leave politics to men of practical
ability. As one grows older, one thinks more of the πρακτικὸς
βίος so it was with Aristotle, Mill, Lightfoot, Westcott.

To THE SAME
29 *October* 1914

You tempt me to write again: and, as I have no lecture tomorrow, I do so.

You may well be proud of the abolition of Purchase in the
Army: I often think of it and bless you. Where should we be
now, if we were still under the early Victorian system?

When Hal became a soldier, I was astonished to find how good
the soldier's life is. He went to India at 19, a mere boy, after
a year in the militia. When he came back at 24, it seemed to
me that he had had the best possible *education*. He had learnt
to make up his mind judiciously, to take responsibility, and to
act without fuss or flurry. He had a burning zeal for his profession and for all that concerned it. (At first I thought that his
ambitions were purely regimental: but this is not so.)

I could not help contrasting my own unreadiness at his age.
For at 24 I still had to find my business in life: all I knew was

that 'I would *not* be a Cambridge don.' Years afterwards George Howard reminded me that I had said this.

I hope that many good things will come from this war: and I think that one of them will be the introduction of an element of military discipline into ordinary education. I should have hated it—but it would have been good for me.

Yes: Hal is the boy whom you saw at my rooms more than 20 years ago, in the quite early nineties.

I have a lively recollection of walking with you on the Barton road, where a brook passes under it. We talked about courage: and I remember confessing that I had a horrible fear that I should be horribly afraid if bullets were flying about. Now, in face of German ideas, I think that we ought all to be taught from early years that fighting for the Country is always a possibility of the day's work. It is a pity that we of our generation are too old to learn the lesson. All honour to the younger men who have learnt it and are learning it.

To PROFESSOR J. A. PLATT
31 January 1915

At Cambridge we are in darkness: no gas in the streets or courts; few electric lights and those shaded; candles on the high tables. The roads into Cambridge were blocked to prevent the approach of motors such as those which guided the East Coast Zeppelins. Rumour says that an attack on Windsor Castle was expected last week.

From COMMONPLACE BOOK. *A typical entry*
24 April 1915

264th day of the war. Hal here. Of late I have made no notes about public affairs. In France and Flanders we make no progress. In the Dardanelles we are at a standstill. The army does not grow as it ought. We have not got ammunition for the existing army. The Germans have been preparing villainies for years, and we cannot condescend to their methods. I shrink from saying even to Hal how disheartened I am. But sick as I am, I do not hesitate. We must go on at all hazards. From quite early days I have wondered that we gave guarantees for Belgium, just as I have wondered that we allowed land tax to be redeemed: but honesty comes first, and I do not repent the declaration of war. It is better that we should be smashed than that we should

[98]

break our word: better that we should lose our status and our colonies than that we should imitate those Prussians. I am 76, and I shall not live to see the world right itself. I pray that Hal and Horace may see honesty reestablished, and I hope that my successors may never forget the dishonesty and the black-guardism and the caddishness which Prussia has imposed upon Germany. God help us and keep us. I wish I could be useful to the country and to honesty. But we must hope and we must be cheerful and we must make the best of things.

To F. J. H. JENKINSON
Bournemouth
4 *August* 1915

I am very grateful to you for sending me the Potsdam diary. It is a valuable record in many ways. Some of the quotations show the German creed of brutality: some of them show our own blindness: some of them show our unwillingness to quarrel, and our desire to make the best of these ruffians. But it is very sorrowful reading. I am not sorry to have a record of the manifesto of E. G. Browne, Foakes Jackson and Co. I can quite understand that people like Haldane, hoping the best, said all they could to maintain a good understanding: but when they did so, 'saying Peace, Peace, when there was no peace,' they showed themselves rotten politicians, and they ought now humbly to eat dirt. *The* man to come well out of it is Lord Roberts. All my life I shall think of him as a *vox clamantis*, when no man would listen. My own feeling was one of despair. But there is no good in growling now, just as there was no good in growling then. But I think that you and I agree: so I indulge myself.

I expect that you rejoice as I do that—failing Kenny—Seward succeeds Howard Marsh at Downing. I respected Marsh much, partly because I have an old attachment to Bart.'s, where I was at home when my brother was dresser and house surgeon in 1865, 1866, and where my father was student in 1829, 1830.

To G. P. BIDDER
6 *May* 1916

I am sorry to hear of your illness last term, and of your new responsibilities[1]. For it will be hard to sacrifice sponges and the

[1] Chairman and Managing Director of Cannock Chase Colliery Co. after having left the Board eight years.

work for the Admiralty. (By the way Plato explains that σπογγιστική and φθειριστική are just as respectable as στρατηγική, inasmuch as they too may exhibit scientific method. σπογγιστική is for you, φθειριστική is for Shipley. Forgive this ribaldry.)

It will be consolation to you that by taking the chairmanship, you are setting your cousin free for the national service.

I am grateful to you for telling me about your brother[1]. I had not remembered that you too have a special interest in the Bedfords. I respect it greatly. Did you know Monteith?

I hope that Hal will recover from his wounds—the two bones below the knee fractured by a bullet. But convalescence will be slow: and he is fretted by his absence from the battalion. I believe that, when he was hit, he was patrolling his trenches and the space between our trenches and the enemy's. This seems to have been his custom. I fancy that he has been very useful with his inexperienced battalion, about which he is *enthusiastic*. But you say 'the other day their attack under him received praise.' I don't know what you refer to. I went to see him last Monday at a house in town converted by its owners into a hospital for officers. I found him with six quite young fellows. He seemed comfortable, and he was well supplied with books. We compared notes about Rupert Brooke, and agreed that this handsome and attractive young fellow was not as great as Tennyson. What do you say?

Do you ever read books about school life? If you do, read E. F. Benson's *David Blaize*. Horace says 'He knows more about it than any one not a professional school-master ought to do.' Horace has done his time at Lincoln's Inn and Hampstead and is now at Berkhampstead.

The affairs of the last fortnight are distressing[2]: but how Mahaffy must have enjoyed making war from T.C.D.! Just think of Stephen's Green occupied by insurgents and the Shelburn in a state of siege. I had thought that the Sinn Feiners were visionaries or cranks and that their hostility to the nationalists made them innocuous. But I suppose that the careful Teutons got at them. Damn Sir Roger Casement! I am sorry for Birrell, because I think that in the main it is right

[1] H. F. Bidder commanded 2nd Bedfordshires after Col. Monteith's death at Hulluch.

[2] The Irish Rebellion.

not to take Ireland too seriously: but in this case he has miscalculated and he must suffer, unhappily. There was a time when I shrank from taking life, and *might perhaps* have become a conscientious objector. But in 1889 I learnt to kill mosquitoes and I regret that I am now too old to try to kill a German or two. My respect for Judge Lynch grows. Who was he?

To THE SAME
18 *August* 1916

I think that 'To France, August 1916' is, so far, your best, and I congratulate you. For myself, I wish that I could make either poetry or rhetoric: but I cannot achieve either the one or the other.

It makes me sick to think that I cannot do anything effective against cultured barbarism.

To A. O. PRITCHARD
27 *May* 1916

I am rheumatic and gouty, and good for nothing except for lecturing to our handful of Classical men.... You must have known Tony Welsh, who so soon followed his friend Erasmus Darwin. It is good to think of these young Galahads.

From COMMONPLACE BOOK
30 *June* 1916

83 Cadets dined with us as our guests. They are to leave for commissions on Monday. God keep them, God bless our Country, God preserve the liberties of the world.

25 *January* 1917

It occurs to me tonight to write a few lines. Things here are sad and sorrowful. Many friends are dead. Few are left here. I am anxious about the home people. Gout and rheumatism punish me. Deafness incapacitates me. And there is always the war, the war. Two days ago President Wilson produced his impudent speech. But I like to hear the O.T.C. [the Officer Cadets] drilling in Nevile's Court: the words of command of the officers and the tramp of the men. I thank God for them and I pray Him to bless and keep them. Hal expects to go soon to Havre and then to have 30 hours journey to Marseilles, and then to the East. Horace is now on the way from Havre to the front. God keep them both. On the 10th was the explosion at the chemical factory of Brunner and Mond opposite Woolwich.

HENRY JACKSON

Sexcentenary of King's Hall, 7 July 1317. Garden party in
Bowling Green: dinner in hall. I cut Lapsley's lecture, and the
service and sermon in Chapel. The 'privately printed' papers
about King's Hall were edited by W. W. Rouse Ball. E. C.
Clark was in the Bowling Green in a bath chair. He looked very
ill and died not long afterwards. I was with him for a few
moments.

To SIR G. O. TREVELYAN, O.M.
12 *March* 1916

I need not say that I am very sick about the pacifist party in
Cambridge, and all its works. I grieve more than I can tell you
that my young friend ——— has cast in his lot with them.
When the country is in danger, I think that those who are not
prepared to come to the rescue should lose their citizenship.

I must look up the article in the New York *Nation* of March 2
to which you refer me. As to Cambridge, bear in mind that
four-fifths are helping the Country, and that amongst those
who remain disloyalty is over-represented.

Last Sunday, there was a church parade in the Great Court,
3216 men in khaki, a great sight. Khaki is always in evidence in
hall. Khaki appears in the lecture-rooms. I am glad to have
known Cambridge in war time, and very sad to think that our
juniors are dying because we, their seniors, were foolish enough
to believe what we were told as children, that, after the Napoleonic wars, a great war was impossible. Ever since the S. African
war, I have been anxious and the Country's deafness to Lord
Roberts' appeals dismayed me. (I am glad to think that my Hal
was one of the aviators who watched over him in Flanders.)

The present situation makes the politics of the end of the
xviiith century more intelligible.

To THE SAME
20 *May* 1916

Best thanks for your welcome letter. But you do not (as you
generally do) send me news of your patriotic and philanthropic
George, and I miss it.

Have you read
(1) *Some Naval Occasions,*

THE WAR

(2) *A Tall Ship and other Naval Occasions*, by Bartimaeus, (Blackwood),

(3) *The First Hundred Thousand*, by Ian Hay—i.e. one Beith?

If you don't know them, read them.

You say nothing about the miserable affair in Dublin. I am very sorry for Birrell. His policy of inaction does not surprise me. I had not expected Sinn Fein to take this new direction. I had thought that they would be content to get their knives into the nationalists, and to preach 'Ireland for the Irish' in a visionary way, and I do not wonder that Birrell trusted Redmond and Dillon—in particular, Dillon, whom I know and like not a little. But I cannot help thinking that he made a grave mistake in absenting himself from Dublin and shutting up the Chief Secretary's lodge. And some of the recent doings were such that he ought to have been alarmed. It is some time since I saw 'Sir Antony,' but I cannot imagine that he has approved Birrell's recent policy. Do you know much of 'Sir Antony'? He is very indiscreet, but for all that a strong man: and strong men attract me.

What are you reading nowadays? You read as a man should, that he may enjoy. I read (1) that I may get and utilise professional information, (2) that I may relax. This is better than not reading: but it is not as good as reading to enjoy. Lord Macaulay understood the right way.

I am just now expecting, for a week end, my younger boy, who has left schoolmastering at Winchester that he may train for the war. One of my three daughters is nursing in France. The classical Tripos is almost microscopic. There are only 555 undergraduates in residence, out of a peace figure of approximately 3333. Confound —— 'et tous ces garçons-là.'

To THE SAME
20 May 1916

Best thanks for your letter and for the sight of George's paper. I return it herewith: for I am always afraid of losing borrowed property. It has one of the qualities which the war has bred in us: gaiety. We are learning on the one hand to take things seriously—very seriously: and at the same time to make the best of things, however bad they may be. I am prouder to be an Englishman now than I was before the war. We have all learnt much.

HENRY JACKSON

I thank you for what you write about my Hal. When he was quite small, he proposed to sleep on the floor in order to harden himself for the soldier's life. In those days I did not take his ambition seriously. But there is no mistake about his devotion. I have good news of his progress.

I am glad to have lived to see the revival of the soldier man, and I rejoice to think of the many men who in hospitals and ambulances and factories are helping the nation.

I suppose that Sinn Fein has changed its character. A few years ago, when I often went to Dublin for University Commissions, they seemed to be cultivated people who wanted to get their knives into the Nationalist M.P.s, so I did not think them dangerous. It surprizes me that Dillon, the most serious Irishman whom I have known, should have allowed Birrell to delude himself. Birrell ought to have been oftener at Dublin. It is some time since I saw 'Sir Antony,' a man who, in spite of his indiscretions, impresses and interests me. I cannot suppose that he approved Birrell's tolerance of Carson's doings.

I much enjoyed my work in Ireland. It greatly amused me to find how very different the Irishman is from what we English suppose. I framed a few generalizations.

(1) Everything in Ireland is a secret, but the secret is known to every one.

(2) Every Irishman suspects every other: and 'they are right' an Irishman said to me.

(3) He does not suspect an Englishman, because he thinks him a damned fool: myself, for instance.

(4) All good Irish whiskey stays in Ireland.

The people greatly interested me: Chief Baron Pallis, Archbishop Walsh, Sir Wm Butler, and one or two Nationalist M.P.s not of the first rank, Dillon. Their knowledge of Irish history amazed me.

But I must not go on gossiping about a past stage in my existence.

I once looked into Schiller's *Thirty Years' War*, and it seemed to me so dull and stodgy that I cut it. But my inquiry was anything but adequate: and I may be quite wrong. On the other hand, let me strongly recommend a forgotten English book: *The Life of Wallenstein* by Lieut. Col. Michell. Also his *Fall of Napoleon*. He knew how to write history, but I never knew anyone except my father who had heard of him.

THE WAR

. . . . . .

It shames me to remember how little fifty years ago we appreciated the realities of life: how sublimely unconscious we were
that the country might one day have to fight for its very existence. We did not believe in the Devil. Now, when at last
we are awake, my heart goes out to the fighting generations, to
the men who are serving the country in the navy, at the front,
and in hospitals, and in factories. You people are doing the
work which we were not called upon to do. We missed a great
deal of education in not having to do it: and it is sad for us that
we have to be educated vicariously.

Now and then I have a letter from your father: and I think
that his feelings about the war are just like mine. No one else
writes to me in the same way. For myself, I grieve to think
that I have not been able to do a small something for our
Country, nor a small something against its enemies: and I never
cease to respect and admire the generations who have borne the
brunt. It is sorrowful, but it is good to read of the many young
fellows who have given their lives for the Country.

It was a blow to me when Hal at 18 declared for the army.
I did not then know that it was a fine profession. When he
came back from India at 24, I realized that he had had an
admirable education, a far better one than can be got at a
University. But even then I hardly understood the patriotism
which was at the root of all his ambitions. Patriotism is a fine
thing, and the nation which in its selfishness desires to destroy
alien patriotism is the very Devil. I echo what you say 'May
God steel our hearts without hardening them.' I should like
to survive the war, and to have a hand in the reconstruction
which will follow. There will be things to do here at Cambridge.
But until the war is over, it would be a mistake to try to formulate them. Premature schemes of reform stand in the way of
better ones, we don't know what we shall want. In my little
sphere I am a reformer still, and ready to back some great
changes.

. . . . .

As you say, the sanguine prophecies of the newspapers are very

[105]

distressing. But the pluck, and good humour, of the army, and of the nation, are things we may well be proud of.

Some years ago French expounded to me the difference in scale between Waterloo and Mukden. The other night he said that the difference between Mukden, and the present war, was still greater.

You say nothing about English and Irish politics: and I suppose that that is the wisest course. The recent developments of Sinn Fein took me by surprise: for in 1908–1910, when I was often in Ireland—or rather in Dublin—the Sinn Feiners were educated visionaries, chiefly concerned to make things unpleasant for nationalist members of Parliament.

To THE SAME

20 *March* 1917

'Cadet Corps' are schools for the training of officers. There are 5 or 6 such schools: Oxford, Cambridge, Lichfield etc., each with preparatory schools. The cadets are of different sorts:

(1) Men who have had *no* previous training; e.g. my Horace joined the Inns of Court O.T.C. as a private, then went to Hampstead Heath, then to Berkhamsted, then to Lichfield, then commission in the 6oth, The King's Royal Rifle Corps, then Sheerness, then the trenches. (He is now in the London Hospital, wounded in the shoulder in an attack on Le Petit Miramont).

(2) Some men have had their training as privates in school O.T.C.'s and come here to learn the duties of an officer.

(3) Nowadays most of them have had six months as privates in the trenches, and come here to learn the duties of an officer. I am afraid that nowadays the time is too short. As it happened Horace had nearly a year or quite a year.

There are about 2000 in Cambridge. At Trinity we have 500 or 600, living in college, dining and breakfasting in hall, drilling in the cloisters. Their officers dine at the high table. When they leave us for their commissions, we have a little dinner party and dine them. St John's, Pembroke, Clare, King's, are other centres. You would like to see and hear them drilling in the cloisters. I have seen church parade in the great court when it was nearly, but not quite, full of khaki. I have seen a man in khaki, with a sword at his side, admitted to his fellowship. I have seen in the chapel a coffin covered with a union jack and

[106]

I have heard the measured tramp of the guard of honour. All this is strange: but I like to think that Trinity is doing its duty in a quiet way. Last Sunday we heard of the death of a fellow and classical lecturer: C. E. Stuart, married 30 Dec^r, wounded March 12, died March 15. We lost another, Keith Lucas, a mechanical genius, by an aeroplane accident some months ago.

Twice I have presided in hall when we were saying 'good-bye' to cadets who were leaving us. I told them that I did not join the rifle corps when it was started, and that now I am heartily ashamed of my indifference. We knew nothing then of the nation in arms.

When Hal took over his head quarters in a French château, he wrote to his mother—'you would have laughed to see me putting all the small children through their gas drill the day after we arrived. Poor little kids. The French gas mask is in two parts, and takes some putting on. Please God! they will never need them.' Somehow I had been unable to conceive the necessity of protecting small children against gas. What pigs the Germans are! It is a sacred duty to hate them. In this I am glad to take a lesson from them.

I have been reading again, with great joy, your extracts from your uncle's marginalia. Do you know *The Table Talk of S. T. Coleridge?* Do you know *Scaligerana?* These scrappy jottings greatly delight me. They are like good talk, than which nothing can be better.

It is good of you to write to me: for there are not many of the old friends left with whom I can talk, and with the young friends, much as I value them, there are limitations.

To J. M. IMAGE
26 *March* 1917

We are virtuously obedient to the controller of food: fish and potatoes but no meat on Tuesday and Friday; meat but no potatoes the rest of the week: bread rolls half their old size: portions strangely dwarfed. Don't mistake me! I back Lawrence's policy. Another party of cadets leave at the end of the week. I hope to go to Bournemouth on Thursday or Friday: but I don't like the thought of the journey. The magnificent distances of Waterloo punish the rheumatic, and the upset of the time tables is a nuisance.

HENRY JACKSON

Speech at A CADET DINNER
1917

Gentlemen,

We are met here tonight to say goodbye to 53 young friends who are to leave us tomorrow to serve the country. The Master with his unrivalled gifts as an afterdinner speaker would have liked to be here. As it is I must ask you to bear with a few plain words from myself.

Gentlemen Cadets, we who represent the College hope that during your stay amongst us, you have learnt to understand our affection for what has been our home for many years: and we hope that you will yourselves carry away pleasant recollections of our courts and cloisters and walks. We who have been here perhaps 50 years think of our youth when the Napoleonic wars were comparatively recent, and when we thought that never again could there be a great European War. We have had a terrible awakening. 100 years ago our fathers were up against the ambitions of an unscrupulous scoundrel. Now we are up against what is worse, the ambitions of an unscrupulous nation— a nation which has not shed its barbarism, has no generous instincts, has highly cultivated itself for evil, is brutalized by the lust for domination.

Gentlemen Cadets—we of the older generation congratulate you on your opportunities of helping the country—we admire the loyalty and the devotion of the noble generation to which you belong—and we wish you with all our hearts God speed. God keep you, God bless our Country, God preserve the liberties of the world.

To G. A. HIGHT
10 *October* 1917

I have been very idle all this summer. A man who is too old for war work is apt to feel slack, except so far as necessary routine is concerned. In all probability I shall have no Part II candidates, and shall try to make myself useful by giving Part I lectures in place of some absentee. I try to fancy that in this way I do my mite in helping the war. Whether we win or lose I am glad that we fought. Honesty required it.

To SIR G. O. TREVELYAN, O.M.
13 *October* 1917

. . . . .

I had guessed that you were in correspondence with good

THE WAR

Americans who felt with us about the unspeakable Hun. My principal American friends are dead. In particular I miss W. W. Goodwin of Harvard—Greek Professor—with whom I constantly corresponded from 1868 till his death four or five years ago.

There are some 25 undergraduates in the College, which is chiefly occupied by cadets. I have read that there are about one eighth of the normal number of undergraduates in the University. It was ungrateful of me to leave your letter so long unanswered: for, as the years pass, I value more and more the old friendships, and the old friends are fewer and fewer.

Please send me news of yourself.

From COMMONPLACE BOOK

29 November 1917

My father's birthday. I thank God for my good and wise father. I wish that he could have known me later. I wish that he could have known my children and in particular my soldier son.

INSTALLATION OF THE MASTER

To G. P. BIDDER

10 March 1918

I am glad that you thought the ceremonial dramatic. There is an excellent document prepared in 1841—it is said by Welsford (otherwise Mephistopheles) the Chapel Clerk,—which fixes all the details. The V.M. 'commands' the porters to open the Great Gates: then welcomes the M.C. and presents him to the fellows (*not* as the Chronicle says 'presents the fellows to him'). To the Chapel the V.M. takes the right hand, the M.C. designate the left. The V.M. says the formula of admission at the M.C.'s stall, holding his hand. I was glad that the 5th Company of Officer Cadets turned out in force.

I got through the business quite comfortably. I went to the Ante-Chapel early. Prior gave me an arm to the gate, and the M.C. to the Chapel and to the Lodge.

From COMMONPLACE BOOK

13 March 1918

Sir J. J. Thomson was admitted M.C. 5 March in accordance with the ritual of 1841, except that we assembled in the Ante-Chapel instead of the Combination Room.

HENRY JACKSON

At night we dined in hall, the M.C. taking the head of the table and I sitting next him. The M.C. proposed the King. Then I proposed the M.C.

'Gentlemen, by the tradition of the College it is my privilege to ask you to drink the health of the Master. Master, we welcome you, we congratulate you, we wish you all prosperity. This morning it was our duty to receive you as a distinguished stranger appointed by H.M. the King to rule over us. Tonight it is our great pleasure to welcome an old friend in a new capacity. Master, do you remember the admission of your distinguished predecessor? Do you remember the speech which Coutts Trotter made in proposing the Master's health? There was a sentence in it which ought, I think, always to be remembered on such occasions as this. Trotter began by telling us how, when he went to Harrow, Butler was head of the school and Captain of the Eleven, an admirable Crichton, admired and loved by every one: how he had followed Butler to Trinity and found that there too he had carried everything before him. And then came a sentence, which in its opening words made me shiver, and in its concluding words made me shout. "I do not know, no man can know, who would have been Master of this College if the choice had rested with the fellows, but there is this advantage in appointment by royal warrant that it leaves behind it the embers of no controversies and the ashes of no discontents." Master, you find no embers and no ashes awaiting you. Rather we are thinking of your progress from strength to strength. I, for one, think of the promise and the early performance which won for you your fellowship. There are several who remember your election to the professorship in succession to Clerk Maxwell and Rayleigh. And now when you come among us to take your place at the head of the proudest College in the world, the sympathy of every one of us goes out to you in a wireless telegraphy more eloquent than any spoken words. Master, we congratulate you on your succession to William Whewell, Hepworth Thompson, and Montagu Butler. May you prosper, and may Trinity prosper, and may there be peace in your time. Did you ever ask yourself to define a College? I think that I never did till some 20 years ago physiological and zoological congresses were meeting here. There were men from every part of the world—from Tokio in the East to California in the West. I had one of the best times of my life. I met many interesting people, and they constantly asked me "What is a College?" At last I hit upon an answer: "A College is a family of students, who probably know very little about one another's subjects, but at any rate are interested in one another's achievements, and rejoice in one another's successes." To that ideal may Trinity always be true.

And now a word in conclusion. In the darkness of war time, I do not know whether a certain panel over our heads is open, but in any case, Master, we ask you to convey to Lady Thomson our sincere congratulations and our heartfelt good wishes.

Gentlemen, I ask you to drink to the health of the Master of Trinity.'

To SIR G. O. TREVELYAN, O.M.

20 April 1918

I was very glad to see your handwriting. In time of trouble, it is good to turn to the old literature, and to think of Macaulay's poem on the defeat at Edinburgh. The fact is that we are in trouble and must look forward to weeks and months of anxiety and suspense. On April 4 the War Office wired that Horace was 'wounded and missing' since March 21, the beginning of the German 'thrust.' At first I feared that he had been left wounded and that no one knew anything. We now know that he was wounded in the throat and is a prisoner. So we hope that he was brought into our lines, and when we retired, became a prisoner with others. And we hope for news of him: but the hope is 'hope deferred.' It is said that some hospitals were taken over bodily with their doctors and nurses, and we must hope that my boy was one of the more fortunate ones. Hal, my elder boy, is now a Major-General, commanding a division of 20,000; I think near the junction of the English and French lines. He took over the new command on the 23rd, two days after the German 'thrust' began.

To T. W. DUNN

3 June 1918

What you say about the maid servant and the man in the street is true. But my bedmaker cares, now that my boy Horace, not long ago here, is a prisoner, and that my other boy Hal commands the 50th Division in the Rheims corner of the black patch of *The Times Map*. The country is warming up to it, and I hope that we are becoming mulishly obstinate.

HENRY JACKSON

Happily the Germans every now and then remind us what pigs they are. The deliberate bombing of hospitals is really very stupid. We don't forgive.

Some time I must discuss old age with you. It makes one damnably *slow*: not in thinking, but in moving, acting, writing. Can you teach me to keep up to the mark? I am *lazy* and heartily ashamed of it: it has been my besetting sin all my life, and it grows upon me—damn it.

Kindest regards to Mrs Dunn.

To SIR G. O. TREVELYAN, O.M.
23 June 1918

Best thanks for yesterday's *Country Life*. Your history of your beautiful house has greatly interested me, and I look forward to the continuation.

I hope that you have good news of your sons. My family news is mixed. Horace is recovering from his wounds, a prisoner at Schneidermühl, half way between Berlin and Danzig: Hal's 50th Division is resting from the heavy fighting of March, April, May. Cicely has a modest mention as a nurse in Sir D. Haig's May despatch.

I must not write you a real letter tonight.

To THE SAME
4 July 1918

Best thanks for the continuation of your history of Wallington. I have greatly enjoyed it. I had hoped that incidentally you might have told the story of Stoney Bowes but I can well understand that you did not care to meddle with such a wretch.

Have you read vols. 1 and 2 of the memoir of Wm Hickey, son of the man in Goldsmith's *Retaliation*? I should like to know what you, who know the end of the eighteenth century, think of this remarkable book.

It reminds me of the wonderful book, *Casanova*. I think it truthful.

To BERNARD JACKSON
Cambridge
6 October 1918

I have been writing for the *Review* a tiny paragraph about Monty James' translation to Eton. The fashion here is to bewail it. I think it an absolutely right appointment: for I like to see the right man in the right place.

THE WAR

Old Edwin Freshfield is dead—the father of all Wykehamists, myself included. He was a great friend of H. Bradshaw's. Knowing H. B. he asked him to dine with him and enclosed two reply postcards—one Yes, one No—addressed to himself. H. B. posted *both*.

To MRS A. J. BUTLER

30 December 1918

You will wonder what at this time of year I am doing at Cambridge and not at home. The truth is that I am very gouty and rheumatic and in consequence find the journey very trying. At the great London stations, such as Liverpool Street and Waterloo, there are few seats and few porters, and it seemed to me there would be a greater mob than ever. So after thirty years I again dined in College on Christmas Day.

It is indeed a comfort to know that the nightmare of these four years is at an end. England is a better England: but I am an older man, and I have fewer friends left to me.

10 March 1919

I am indeed deeply grieved by your sorrowful news. You may be very sure of our sympathies[1]. It is small consolation to say that he has died in a good cause.

But one must always thank God for the young men and the boys who have saved the world from the worship of the devil.

CLOSING YEARS

To V. H. RENDALL

22 July 1917

I miss [A. J. Butler] horribly: for he was the last of the people with whom I consorted in the late sixties: and that period of my life is now a closed book for me. It had been a very good time for me and I think for some others. I had plenty of work to do: but there was plenty of merriment; and my next period, the early seventies, was more severe. Forgive this egotism. The times of merriment are very precious, and they drop out when no one is left with whom to remember them.

To G. A. HIGHT

28 December 1918

I have said that I am gouty and rheumatic. I ought in honesty to add that I am also blind and deaf. So I am no good as a man

---

[1] On the death of her son William Martin Butler.

of business. Perhaps this is a good thing: for in my time I have
had my turn at affairs, and I am not sorry to be sent back to my
books. The bother is that I am now a slow worker, and wonder
at some old performances. This will seem to you very egotistical.
Forgive me.

1919–21.

THE story of the last three years must be briefly told. In
July 1919 the address, printed on the next page, was presented
to him by the College, with a reproduction of 'Porson's'
tobacco-jar. His letter shows with what feelings he received it.
The armistice relieved him from the most pressing anxieties of
the war, both public and personal. His son Horace, who had been
wounded and taken prisoner in March 1918, returned home. The
marriage of his eldest son in December 1918 with Miss Dorothy
Seymour was a source of great happiness to him: and not long
after his daughter Cicely returned from her service in the
hospitals in France. The death of his sister-in-law, widow of
Dr Arthur Jackson, occurred in the spring of 1919 and occasioned
the last considerable journey he took, a visit to his native town
to wind up the family affairs. After this visit, and except for an
occasional journey to Bournemouth, he became more and more
closely confined to his rooms. For the last few months he was
lovingly tended there by one or other of his daughters. He
persisted in his endeavours to carry on his classes till within a
few months of the end; but the effort became steadily greater.
His increasing difficulties of eyesight and hearing restricted his
opportunities of social intercourse: but he still enjoyed the visits
of old friends, such as Sir Clifford Allbutt, Baron Anatole von
Hügel, and Dr G. P. Bidder. At last, in August 1921, he
became intensely anxious to rejoin his wife and family at
Bournemouth; and the last five weeks of his life he spent there.
He died on 25 September 1921. The funeral service was held
in the College Chapel on 28 September, amid a great con-
course of members of the University and friends from a distance. The burial took place in the cemetery of St Peter and
St Giles on the Huntingdon Road.

ADDRESS OF THE MASTER, FELLOWS, CHAPLAINS AND ORGANIST TO DR JACKSON ON THE OCCASION OF HIS EIGHTIETH BIRTHDAY

Trinity College
14 *July* 1919

Dear Jackson,

The present year, in which your eightieth birthday has been followed by your retirement from the office of Vice-Master, affords the Fellows of your College a suitable opportunity of expressing in symbol their affection for yourself and their sense of your services to the foundation which received you more than sixty years ago.

We therefore ask you to accept from us, as some token of these feelings, a copy of a vessel from which your most illustrious predecessor in the Chair of Greek is thought to have derived a solace not unknown or unwelcome to its present occupant; and we trust that the figure of Porson's tobacco-jar may often meet your eyes, and bring us before your mind, in moments tranquillised by its contents.

Our tribute carries with it the personal affection of friends and the gratitude of a community. From the day when first you were elected a Fellow of the College, no measure has been undertaken for the promotion of its welfare or the increase of its efficiency which has not been furthered by your zeal or due to your initiative. In Trinity, in Cambridge, in the whole academic world and far beyond it, you have earned a name on the lips of men and a place in their hearts to which few or none in the present or the past can make pretension. And this eminence you owe not only or chiefly to the fame of your learning and the influence of your teaching, nor even to that abounding and proverbial hospitality which for many a long year has made your rooms the hearthstone of the Society and a guesthouse in Cambridge for pilgrims from the ends of the earth, but to the broad and true humanity of your nature, endearing you alike to old and young, responsive to all varieties of character or pursuit, and remote from nothing that concerns mankind. The College which you have served and adorned so long, proud as it is of your intellect and attainments, and grateful

HENRY JACKSON

for your devotion, is happy above all that in possessing you it posseses one of the great English worthies.

We are

Your affectionate friends

J. J. THOMSON	J. ELLIS MCTAGGART	T. C. NICHOLAS
H. M. TAYLOR	C. DAMPIER WHETHAM	R. V. SOUTHWELL
J. M. IMAGE	J. W. CAPSTICK	F. R. TENNANT
J. W. L. GLAISHER	H. MCLEOD INNES	J. R. M. BUTLER
A. F. KIRKPATRICK	W. M. FLETCHER	S. CHAPMAN
V. H. STANTON	F. M. CORNFORD	E. D. ADRIAN
A. H. F. BOUGHEY	E. HARRISON	W. L. BRAGG
W. W. ROUSE BALL	G. H. HARDY	R. H. FOWLER
J. WARD	R. VERE LAURENCE	DENNIS ROBERTSON
R. D. HICKS	G. T. LAPSLEY	N. K. ADAM
R. T. GLAZEBROOK	DENYS A. WINSTANLEY	J. BURNABY
FRANCIS JENKINSON	F. J. DYKES	J. PROUDMAN
J. P. POSTGATE	A. S. EDDINGTON	P. A. BUXTON
J. G. FRAZER	J. E. LITTLEWOOD	O. D. SCHREINER
R. ST J. PARRY	H. F. NEWALL	H. F. STEWART
R. A. HERMAN	H. A. HOLLOND	E. RUTHERFORD
J. D. DUFF	D. S. ROBERTSON	J. C. H. HOW
A. N. WHITEHEAD	F. G. HOPKINS	R. H. KENNETT
J. N. LANGLEY	A. E. HOUSMAN	ALAN GRAY
A. A. BEVAN	F. A. SIMPSON	

Trinity College, Cambridge
19 *August* 1919

My dear Master,

I do not know how to express my gratitude to you and to the Society not only for your good wishes on my eightieth birthday but also for the unceasing kindness which I have had from the College throughout my life.

From early years it was my ambition to find a home at Trinity. At first I hardly hoped to achieve it: but the College has been very good to me; and for more than half a century I have lived within the walls. With all my heart, I thank you, Master and brother Fellows, for admitting me to the privileges of our goodly heritage and for honouring me by associating my name with that of Porson.

I am, yours affectionately,

HENRY JACKSON.

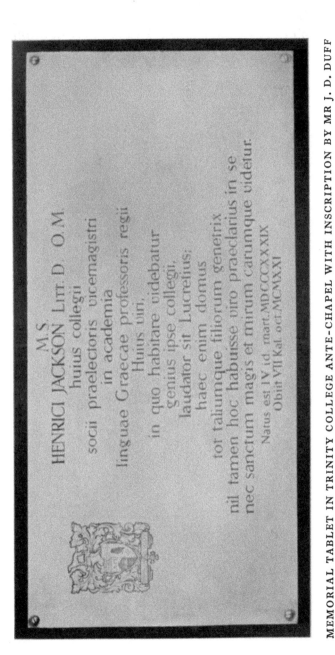

M S

HENRICI JACKSON Litt·D O·M

huius collegii

socii praelectoris uicemagistri

in academia

linguae Graecae professoris regii

Huius uiri,

in quo habitare uidebatur

genius ipse collegii,

laudator sit Lucretius:

haec enim domus

tot taliumque filiorum genetrix

nil tamen hoc habuisse uiro praeclarius in se

nec sanctum magis et mirum carumque uidetur.

Natus est IV id·mart·MDCCCXXXIX

Obiit VII Kal·oct·MCMXXI

MEMORIAL TABLET IN TRINITY COLLEGE ANTE-CHAPEL WITH INSCRIPTION BY MR J. D. DUFF

LIST OF BOOKS
DEDICATED TO HENRY JACKSON

DATE	TITLE OF BOOK	AUTHOR	DEDICATION
1881	Select Elegies of Propertius*	J. P. POSTGATE, Fellow of Trinity College, Cambridge	HENRICO JACKSON. τροφεῖα
1883	Aristotelis Quae Feruntur Magna Moralia	FRANCISCUS SUSEMIHL (Leipsic)	HENRICO JACKSONI et HENRICO OMONTO, D.D.D.
1892	The Odyssey of Homer	ARTHUR PLATT, late Fellow of Trinity College, Cambridge, Professor of Greek, University College, London	To HENRY JACKSON, Litt.D., is dedicated with affectionate admiration and gratitude this edition of Homer begun under his auspices
1895	Euripides, The Rationalist	A. W. VERRALL, Fellow of Trinity College, Cambridge	To HENRY JACKSON, Litt.D., this book, written in response to his suggestion, is offered as a small acknowledgment of many debts
1897	Some Observations of a Foster Parent	JOHN CHARLES TARVER, King's College	Epistle, Dedicatory and Prefatory, of ten pages
1897	The Republic of Plato	JAMES ADAM, Fellow of Emmanuel College, Cambridge	Studiorum Platonicorum egregio antistiti fautorique HENRICO JACKSON, Litt.D., hoc opus beneficiorum memor dedico
1902	The Greek Grammar of Roger Bacon	The Rev. EDMOND NOLAN, Trinity College, Cambridge	HENRICO JACKSON, Litt.D., grato animo Edmundus Nolan
1904	The Chapel on the Hill	ALFRED PRETOR, Fellow of St Catharine's College	To my friend HENRY JACKSON greeting and thanks
1904	Demosthenes on the Crown	WILLIAM WATSON GOODWIN, Eliot Professor of Greek Literature in Harvard University	To HENRY JACKSON, in token of a friendship of more than thirty years
1905	Translations into Greek Verse and Prose	R. D. ARCHER-HIND, Fellow of Trinity College, Cambridge	Veteri amico HENRICO JACKSON, Coll. ss. Trin. Socio, φιλοσόφῳ, φιλοκάλῳ, φιλοφίλῳ
1905	Cantabrigia Illustrata by DAVID LOGGAN (reprint)	J W. CLARK, Registrary of the University of Cambridge, formerly Fellow of Trinity College	HENRICO JACKSON, Litterarum Doctori, Collegii sacrosanctae et individuae Trinitatis socio, scriptorum meorum scrutatori diligentissimo castigatori interdum impavido, dilectissimo denique sodali amicitiae jam longae pignus hasce schedas dedico

* In a letter accompanying this book Dr Postgate writes: 'I want you to give the phrase of the dedication the broadest and most extended interpretation, and to view it as a poor acknowledgment of a debt which I cannot repay.'

LIST OF BOOKS
DEDICATED TO HENRY JACKSON (*continued*)

DATE	TITLE OF BOOK	AUTHOR	DEDICATION
1907	*Aristotle De Anima*	R. D. HICKS, Fellow of Trinity College, Cambridge	To HENRY JACKSON, who has inspired many with his own love of Greek Philosophy
1909	*Schoolboys and School Work*	Rev. THE HON. E. LYTTELTON, Headmaster of Eton	Dedicated to HENRY JACKSON, Professor of Greek at the University of Cambridge
1910	*The Works of Aristotle* Vol. IV. *Historia Animalium*	D'ARCY WENTWORTH THOMPSON, Trinity College, Litt.D., C.B., F.R.S., Professor of Natural History in St Andrews University	HENRICO JACKSON, Philosophi discipulo condiscipulus philosophiae tirunculus primipilari
1911	*Roman Stoicism*	E. VERNON ARNOLD, formerly Fellow of Trinity College, Cambridge, sometime Professor of Latin, Bangor	HENRICO JACKSON, Litt.D., dilectissimo Praeceptori
1913	*Antigonos Gonatas*	WILLIAM WOODTHORPE TARN, formerly Scholar of Trinity College	To HENRY JACKSON, O.M., Litt.D., Regius Professor of Greek in the University of Cambridge
1921	*Apollodorus* *	SIR JAMES GEORGE FRAZER, Fellow of Trinity College, Cambridge	To my old teacher and friend HENRY JACKSON, O.M.

* On the first page is written: '*To* HENRY JACKSON, O.M., *with most grateful and affectionate regards from his deeply obliged and attached old pupil and friend*, J. G. FRAZER, 29*th July*, 1921.'

BIBLIOGRAPHY

1. *Translations*, by R. C. Jebb, H. Jackson and W. E. Currey. Cambridge, 1878.
2. *The Fifth Book of the Nicomachean Ethics.* Cambridge, 1899.
3. *Passages in the Eudemian Ethics* (a pamphlet addressed to Prof. Susemihl on the occasion of his jubilee). Cambridge, 1900.
4. *Texts to illustrate a course of Elementary Lectures on the history of Greek Philosophy from Thales to Aristotle.* London, 1901.
5. On the Parmenides of Plato in *Festschrift*, dedicated to F. Gomperz (Vienna 1902): privately printed in Cambridge, 1901.
6. Praelection on Plato's *Cratylus*, in 'Praelections delivered before the Senate of the University of Cambridge, 25, 26, 27 January 1906.' Cambridge, 1906.
7. *Journal of Philology.* Papers on Plato's Later Theory of Ideas.
   Vol. x, i. The *Philebus* and Aristotle, *Metaphysics*, 1, 6.
   Vol. xi, ii. The *Parmenides.*
   Vol. xiii, iii. The *Timaeus.*
   Vol. xiii, iv. The *Theaetetus.*
   Vol. xiv, v. The *Sophist.*
   Vol. xv, vi. The *Politicus.*
   Vol. xxv, vii. The supposed Priority of the *Philebus* to the *Republic.*
   Also Vol. x. On Plato's *Republic*, vi, 509 D *sqq.*
8. *Encyclopaedia Britannica.* Articles on Parmenides, Socrates, the Sophists, Speusippus, Thales, Xenocrates, Xenophanes, Zeno of Elea.
9. *Cambridge Companion to Greek Studies*, iii, 2. Philosophy to Aristotle. Cambridge, 1905–1916.
10. Various contributions to the *Journal of Philology* (especially on text of Clement of Alexandria), the *Proceedings of the Cambridge Philological Society*, and the *Classical Review.*
11. *About Edwin Drood.* Cambridge, 1911.
    Cambridge Review. In memoriam notices of E. S. Shuckburgh (1906), Wm. Everett (1907), W. E. Currey (1909), R. D. Archer-Hind (1910) and J. E. Nixon (1916). *Reviews and notes*: 'Junius Unveiled' (1909), 'Esmond' (1910), 'The Mystery of Edwin Drood' (1914, 1915), 'Some Textual Difficulties in Shakespeare' (1915), 'Cambridge Fifty Years Ago' (1910).

END OF PART I

PART II

OBITER SCRIPTA

OBITER SCRIPTA

I T is hoped that a good idea of Jackson's many interests, intellectual vigour, and sound and independent judgment may be gathered from the extracts from his correspondence which follow this memoir. They may be taken as representing, not inadequately, his opinions on many subjects, and to a considerable extent his manner of expression and familiar conversation among friends. To many they will recall delightful memories of the great room in Nevile's Court, where after dinner in Hall, Jackson was always ready, in degrees of undress varying with the thermometer, to welcome all comers, and to talk on all subjects, far into the night. Something of the quality of those talks may be recaptured from these extracts.

A.D.C. (AMATEUR DRAMATIC SOCIETY)

To W. DURNFORD
22 *February* 1905

I am heartily sorry that I cannot be present at the A.D.C. Jubilee. Unluckily I have an absolute engagement made more than three months ago. I should have enjoyed much the revival of the memories of the early sixties and of the years intervening since that time. Thanks to Clark's loving care and a succession of good actors, the Club is now a better exponent of the drama: but it is pleasant notwithstanding to think of the rollicking unconventionality of its youth.

J. W. has shown me in confidence Jebb's admirable epilogue. It is absolutely perfect.

ACTON, LORD

To F. J. H. JENKINSON
14 *July* 1902

Your question 'have you seen Grant Duff's long letter in the *Spectator* about Lord Acton?' gave me a piece of information which I much wanted. Last Tuesday (the 8th) there was an article in the *Daily News*, signed 'Verax,' on the 'hoarding of knowledge.' It was from end to end an ignorant and ill conditioned depreciation of Acton. In it 'Verax' quoted Grant Duff once or twice, without saying where his notice had appeared. With your help I have traced it to the *Spectator* of July 5th, and have read it. Am I completely mistaken, or was Acton

OBITER SCRIPTA

utterly unlike what 'Verax' and Grant Duff conceive him to have been? For apparently Grant Duff regarded him as a mere *heluo librorum*. Now to me it seemed, that whatever he saw, heard, or read, he formed a keen, and sound, and above all independent judgment upon it. It is true that he was slow to produce these judgments unless, either he was directly challenged, or he was moved by righteous indignation. But when he felt righteous indignation, it was righteous *wrath*: and when he was challenged, he seemed to me always to have a decided view. I sent a few lines to the *Daily News*, Friday the 11th, in protest against 'Verax's' onslaught.

ACTON'S LETTERS TO MRS DREW

To F. W. MAITLAND
27 *January* 1904

By the way, the night after I read Acton's letters I was at the Bournemouth theatre where Benson's Company was doing *Julius Caesar*. 'Brutus' was to me throughout a perpetual reminder of Acton's views about the morality of statesmen.

7 February 1904

I have now read the Acton letters for the second time.... To me they are more than ever interesting, because I can fit sentence after sentence to what I knew of the man. But I begin to wonder whether the man in the street will see that a reticent man is revealing his enthusiasms. If he does not, he will be more bewildered than ever, and will think that some of us are insane. ...Between ourselves I will confess that whilst I can heartily applaud Acton's enthusiasms for lost causes, I am a little dismayed to find that he erected Mr G. into a sort of God, and George Eliot into a sort of Goddess. When Mr G. does not come up to this mark, the letters become painfully sad: and this is the man whom that jackass Manning called 'cold.'

11 March 1904

I should have been sorry to be consulted about omissions, but I cannot help wishing that you had edited. I don't know whether Paul knew Acton well enough to sympathise with him, and to realize that he wanted to do the right thing, the chivalrous thing at all costs: and that what attracted him in Mr G. was his conviction that Mr G. would sacrifice everything, party included,

[124]

for an ideal. There is *nothing* in the letters which surprises me except the unrestrained admiration for George Eliot, and perhaps the intensity of his trust in Mr G.: but these enthusiasms a little weaken my confidence in Acton's judgment. George Eliot was a considerable personage: but I don't feel sure that, if Mrs Oliphant had begun to write a few years earlier, she would not have had George Eliot's place; just as I don't feel sure that, if Charles Darwin had not been warned that Wallace was about to publish, Wallace would not have had Darwin's place in the great world.

To C. E. SAYLE
11 *August* 1905

I cannot remember what I wrote to you about Acton's letters. They are to me amazing as a revelation of Acton. I agree with you that he wrote them, not for posterity, but for Mrs Drew, and that he deliberately gave her of his best. But I think that he wrote to her with a strong sense of responsibility for his words, because what he wrote might reach Gladstone. For, even if Acton would not confess it, he must have known that 'Mr G.' was open to influence and was deficient in insight: (he acknowledges that G. was a bad judge of men:) and that if he, the theoretical statesman, could win Mrs Drew, he might determine Mr G.'s practice in the right direction.

But the estimates of Gladstone and George Eliot shock me. They lower my estimation of Acton's judgment. 'The hanging judge,' as Maitland used to call him, seems to me to lose his head as soon as he thinks of these two. In my opinion Gladstone was a great politician, a considerable orator, a superb debater, and a consummate parliamentarian: but I cannot think him a great *statesman*. It is at once pathetic and ludicrous to find Acton, the irresponsible student, recognizing that Home Rule was inevitable, and rejoicing that Gladstone, the professional politician, was *unconsciously* moving in that direction.

I believe that what warped Acton's judgment was his sense of Gladstone's transparent honesty. I think that Gladstone was the honestest of all statesmen, but it does not follow that he was the greatest. In fact he was a hand-to-mouth politician. The nuisance is that this overestimate colours the whole book: and whilst Acton's regard for Mrs Drew seems to me always absolutely unaffected, his language is inevitably influenced by the habit of thought of his correspondent and her family. Granted the sentiment, the panegyric on Mr G. seems to me a superb piece of literature. You ask me whether I can tell you of some book which is fit to put alongside or to take precedence of it, some book which you have not read. If you mean some book which in some way resembles it, I would suggest Diderot's letters to Mlle Volland, though of course in them you will not find the learning, the morality and the earnestness.

ACTON'S LETTERS—MACAULAY

To J. M. IMAGE
8 *July* 1911

In the phrase which you quote from Acton, I note the word 'writers.' For myself, much as I admire Macaulay's businesslike style, which seems to me the norm which guides us all, I cannot put him amongst 'the greatest of English writers': I cannot put him in the same class as (say) Sir Thomas Browne.

I am sorry to say that the letters to Mrs Drew lowered very much my respect for Acton's judgment. I began to read them at 10 o'clock one night after our domestic bridge here: and though I tried to go to sleep, I had to light my candle and go on to the end. But his conclusions, that Gladstone was the greatest of 'statesmen,' and George Eliot of women writers, shocked me exceedingly. The judgment about Mr G. seems to me to confound 'statesman' with 'parliamentarian' and that about George Eliot seems to me to overlook the ephemeral quality of her work.

Someone asked me to write an article about the letters and I was very much tempted to try: but these two pronouncements stood in the way. I think that I know what made Acton over-rate Mr G.: and I can see that, writing to Mrs Drew, he was tempted to overstate in order that he might influence, and he gave way to the temptation. But with me the 'statesman' is the man who can look ahead and it seems to me that Mr G. never saw an inch in front of his nose.

Forgive me for pouring out these commonplaces.

AESCHYLUS

To PROFESSOR J. A. PLATT
10 *July* 1910

I am sorry if I shocked you. Please do not think that I want to run down Aeschylus! But I think quite seriously that in his day, as now, the writer of what was intended to be sung allowed himself licenses, slovenlinesses, and extravagances, which in other literary productions would have been intolerable, and are tolerable, when they are sung, only because the hearers are indifferent to the meaning of the libretto. This being so, I think that Aeschylus would be surprised to hear that we get grammar and sense out of his choruses. It is as if we were to regard as admissible English—'the marvellous world beholds amazed the glorious hierarchy of heaven.' But, if I sometimes scoff at the damned scholiast, it is because I am wholesomely conscious that I am a damned scholiast myself. Eudemus was by no means a fool and I try to clear up some of the messes which make you think him one. It amuses me, and it does not hurt him.

ANTHROPOLOGY

To G. P. BIDDER
27 June 1902

Nor do I know anything about Whitsuntide and Monte Vergine. There is an inclination nowadays to connect all festivals in spring and autumn with seedtime and harvest: so that it becomes easy to identify all spring festivals, and again all autumn festivals: for things which are equal to the same thing etc. I do not believe in a master key to all mythology.

APPULEIUS—PETRONIUS

To PROFESSOR J. A. PLATT
16 *August* 1900

'If you haven't read Appuleius': I have never read him from cover to cover: for, to tell the truth, Psyche bored me. But I have 'read in him' a good deal over and over again, in spite of his disgusting jargon. His vocabulary puzzled me much. Plainly he could write idiomatic Latin; whence then this horrible affectation? At last Pater's *Marius* came out, and provided the key. Appuleius was plainly recognised by Pater as his forerunner: Appuleius was in fact an African aesthete, and the author of the *Pervigilium* was another. Do you mean that you have never read Petronius? If there is too much of Appuleius, there is far too little of Petronius. In spite of the filth, which is very bad, it is, in my opinion, well worth reading. Surely a novel of contemporary life must always be more interesting than a historical romance such as Livy's great work.

OBITER SCRIPTA

AQUINAS—ROGER BACON

To SIR CLIFFORD ALLBUTT
2 November 1900

I have never tried to make out whether Albertus knew Greek himself. I see that F. Ueberweg (*Grundriss der Geschichte der Philosophie*) speaks of him as knowing Greek writers through Latin translations from the Arabic and the Greek.

Aquinas sent people to Spain to make versions from the Greek for his use. In his commentary on *Ethics* vi. 14 χεῖρον δὲ ὁ ἀπεσχεδιασμένος sc. νόμος, he writes 'alias vero dicitur lex aposchediasmenos (sic) ab a, quod est sine, et poschedias quod est scientia, et menos, quod est perscrutatio, quasi lex posita sine perscrutatione scientiae, vel schedos, quod dicitur dictamen ex improviso editum, inde schediazo. i.e. ex improviso aliquid facio, unde potest dici lex aposchediasmenos, id est quae caret debita providentia.' This presentation of the right reading misspelt and of a ludicrous etymology side by side with one which is very nearly right, seems to show that whilst he had beside him people who knew Greek, he had himself no real knowledge of it.

Roger Bacon however was plainly a competent Greek scholar. Nolan's book will show this conclusively. Indeed there is already proof of it in the *opera inedita* edited by Brewer for the Master of the Rolls.

In *Timaeus* 30 D f I translate νοητὰ ζῷα (as opposed to ὁρατὰ ζῷα) 'intelligible animals' just as I should translate αἰσθητά 'sensible.' But I see that Archer-Hind *ad loc.* renders νοητά 'ideal,' and I should think that in non-technical writing this might be the more suitable phrase.

I should much like to know your proofs of Albertus' ignorance of Greek.

18 January 1901

I am too ignorant to take up the cudgels for Thomas Aquinas, though I had given him credit for more initiative than you allow to him. I am very glad that you think highly of Roger Bacon. So do I. It seems to me that Francis Bacon is by his side a very poor creature—no more than a populariser of Ramist principles in a country which did not know Ramus.

[128]

ARISTOPHANES AT CAMBRIDGE

ARISTOPHANES AT CAMBRIDGE

To A. J. BUTLER

1 *December* 1903

The Greek Play was a huge success. Edwards had trained the Chorus, and Durnford the actors excellently. The men knew their parts. The byeplay of the birds was most entertaining. On the last night one of them, as they danced round the stage, dropped a huge egg.

Have you heard that Verrall gave, twice, a lecture in which he maintained that the *Birds* is a satire upon, and a warning against, that Palestinian religion which is now best represented in England, and that what is satirised appears in the Chapels of Jesus, John's, Trinity, and the R.C. Church in Lensfield Road? The lecture was set up for publication in the *Cambridge Review*, when Verrall, the evening before the *Review* appeared, withdrew it. The Editor cleverly revenged himself by publishing the facts, and commenting upon the lecture—'se non è vero, è Verrall.' I will tell you about it when you come here.

ARISTOPHANES, SCHOLIA

To F. W. MAITLAND

27 *January* 1904

I have been spending a lot of time lately very unprofitably in reading the proofs of an elaborate American edition of the Scholia on the *Birds* of Aristophanes. Hitherto I had never done more than dip into them: and, in as much as the commentators on Aristotle are quite splendid fellows whom I read constantly, I had thought that the scholiasts on Aristophanes would have interesting things to say, if one did but read them seriously. Lo and behold, they are no better than the barn-door commentator of this twentieth century. They write down obvious statements derived from reading the text, and very seldom have a scrap of tradition to add. Now and then they are palpably wrong. About real difficulties they know no more than we do, and I trust that most of us have rather more judgment.

OBITER SCRIPTA

ARISTOTLE: MATTER AND FORM

Draft (no name)
2 February 1900

My dear Sir,

I thank you for your kind letter of Jan. 26, which ought to have been acknowledged before this. The truth is that this is a busy time with me. As yet I have only dipped into Father Aherne's article in those places in which he talks about Aristotle. It was however immediately obvious that I must not in any way meddle in the controversy: for seemingly he accuses some modern writers, whose books I do not know, of teaching Aristotle's rudimentary physics. So you must not draw me into the dispute.

If there are such—if there are people who take fire, air, water, and earth to be elemental—surely it is waste of powder and shot to bring against them the whole artillery of modern science. But the title of the article does not express this. Aristotle's antihetical formula—matter and form—must not be confounded with his theory that fire, air, water, and earth are elemental. (Parenthetically I remark that by fire, air, water, and earth A. does not mean our fire, air, water, and earth which we perceive through the senses, for these are all impure compounds.)

(A) Aristotle regards each sensible thing as resolvable in analysis into matter and form. The brazen statue or the brazen sphere has for its matter brass and for its form the shape impressed upon it. The brass again has form and matter: and indeed the shape impressed has form and matter in like manner. So far this is mere definition. (B) In the ultimate analysis of a member of a natural kind (1) primary and ultimate *matter* (πρώτη or ἐσχάτη) is pure potentiality; in actuality nothing, but potentially capable of receiving any form whatsoever, (2) *form* is that which belongs to the member of the natural kind as such, (3) *accidents* are those characteristics which belong to the individual, not as member of a natural kind, but as an individual actualised by the combination of the specific form with primary or ultimate matter. This is the metaphysical statement of the doctrine of natural kinds. (C) In the *de anima*, stopping short of his final analysis, Aristotle regards body as the matter of the animal, soul as its form. But unluckily he has confused his statement, by speaking of soul as the form, not of the animal, but of the body. This is contrary to his usual practice, and it has made

[130]

ARISTOTLE: MATTER AND FORM

a good deal of confusion: e.g. Spenser writes (*Hymn in Honour of Beauty*) 'For of the soul the body form doth take, For soul is form, and doth the body make.' Rather, soul makes inanimate body into animate body or animal. This however is here wholly irrelevant. (D) Aristotle uses his antithetical formula as the basis of his theory of the elements and their transformations, for which see *de gen. et corr.* II, ii–iv. The elements, i.e. the constituents of material things, are fire, air, water, and earth: and fire, air, water, and earth are produced by the combination, with the primary or ultimate matter, of the primary qualities, hot and cold, wet and dry. Fire is hot and dry, air is hot and wet, water is wet and cold, earth is dry and cold.

So far as I see, Father Aherne is elaborately disproving my (D), the theory of the elements, which is not worth disproving: but in his heading he opposes modern science to A., which is, as after all he has to admit, an analysis of things capable of being used in conjunction with any physical theory whatsoever. This is surprising, and the confusion is worse confounded when at pp. 322, 323 he takes as 'materia prima' not pure potentiality, but pure potentiality already informed. In a word, he gravely misrepresents Aristotle, and as far as (from my standpoint of ignorance) I can see, he seriously confuses the issue. In short, (1) Father Aherne's own modern science in no way excludes 'Form and Matter.' But (2) I should be surprised to learn that there is anyone who regards fire, air, water, and earth as elemental. You will see from what I have written, that I know nothing about the bearings of Father Aherne's article.

ARISTOTLE, *POLITICS*

To PROFESSOR J. A. PLATT
16 *August* 1900

Last Easter I read the greater part of the *politics*: last month I read the whole of it. For some time I had put it aside. It is an amazing book. It seems to me to show a Shakespearian understanding of human beings and their ways, together with a sublime good sense.

To G. A. HIGHT
20 *December* 1918

Have you ever read Aristotle's *politics*? I am going to lecture on parts of it next term. It is a great book, and seems to me to have a Shakespearian appreciation of human nature.

OBITER SCRIPTA

MARCUS AURELIUS

To V. H. RENDALL

22 *July* 1917

I like people who like Marcus Aurelius: but I don't altogether like Marcus Aurelius himself. I have headed my copy of the Text—'A Prig, by himself,' and I doubt whether I should have got through it if I had not had the interleaf on which to vent my irritation....By the way, does it not surprize you that Marcus Aurelius writes such unkempt Greek?

A. AUSTEN LEIGH OF KING'S

To F. BRANDT

31 *July* 1906

I posted your letter to Mrs Austen Leigh. I think that the memoir is a great success. It at once commemorates Augustus and records what happened at an important crisis in the history of King's. My feeling has always been that, if he had been *less* sympathetic and tactful, people would have better appreciated the work which he did for the College. He did it so well that they do not realize that it was great and difficult.

BAGEHOT

To PROFESSOR J. A. PLATT

3 *October* 1904

I am certainly not a person who cannot read Bagehot. If I were to make a list of books, which have been suggestive to me, I should put down *Physics and Politics* in that red series of popular scientific books. The title is rotten, but the book is excellent. And I delighted in the old magazine which he edited and wrote for: was it *The National Review*? It soon died, and so did he. But I have never read the *Literary Essays*, nor yet *Lombard Street*.

BOOKS

16 *August* 1900

You say 'If I talk any more about books may I meet the doom of Solon ἀσκὸς ὕστερον κ.τ.λ. (*sic*).' Why stop talking about books? I thought that you, at any rate, like Macaulay, appreciated books. That at your time of life you should even in appearance scoff at them, dismays me. For me, as years go by, I value books more and more.... To me he (Macaulay) seems always to be, not historian, nor orator, nor politician, but the book-lover, and I respect him as such.

[132]

BRIDGE

BRIDGE

To PROFESSOR J. A. PLATT
15 *September* 1909

As to Bridge—the other night we were playing either Bridge, or what we call cut throat, i.e. three-handed Bridge. One of my twins dealt and made no trumps. Her sister doubled and we made grand slam. The fact was that we had all the black cards and the dealer had all the red.

BRITISH ACADEMY

To SIR G. GREENWOOD
3 *April* 1903

Thanks for your congratulations. I have long thought that either the Royal [Society] should revert to its older practice or a new institution should be started: so I am glad to have been elected.

W. H. BROOKFIELD

To PROFESSOR J. A. PLATT
2 *April* 1906

I have just finished *Mrs Brookfield and her Circle*. The book had a certain interest for me. W. H. B.'s father lived within about 200 yards from my grandfather's house in Sheffield, and W. H. B. and my father were intimates in early years. I knew him from childhood; and after Thompson became Master, when Brookfield was staying with him, he would come and smoke in my rooms and imitate the Trinity people of 1830. I am sorry to say that C. Brookfield and his wife have printed too many letters, and that W. H. B.'s letters are not as good as his talk. And I am bound to confess that he was too much the *society* talker to be quite first rate. But the book gives glimpses of interesting people, some of whom I knew.

BROWNING AND MEREDITH

To J. M. IMAGE
11 *July* 1911

I have to acknowledge that I used greatly to over-rate Browning and Meredith, very much as our predecessors had over-rated Wordsworth and Carlyle. But I suppose that in future there will be no place for private judgment, and that our literary likings and dislikes will be settled for us by the Academic Committee of the Royal Society of Literature. Fancy a 'xxxix Articles of English Literature' drawn up by Arthur Benson, Gosse and Co.!

R. BROWNING

To SIR G. GREENWOOD
22 June 1902

I have been reading *Any Wife, etc.* once more, and I come round to something which is very near your view, i.e. that the wife objects to any relations with other women, whether marriage, flirtation, concubinage, or promiscuity. But with this general interpretation it becomes necessary to explain 'must it be by stealth?' I suspect that R. B. wants to say—though he has not said—'is there any reason why I should be ashamed of it?'

The truth is that, whereas Ruskin can always explain in simple, intelligible, words, whatever he wants to say, Browning constantly fails to do so, and it is only by taking the context into account that we get at what is in his mind: e.g. xii, 1 'Is it true' thou'lt ask 'some eyes are beautiful and new.' 'Is it true' means, 'don't you know that,' 'you must admit that'—in fact, it stands for 'is it not true': and even that phrase would not be exactly appropriate. Again ii, 3 'its place' = 'it,' xviii, 6 'I know,' xxv, 5 'is it to bear?—if easy, I'll not ask,' xxi, 3 'all of thee,' Browning finds himself beaten by the difficulties of versification, and, in order that he may have something that will scan, writes what will not construe. This inability to deal with his material goes far to justify the doubt whether R. B. is a poet; and the fault is all the more apparent, if, as sometimes happens, the versification also is poor. In xvii 'only why should it be with stain at all' is paraphrased by the lines 2, 3 'Why must I be, etc.' In fact she regards both second marriage and flirtation, however trifling, as 'stain.' The word is not a good one, but he has made a verse. And now coming back to v, 6, I think (1) that I can strengthen my former interpretation. 'And gain the sky' does not echo 'the next world after this': it is, by anticipation, antithetical to 'and thou wilt sink' in vi, 2 and means 'rise to the height'; (2) that 'couldst thou repeat a stroke' means 'if you would make one more successful stroke': as if you were to

BYRON

say to a tennis player at 40 'one more such stroke and the game is yours.'

BYRON

To THE SAME
22 *June* 1900

Don Juan, iii, 103. Most certainly I leave 'O that face most fair!' In the 1833 edn. of the life and works, 17 vols., this passage is printed

> Ave Maria! oh that face so fair!
> Those downcast eyes beneath the Almighty dove—
> What though it is a pictured image—strike—
> That painting is no idol,—'tis too like.

I think that after 'strike,' there should be either a full stop or a note of exclamation. The absolute use of 'strike' is very harsh and shows that Byron was sorely put to it for a rhyme. But when you have got over these difficulties, what do you make of the whole of the four lines? From 102, 5 to 103, 2 he is talking about the hour and the bell, and we naturally conceive ourselves to be outside the church or monastery, listening to the bell, which announces at once 'the hour of prayer' and 'the hour of love.' Then in 103, 3, 4 there is an unmeaning ejaculation. Then in 103, 5–8 we are looking at a picture of the Virgin, presumably *in* the church or monastery. This picture has nothing to do with 'the hour of prayer' which is 'the hour of love'; and what we are told about the said picture is that it is 'too like.' 'Too like' what? Read on, and the general ineptitude is still more obvious. I maintain that this stanza is very bad.

To THE SAME
(In continuation of the preceding letter)
26 *June* 1900

Thanks for your letter. I have not got a Byron here to refer to, but I want to say a word in explanation. The starting point is that sunset is the hour of prayer and the hour of love, so that the bell is a summons to both. It is however love, not prayer, with which Byron is here concerned. When then, leaving the bell, which marks incidentally the hour of love, he talks about the furniture of the church or monastery which owns the bell, his remarks, however beautiful, are completely irrelevant. They are, in fact, 'matter out of place' or 'dirt.'

'Too like,' you say, means 'too like the reality of which it is a copy.' (1) The subaudition of the words which you supply seems to me slovenly. (2) When is a copy *too* like its original? Only, I imagine, when it follows exactly an original which it ought not to have followed exactly, because that original has defects, which should not be reproduced. In a word, 'too like' in the sense of 'very like,' seems to me, though a ladylike, a hateful colloquialism. You are at liberty to call this hyper-criticism. Byron lends himself to it. 'A palace and a prison on each hand,' i.e. two palaces and two prisons. It is as bad as Ovid

> hic fuit ille dies in quo Veientibus arvis
> ter centum Fabii ter cecidere duo.

To BERNARD JACKSON
9 January 1903

Have you ever lately read any Byron? For years I have kept clear of his verses, having ceased to regard him as a real poet as long ago as 1868, when I read *Childe Harold* in Italy, and concluded that its proper function was to provide banale quotations for Murray's guides. Horace has got *Childe Harold* for one of the subjects for an English Examination: so I am reading it once more. The notes, which don't pretend to be more than prose, are good prose and often interesting. But the verses seem to me only bad prose, and their substance the sheerest twaddle. Very rarely there is a stanza which has some tolerable rhetoric in it: but it is rhetoric, rather than poetry. Moreover I observe that the stanzas which I pick out as above the average are those by which he is best remembered: so that my judgment does not differ from the popular judgment as to what things in him are best, but only—though this is important—as to the positive value of what is best in him. I suppose the closing of Europe during five and twenty years gave a special interest to this sentimental rubbish about continental countries. But, whatever excuse may be made, it is surprising to me that people should have taken washy fluency for good technique, and tawdry claptrap for real feeling. Do you remember Macaulay's celebrated sentence about British caprice, as shown in the popular treatment of Nelson and Byron? It is my conviction that though people abused Byron, they were attracted by him, and that the attraction which his personality exercised upon them completely perverted their literary judgment. What riles me is

[136]

BYRON

that Germans and Frenchmen regard Byron as one of our
greatest poets.

I ought to guard myself. I have never abused Byron when he
aspires to nothing more than wit. I think *Beppo* and such like
excellent; at least I used to think so, and I don't imagine that,
when I read them again, I shall find that I have changed my
mind. What I deny to him is the poetic faculty. I think that
he must have been really a very hateful person—treacherous,
insincere, inordinately vain, a 'poseur'—but that he must have
been a very entertaining companion. He had read: he was
witty: and when he was not posing, he could talk first-rate good
sense. He was eminently sane, all the time that he pretended to
be morbid to serve his own ends[1].

To PROFESSOR J. A. PLATT
1 *January* 1904

I have looked into the new Byron only so far as concerns the
residence at Diodati in 1816. I must look up the part about
Jane Clairmont to which you refer me. As to your further
remark—I could imagine Lady B. saying—'he is not mad, and
therefore his conduct, in forcing a liaison with a young girl
just at the time when he is professing a desire for a reconciliation,
is inexcusable.' But of course, if the dates will not do, that is a
different matter. By the way there is a letter from Diodati to
Mrs Leigh which shows (1) that Jane and Byron met at Sécheron
by agreement, and (2) that by the end of the summer Byron
was heartily sick of her. It suggests further that Byron's interest
in her was cooling *before* they met at Sécheron. This is important
as regards chronology.

BYRON, SHELLEY, ETC.
To R. ST J. PARRY
4 *August* 1909

I dipped into the new Lord Broughton a few weeks ago, and
wondered how much of it had appeared in the old book. There
was nothing new about Shelley, Byron, and the Montauvert
album—a matter which interests me. Some day I will tell you
the true story. I think that Cam Hobhouse was Byron's most
respectable friend, and that Byron kept him in the dark about
his misdoings.

[1] See pp. 221, 222.

[137]

OBITER SCRIPTA

CAMBRIDGE FIFTY YEARS AGO

From the 'CAMBRIDGE REVIEW'

2 June 1910

LONG VACATION RESIDENCE

In my undergraduate period permission to reside during the Long Vacation was seldom granted at Trinity to any one who had not been placed in the first class in some college examination; but very nearly all who could obtain permission availed themselves of the privilege, and resided during July, August, and the early days of September. All the better mathematicians were here, because they depended upon 'coaches': and, though a few of the Classical men made up reading parties at such places as Festiniog, Keswick, Oban, most of them came into residence as a matter of course....Most 'coaches' charged £7 for the Term, and £12 for the Long Vacation: but Richard Shilleto charged £10 for the Term, and £20 for the Long Vacation.

THE STRENUOUS LIFE

Mr Conybeare had asserted that 'the Cambridge of 1860 looked, for the most part, with suspicion and dislike upon the strenuous.' Dr Jackson replies:

Now I am aware that there were in the generation which preceded Mr Conybeare's some men who were not judicious in the disposal of their time. I am myself very conscious that I did not spend my time to the best scholastic profit; in particular, I have unceasingly regretted that, taking advantage of the legislation, then recent, which made the classical tripos an avenue to a degree, I dropped mathematics. But I altogether dissent from Mr Conybeare's assertion [quoted above], and that 'the percentage of men who read hard, and the percentage who rowed hard both alike were considered legitimate objects of satire, as was also the small handful of Dons who had the bad taste to teach hard.' I can say confidently for myself, that, though the libraries of the University, the College, and the Union, and those nightly talks to which some of us owe so much, made serious inroads upon hours which I ought to have spent on the proper studies of the place, it was the man who read hard, the man who rowed hard, and, let me add, the man who did both, whom I and my contemporaries respected and admired....The Cambridge which I have known continuously

[138]

as undergraduate and graduate since 1858, was then, is now, and, I hope, always will be, strenuous.

From DR VENN

8 *May* 1910

Dear Jackson,

As I read your speech at the Discussion, you are rather sarcastic on Antiquaries—at least so it strikes the late president of our socalled society—for, after intimating that you propose to take an antiquarian view of the 'Caput,' you proceed to state that you know nothing about it.

I think there is some interest in considering what the old method was. So far from the 'Caput' being a 'Committee of the Heads' there was not necessarily any Master of a College upon it: except the V. Chancellor, and even he, by ancient rules, was not necessarily a Head. There were some good points about the old system. I should describe the body as 'representative' in distinction from 'elective': i.e. a small body was chosen by *rule* (not by election) to represent the aggregate of each of the principal different classes of graduates.

It comprised the V.C.; the senior doctors of the three faculties of Theology, Law, and Medicine; and the senior non-regent and regent M.A.'s. This was the law for very many years—down, I believe, to my own days.

One odd result of historical enquiry is to show the extreme youth, as we should now reckon it, of the acting members. Take the year 1588–9, the last year of Grace Book Δ on which I am now engaged. Reckoning the ages in the usual way, where I can't give a known date of birth, I make the body as follows

V.C.	Dr Nevile, age about 43	
Sen. D.D.	H. Tyndall	„ 39
Sen. LL.D.	J. Cowell	„ 33
Sen. M.D.	S. Perse	„ 40
Sen. non-regent	Mr Farr	„ 39
Sen. regent	F. Burgoyne	„ 27

i.e. the oldest of this Caput was many years younger than the youngest of the present Council.

The real vice of the system, at least in its later developments, had I apprehend no connection with its constitution; but was rather due to the rule, or custom, which gave an absolute veto to each separate member. Excuse my correction; but you see

I am editing a Grace Book and am therefore rather stuffed with the facts of the far past.

Yours truly,   J. Venn.

P.S. The earliest reference I have seen to the thing *Caput* is in 1526: the earliest to the name is in 1547 ('in capite ut vocant'). Its official designation was *Caput Senatus.*

To DR VENN (*Draft*)

9 *May* 1910

Dear Venn,

I am very grateful for your letter, and rather sorry that you did not take me to task on the spot. I think that you have misunderstood the spirit of my remarks, and I fear that others may have misunderstood me in the same way.

There was no sarcasm whatever in what I said. I disclaimed all knowledge of the older constitution, and in particular of the Caput. But being ignorant I ought not to have said what I supposed the Caput to have been.

What I wanted to say was that the existing constitution dates from 1856 only, that it has serious defects, and that those defects ought to be corrected in the light of the experience of half a century. Now there are some people here who resent all reference to the past history of the University as an irrelevant pedantry; and it was to guard myself against such that I confessed myself an antiquarian. Apparently I did not make clear my meaning: my notion is that, when a system is not working satisfactorily, it is worth while to examine its origin and development, and to ascertain how and why it has failed.

As to antiquarian studies as such, I am ignorant: but I can assure you that I deeply sympathise with those who pursue them, and that my ignorance of them is largely due to my fear of being fascinated by inquiries which would take me off from more pressing work.

What you write me about the Caput has interested me much. I shall now have to make out how I had got the impression that before 1856 the University was administered by a Committee of Heads.

With sincerest thanks,

I am,

Yours very truly,
Henry Jackson.

[140]

CHRISTIANITY AND PLATONISM

CHRISTIANITY AND PLATONISM

To F. W. FELKIN

29 April 1894

I told you that I would try to answer your letter of Jan. 25 during the Easter Vacation: but it was not till April 20 that I began to write and I had to break off in the middle to make preparations for my return. For several reasons, but principally because I hope that we may have an opportunity before very long of meeting and talking, I shall confine myself to a few bald remarks.

I most certainly think that Platonism, broadly understood, is reconcilable with Christianity: and more, that Platonism provides a metaphysical hypothesis which is sufficient for the purposes of the Christian.

We want, I think, *outside Theology*, a hypothesis of the universe, which shall enable us to conceive, however vaguely, Being and the development of Becoming, Perfection and the development of Imperfection. That it can be no more than (2) a hypothesis is clear: for how can the conditioned understand the unconditioned? But (1) some sort of hypothesis of Being we must have, unless we are to fall back upon (3) the more difficult hypothesis that $\mu\grave{\eta}$ $\mathring{o}\nu$ $\mathring{\epsilon}\sigma\tau\iota$ $\kappa a\grave{\iota}$ $\mathring{o}\nu$ $o\mathring{\upsilon}\kappa$ $\mathring{\epsilon}\sigma\tau\iota$.

These preliminaries are quite Platonic. In particular I might appeal to (1) various statements about the myth, and especially one in the *Phaedo* c. lxiii, (2) the passage in the *Parmenides* about the separation of God and men, (3) the hypothetical treatment of $\mathring{o}\nu$ and $\mu\grave{\eta}$ $\mathring{o}\nu$.

Now for the chief points in the metaphysical hypothesis which Plato offers us. When he says that $\mathring{\epsilon}\nu = \nu o\hat{\upsilon}\varsigma = \mathring{a}\gamma a\theta \acute{o}\nu$, he seems to me to say all that can be said about God without bringing in 'mythical' details, valuable perhaps to some or rather to all, but of which there can be no assurance. As for this fundamental equation, I sometimes think that it is tacitly assumed even by those who deny it. Do we not postulate $\mathring{o}\nu$, when we affirm $\gamma\iota\gamma\nu\acute{o}\mu\epsilon\nu o\nu$?

Plato's conception of the thought of God, evil and matter being the results of the pluralization of unity in thought, seems to me the only explanation of the good and bad in things. For, the belief in $\mathring{\epsilon}\nu = \nu o\hat{\upsilon}\varsigma = \kappa a\kappa \acute{o}\nu$—i.e. that belief in the devil, which seems to be the first article in some people's creed, is surely impossible.

[141]

OBITER SCRIPTA

This seems to provide the philosophical foundation which Christianity wants, at any rate when one comes to it, or comes back to it, from Agnosticism or Paganism. And I am glad to get it from Plato: for I abominate the notion, dear to so many, that the knowledge or quasi-knowledge of God is an aristocratic privilege enjoyed by a selected few. It may be absurd of Numenius to say τί γὰρ ἦν Πλάτων ἢ Μωυσῆς ἀττικίζων; but I sympathise heartily with Clement of Alexandria's liking for finding Christianity in heathens. It seems to me that (1) the attempt to restrict revelation to Christianity, and (2) what I may call devil worship, are two unchristian elements which have done Christianity incalculable harm with many thinking men.

As to the details of Christianity, when people urge that the historical evidence is of necessity insufficient here as in all other cases, I am inclined to quote from the *Phaedo* τὸ μὲν οὖν ταῦτα διϊσχυρίσασθαι κ.τ.λ.[1]: for Christianity gives me a working hypothesis, and that is what I require.

Is what I have written to the point? If not, let me know. I have no desire to shirk, and on the other hand I fear to dogmatise. Probably you have got things to say to me which I should like to hear. Some parts of your letter I have not touched, thinking that, at present at any rate, I had better limit myself to giving you something to criticise.

CLASSICAL TRIPOS, SECTION B (ANCIENT PHILOSOPHY) AND PRINCIPLES OF TEACHING

To R. ST J. PARRY

10 *July* 1904

Please understand my position. Personally, I should think it wrong to interfere in the choice of a section, because I think that the section for which a man has a leaning is for him the right section. But I can quite understand that other people may think this or that section mischievous, and may be moved to denounce it. I have nothing to say against this, and do not desire to make any complaint: but when lecturers boycott me, I think that the *tutors* ought to know.

Possibly it may be thought that my teaching is 'narrow,' in the sense that I teach my own heresies. I teach on my own lines because I have a definite conception of the development, and

[1] See p. 71.

[142]

a definite scheme helps the learner: but I do my best to make my pupils criticize and hold their own, and in this I think that I succeed.

CLASSICS

To V. H. RENDALL
17 December 1916

What you say about the Classics, that they have gained position in the war, surprizes me. My notion is that when the war is over, mechanics, engineering, electricity, and medicine, will have it all their own way. There will be innumerable problems to be solved. In Classics there is *one* great problem—pre-Hellenic civilisation: but what can be done with it? Elsewhere we 'hunt old trails.'

Classics have been a happy hunting ground for the Huns, and we have worked on their lines. But I think that is over now. Of course there may be a revival of the interest in the literatures. For example, George Trevelyan, senior, reads his Classics as zealously as Macaulay did. The old folks last, I think, because they are compact and concise, and give you things to think about. 'If you were to be in the desert, and to be allowed three single volumes—Bible excluded—what would you take?' H. Sidgwick and I both said Shakespeare, Plato and Aristotle.

CRICKET

To PROFESSOR J. A. PLATT
15 September 1909

By the way, not long ago the *Morning Post* had a cricket dream— 'England Past and Present at Lord's.' Of course the people in Nyren represented England Past. The article was all right for me: for I know my Nyren. When the Past were in 'Lilley was behind the sticks, and A. O. Jones *in the box*.' What does 'in the box' mean? If it means 'in the slips' why?

DANTE

To R. ST J. PARRY
26 September 1909

I do not know the *Paradiso* well enough to compare it with the *Inferno*: but I think that we cannot rate Dante too highly. Do you know Munro's sentence in a letter to Billy Johnson (Cory)— 'All other poets—Homer, Vergil, Shakespeare and the rest— are in comparison with Dante like children beside a grown man.' I think that this is almost an accurate quotation. The sentence would draw Billy Johnson: for Miss Coleridge tells in her

MS. notes how he gave back to her a copy of Dante with a contemptuous—'You can take back your Dant' (*sic*). Herbert Paul was quite right in taking Arthur Benson to task for calling Cory 'a good judge of literature.' He was enthusiastic about some literature in a lopsided way—quite a different thing.

DETERMINISM

To SIR G. GREENWOOD
11 *May* 1902

The phrase 'moral responsibility' seems to me to make confusion. Then again much turns upon the meaning which is attached to the words 'blame' and 'punishment.' I distinguish 'punishment' which is ἀποτροπῆς ἕνεκα (*Protagoras*) from 'vengeance'; and 'blame' a sort of 'punishment,' from 'damnation' a sort of 'vengeance.'

So far as I can see (1) the determinist thinks it right and reasonable to provide, artificially, rewards (including approbation) and deterrent punishments (including disapprobation or 'blame') to assist the individual to conquer the weaknesses which he inherits and the temptations to which he is exposed. Why not?

(2) The determinist thinks 'vengeance' (what people absurdly call 'eternal punishment') and 'damnation,' inflicted upon the individual (in consequence of the doings of his predecessors and his contemporaries as well as himself), as the height of injustice. Accordingly I strongly disbelieve in it. The race gets its due in the natural course of events, so that here no question arises. Of all men the determinist should recognize the value of rewards and punishments, the word 'punishment' being properly used. Remember that rewards and punishments are among 'the forces to which he is exposed.' If there is another life, it is reasonable to suppose that there too there is room for improvement.

When I say that a man is 'morally irresponsible' I mean that the act in question is done under such circumstances that the artificial motives of reward and punishment cannot operate upon him: e.g. if he acts under compulsion or suffers from *certain* forms of lunacy. By 'morally responsible,' I mean 'not morally irresponsible': so that he is accessible to the motives of reward and punishment. Forgive my apparent dogmatism. It means no more than the desire to be clear and brief.

[144]

DREAMS

DREAMS

To G. P. BIDDER

27 *June* 1902

(In answer to a postcard recording a dream of reading a letter relating to the illness of a cousin—which proved false.)

For more than a month I have been intending to write my thanks for your postcard and letters of May 20, 21. I hope most sincerely to hear from you that no harm has happened to your cousin, and that your premonition was—as often—a mere hoax. But I quite understand your action in writing to me: and I recognize that the postcard is the very best way of securing evidence.

You assume, I think, that dreams are chiefly built up out of *recent* waking thoughts. This is not my experience. In particular it is rare with me to dream about recent *anxieties*. A grave anxiety makes me sleep like a log. I note also—I think—that, when I *doze* rather than *sleep*, my dreams are specially inconsequent. Your comment about the incomplete sentence is plainly quite sound. You will observe that it was your ignorance as to the concluding word which *caused* the sentence to break at the bottom of the page. I am inclined to fancy that a dream is almost instantaneous, so that successive epochs of time, however short, hardly come into it.

EDUCATION

To H. O. D. DAVIDSON

11 *July* 1910

If you have not read in to-day's *Times* or *Morning Post* Lord Selborne's speech *ad portas* at Winchester on Saturday, read it. The concluding words are—'of the three, muscles, brain, and character—the greatest is character.' By 'character,' Selborne means 'moral courage—the courage which enables a man to defy public opinion and to take his own line.' Is this what you meant? If so, I most heartily agree with you. I have sometimes doubted whether the school and the University did what they ought to do: but I am glad to say as I grow older, I answer emphatically that they do. What we learn is to recognize our limitations, and, although we cannot do this or that, which our neighbours do, to find something which we can do, and to do it with all our might.

OBITER SCRIPTA

It amazes and delights me to see how much excellent work is being done by men whom I have known at Cambridge, and not unfrequently by men who at Cambridge have taken things rather easily: for example, Walter Hely Hutchinson, whom I saw the other day after very nearly forty years.

I think that we learn to do our best in our business, whatever it may be, and not to care what the world thinks about our business. And it seems to me that this is the best lesson which we can learn.

EPICURUS

To PROFESSOR J. A. PLATT

17 *April* 1899

Of course I belong to the Clough time, and it shocks me to find that the young people of the present day find nothing in him....

Is not Epicureanism a better philosophy than Stoicism, ἁπλῶς as well as 'for poets'? Surely Epicureanism absorbs all the Stoicism that is valuable, and leaves room for something else. But I hardly think that Omar FitzGerald was a sound Epicurean. After all there is something in M. Arnold's distinction between Hebraism and Hellenism: the Greek voluptuary is healthy, the Oriental voluptuary is morbid. It seems to me that Epicurus would have turned up his nose at O.F., Jacques, Sterne, 'et tous ces garçons-là.'

ESSAYS

22 *September* 1904

I knew Hallam much as the cannibal knew the missionary: I examined him. He was a very effective—no, an effective—examinee: but his scholarship was made at Shrewsbury in the sixties.

I was sorry to see in to-day's paper the announcement of the death of young Hudson of St John's in Wales. The death toll of mountaineers this summer must have been an unusually long one. People would be astonished, I think, if the statistics of mountain accidents during the last forty or fifty years were to be collected.

Do you know why it is that Essay-writing has to be taught at the Universities? I believe that the reason why so many men fail in power of expression is the penny post. I have been

[146]

reading a lot of letters written in 1828–1830 by my father from Dublin and London to my grandfather about lectures and professors, and hospitals and operations and 'sack-em-ups' and 'stiffies,' and by other medical students to my father. They are curiously different from the letters we write nowadays. They are carelessly but currently written, and very often have interesting things. Obviously the obligation to give the correspondent something for the postage he would pay, was the stimulus.

GAMES

To A. F. SIEVEKING

6 *April* 1912

It is not easy to find a term which will cover what I suppose you to include in your science. Am I right in my supposition? I imagine (1) that you are thinking of the recurrence of the same games in remote places—of hopscotch in Scotland, England, Ireland, Portugal, Goa, Bellinzona, San Remo, Cannes, and of the general resemblance of the scheme: of knuckle bones: of cat's cradle in New Guinea: of the backgammon problem in the Greek Anthology, etc.: and (2) that under the head of Games you include dice, cards, including patience, battledore, cricket, football, fencing, tournaments, running, jumping, wrestling; in a word, amusements, whether they bring people into conflict or not, and whether the skill shown in the amusement can or cannot be turned to serious account. Now I think that a Greek would put together *all forms of conflict* under the head of ἀγωνιστική, but this will not do for you because, as I understand, you are thinking of amusements only. Now παιδία and παιγνία mean 'a game, sport, pastime' as opposed to σπουδή, 'earnest': and you can make from them παιδιολογία and παιγνιολογία, which when written in Latin letters and anglicized will be *paediology*, and *paegniology*. But there is an obvious objection to *paediology*, that it suggests the Greek word παιδεία, 'education.' I think then that, if a Greek name is really necessary, you would do well to prefer paegniology. By the way, the *o* in the middle of the compound is a mere connecting vowel interposed between παιγνί- and λόγ-, these being the effective parts of παιγνία, and λόγος. I reject *athlology*, because it suggests competition for a prize, and in particular wrestling and the like. There are two useful treatises about the non-athletic games of the ancients, written (I think) in the xvith century: one is called, if my memory serves, *Palamedes*, who was the mythological inventor of such pastimes; the other *de ludis*. Do you mean that Paidialogy, Paignialogy and Athlology have been used? They are not happy inventions. The objection to paegniology is that it suggests 'the philosophy of playthings' rather than 'the philosophy of play': but I do not see how to better it. Anyhow it will be well to keep clear of paediology.

Can you throw light upon hopscotch—the French *marelle*, which the Cannois children call *misère*, or, in its more complicated form, *la misère du dimanche*? I once made a small girl explain to me the difference. What puzzles me is that the diagrams in remote places have a general resemblance, though the rounded end which in England is called 'plumpudding' in R.C. countries is 'paradise' and preceded by 'purgatory' and 'hell.' Is the diagram the ground plan of a church?

Where did the tennis court take shape? There must have been some one courtyard which had pent house, gallery, tambour (? a water spout), and grille, just as the buttress in Eton fives was a buttress of the Chapel. By the way, I once had to try to explain to some French people with whom I had played lawn tennis the rules of tennis proper. They knew *nothing* about it; but surely it was a French game? The difficulty of explaining a chase is very great, especially when it comes to 'better than half a yard.' If Eton fives should come within your view, I think that I might tell you something: for there were no written rules till, with Edward Lyttelton's help, I made a protest in *The Etonian*; and I am old enough to remember the left hand return which the printed rules of the present day very properly exclude. Its disuse—even before it was forbidden—altered completely the attitude of the server. But if Eton fives does not appeal to you, what I have written will be 'Hebrew Greek.' Anyhow I bless the buttress of Eton Chapel which gave to Eton fives its characteristics.

You will see from what I have written, that, if you are investigating games in order to make out their resemblances and their differences, and whether similar games have grown up independently or have been transmitted, you are attacking a problem which has for long stirred my curiosity.

It is curious to note how small details affect a game. In the middle of the sixties what was supposed to be an Eton fives court was built at Rugby. The builder spoilt it by indulging his fancy in some of the mouldings. A few years later an Eton Court was built at Harrow, and I pointed out that the mouldings and the angles of the ledges must be imitated exactly. The Rugby Eton court was bad because the player could play upon the larger moulding and the temptation to do this altered the short, sharp, cut of the Eton game.

It is very interesting to watch the changes which take place in a game when its rules are not quite fixed. It is not clear yet what risks should be run at Bridge: that is to say, it is not yet clear to me, and at Bridge too much depends upon agreement as to risks to be run.

To THE SAME

9 *April* 1912

I am very grateful to you for letting me see your articles on football: and I send you a few notes and queries suggested by them.

§ 1. I suspect that football originated in 'Kick about.' This seems to me antecedently probable, and I think that I have read of some town, where on some feast day the populace turned out and kicked a football. This might well be without a division into two sides. I remember how on Sunday afternoons in the late sixties, people stood around a circular space in the Champs Élysées and punted a football into the air, backwards and forwards: and how, an Etonian, half a Frenchman, coming along one of the avenues, and meeting a Frenchman who was running after the ball, charged him and got into a frightful row. I suspect that the larger Roman ball was used in this way: and I have a dim notion—which I cannot now justify—that it was principally used by people who had been bathing, to warm themselves.

§ 2. I venture to say something about modern developments. In the fifties and early sixties several large schools were started, and in the first instance were largely officered from Rugby— Marlborough, Clifton, Haileybury, Wellington. So Rugby football spread. We had it at Cheltenham, when I went there in 1856, though our connection with Rugby was very slight. In 1856 Hughes' *Tom Brown* came out and made the Rugby game known to all the world. I believe that in earlier times each club made its own rules as occasion arose. At the Sheffield Collegiate School in the early fifties we had *no* off-side rule: and when in the late fifties the Sheffield Club was started—according to the Badminton first ed^n the first Club for men—we had no such rule, though Tom Sale and I were familiar with the Rugby theory and practice.

When I went to Cambridge in 1858, old Rugbeans had a game once or twice in the season in memory of the past: but the notion was that football was a game for boys. Then the Harrow men and the Eton men started their respective games. Then they began to learn one another's games. Then 'association' was deliberately invented. I have an impression, derived (I think) from an illustrated MS. notion book, that football at Winchester in the forties was different from what it is now: but I cannot speak confidently about this.

The moral of what I am writing is—Don't assume that exact rules about football are very ancient.

§ 3. I do not pretend to have read your article critically for I have here no books of reference. But I append a few queries.

'Field' p. 599. I think that children and old men indulge in 'kick about,' not in a game. So I am with you about *follis*.

Does 'expulsare' mean 'strike' or 'throw'? Comp. Expulsim in Lat. Dicty.

Martial XIII. 83. Shilleto (?) understood this to mean that the flatterer caught the ball with the right and the left hands, when he ought to have caught it with the left, and that in consequence he deliberately lost points. Translate 'that again and again he may serve to you the catches which he has made (two handed).'

'Polybi sinistras' (epig. 72), q. Polybus' left hand *catches*.

XIV. 45 and IV. 19. When I lectured on Martial I thought that *laxus* here and elsewhere meant *large*. Surely a bladder is not *soft*.

2nd article, p. 92, φαινίνδα. If your derivation is right, say φαίνομαι = I appear, not φαίνω = I show.

Polybus again.

Have you investigated the history of tennis? You will remember it is referred to in *Henry V*, Act I. ad finem[1].

p. 93. Thermis Traiam, q. Traiani.

§ 4. It seems to me that football must infallibly grow up

---

[1] I do refer to 'Tennis' in *Shakespeare's England*, vol. II. pp. 459–62 (art. 'Games'). A. F. S.

everywhere, and that the chief differences in the rules will depend upon two things:

(1) Whether carrying is allowed, (2) how a ball which is caught is to be dealt with.

It does not matter much whether there is an offside rule, or what it is: but of course it largely influences procedure; e.g. carrying and passing in the Rugby game. By the way, it was a delight to me when I saw passing, of which we had no definite notion when I played the Rugby game.

To THE SAME

1 *May* 1912

I am sincerely grateful to you for letting me see the two articles, which I return herewith. It surprizes me to learn that the Italian game had been so exactly organized and so carefully described[1]: and I am astonished to find that at 'Hurling' there was a simple but effective off-side rule (p. 794 at top), and that the theory of 'passing' was well understood. I doubt whether in my disjointed remarks you will find anything which you want to quote: but I know of no reason why you should not use them, if you care to do so.

It is interesting that (1) you trace the organized ball game to Italy, (2) you connect it with the art of war. For the influence of Italy upon the art of war is obvious, and you have proof of it in the transfer of Italian words about war into French: e.g. fantassia, spadassia, alerta. I am convinced that 'qui vive?' is not French, but a transliteration of 'chi vive?' if that phrase is in Italian use: but I should not care to print this without further inquiry.

Your derivations of 'calx' and 'scrum' are very interesting.

I must look up Julian Marshall on Tennis. When you come to 'Fives' please let me know: for I knew the game before the rules were put into writing[2], and for a number of years I played

---

[1] By Giovanni di Bardi in his *Perioco del Calcio* (1585) and by Antonio Scaius in his treatise *della Palla* (1555–7). A. F. S.

[2] Did I say that the disuse of the left wall return of the service completely altered the position and attitude of the server? When I began to play the server had to stand in the middle of the upper court: he could not risk being hit in the face by the left hand return. But when this horrible return was first disused and then about 1876 prohibited, he could stand back into the buttress and did so. H. J.

with the acknowledged authorities of the Eton game such as the Hoares, Lyttelton, the Studds, Launcelot Dent: and I knew also the open court game as played at Rugby and at Cheltenham.

GREEK IN THE PREVIOUS EXAMINATION

To A. J. BUTLER

22 January 1905

You ask for a pamphlet, and I have not time to write one. But I will send you a few jottings and leave you to put them together. I think that in this way you will realise my position.

1° I think both Latin and Greek excellent instruments of education for the right men: but I think also that in this busy xxth century the wrong men ought not to be expected to take *two* dead languages.

2° By the wrong men I mean (*a*) men who have no turn at all for languages, (*b*) men who, for whatever cause, have got sick of Latin and Greek at school. You and I found all our subjects at school interesting: Greek, Latin, Mathematics, French, History, Divinity. None of them bored me. In fact, at Cheltenham, I was first in all, except in Mathematics, and in Mathematics I was second, and in French, which in the top form we did not take. At Sheffield I had been first in all, except history, which we did not take as a separate subject. But there are many boys who are not so fortunate in their likings, and they get horribly sick of the subjects in which they perpetually fail.

3° It is reasonable to require a modicum of Mathematics— at any rate Arithmetic, and similarly it is not unreasonable to require a modicum of dead languages: but for my own part I would rather get a decent modicum of one dead language than ask for a modicum of two and get failure in both.

4° I believe that the present system is pernicious. The boy feels himself always a failure, and because he is a failure in the subject which does not interest him, he becomes a rotter, and does not address himself to anything.

5° Of late years, thanks to open scholarships (which I detest), the better boys have been allowed to specialize for two or three years before leaving school: hence, when they leave, just at the time when they ought to be learning how to work their speciality in the Academic fashion, they have to go *back* to a subject which in the past they hated, and it does them no good at all.

GREEK IN PREVIOUS EXAMINATION

6° It is my conviction from long experience that a man gets inspiration from what interests him and not from what does not interest him.

7° I don't like the argument that 9 boys out of ten must learn Greek in order that the tenth may not risk his opportunity of learning it, because it seems to me immoral: but I do not believe that the tenth boy would lose his chance. Consider how girls have caught on at Greek, in spite of want of encouragement and positive discouragement.

8° The Syndicate's report requires a larger literary acquirement: though it does not make a smattering of Greek a *sine quâ non*.

9° We must remember how much things have changed since the Renaissance, when even a smattering of Greek was valuable, because it was a symbol of the newer studies.

To DR F. MELLAND
23 April 1905

I ought to have written about these things last term: but I was exceptionally busy. You have seen in the newspapers that we were discussing the old 'Greek question' and I was Chairman of the Committee which advocated the abolition of compulsory Greek. So I had a good many letters to write to non-resident voters, I had a heavy correspondence and many talks with the Secretaries, Committee meetings, I wrote circulars and letters to the newspapers, and even three leading articles Meanwhile my lectures were rather heavier than usual. So my private correspondence was neglected, and even now I am in arrears. It was a great disappointment to us to be beaten. It is the fourth time that I have been on the losing side in this matter. What especially pains me about it is that the opposition really rests upon a social prejudice, and this social prejudice is intensified by the existence and growth of the provincial universities. People say—'Let us keep compulsory Greek at Oxford and Cambridge, to distinguish them from the provincial universities'—in my opinion a very mean and illiberal sentiment. For my part I am sure that there is plenty of room for the new universities as well as for the old: and I am particularly glad to know that Sheffield has got its charter and that they are to open sometime in July. I am very glad that you sympathise

[153]

with me in this matter. Of course just now we are in a period of reaction, or else we should not have Chamberlain's fiscal scheme before us and Arthur Balfour in power. And no one can tell when the tide will turn. But when the tide turns in Imperial politics, we may hope for better things in University politics also. Till then we must keep up our spirits as best we may. The nuisance is that in times of reaction the younger men grow up either as Tories or as fanatics, with no notion of practical action.

GREEK LITERATURE

To A. O. PRITCHARD

22 *August* 1910

It is curious what a difference there is between the beaten tracks, and the out of the way regions, of Greek literature. I have spent many hours on Aristotle, *Eud. Ethics* 1246ᵃ 26–1248ᵇ 7, and I expect that what I am writing about the two chapters will fill perhaps 60 pages of the *Journal of Philology*. People have tinkered particular phrases, but they have made no attempt whatever to set out the argument. It seems to me that the old fashioned Latin translations did a good deal to prevent clear thinking. Men put the Greek into Latin, and did not always realize that what they wrote in Latin was not sense. Nevertheless, it is a comfort that there are things in Greek which have not been swept and garnished: and I am looking forward to the reading of your notes and queries. The fact is that a real difficulty interests me because there is something to be tackled, and in the out of the way regions there are plenty of real difficulties. But I do not care for what is fashionable nowadays: such as the conversion of Greek Tragedy into something resembling Bernard Shaw, or the rewriting the history of the Peloponnesian war on the assumptions (1) that what was likely to happen could not possibly happen, and (2) that Thucydides was such a fool that, if he says anything, it cannot be true. Here it seems to me that the old is good enough, and the new is worse. But even in the beaten tracks there are many things which seem to me far from a settlement: for example, *Nicomachean Ethics* vi, and the *Protagoras*.

GREEK PHILOSOPHY

GREEK PHILOSOPHY

To SIR G. GREENWOOD
24 November 1901

I never forget our evenings together over a chapter at the end
of Bain's *Mental and Moral Science*, which chapter was afterwards acknowledged to be George Grote's. I mean the chapter
which paraphrases Aristotle, *metaphysics* A 9—the criticism of
Plato. Book A is the one subject which I repeat every year: so
that by this time I have a considerable familiarity with it. In
those days, in my history of Greek philosophy, I was largely
dependent on Schwegler. Now, I have a lot of views of my own.
I think I said that Socrates was 'intellectually a prig, socially
a bore, physically ugly, otherwise wholly unobjectionable.' The
remark was based upon Ferrers' (the present Master of Caius)
description of the then Master, Guest, 'intellectually a fool,
socially a snob, physically dirty, otherwise wholly unobjectionable.' You distorted my bit of epigram; and when I tried to
reproduce it the other day, after so many years, I forgot to
use the word 'prig,' which is all important.

To G. A. HIGHT
23 June 1901

My dear Hight,
(I drop the formal M^r, trusting that you will drop the D^r
in like manner: common studies ought to put an end to for-
malities)....It will be a real pleasure to me if I can give you
any help in the October Term. I am very glad that you have
been reading the *Memorabilia*, both because the book is to me
a very interesting account of a very interesting personality, and
because I am sure the study of it will be a help to you in the
current reading of Greek. By the way, I hope you make a point
of re-reading *soon* all the Greek which you read. The second
reading takes only a short time; and whilst the first reading is
fresh in the memory, you are free to think of the substance of
what the author writes.
About τὸ τί ἦν εἶναι—you say 'I neither understand the
question nor how it can be answered, except by mere words and
classifications which bring us no further.'
To begin at the beginning, τί ἦν εἶναι is (in my opinion)
short for τί ἦν τούτῳ ὥστε εἶναι τοῦτο—'what in reality
has this thing to make it what it is?' τὸ τί ἦν εἶναι 'the what

made it so' is the answer to this question. As by assumption τὸ τί ἦν εἶναι is primary, it is impossible to explain by analysis of the thing in question into elements. Hence, both according to Plato and according to Aristotle, the only way of giving an account of the primary thing is to fix its resemblances to and differences from other primary things. In a word, according to both of them, the objects of knowledge are 'the what made them so's' of nature's kinds, and what we can know about them is their resemblances and differences, which resemblances and differences are comprehensively stated in a classification. But are you sure that the classification which comprehensively states the resemblances and the differences of what are assumed to be fixed natural types, is 'mere words' and 'brings us no further'?

Hicks brought me your letter of April 22, in which you asked him whether 'Plato or any other Greek philosopher had any inkling of what we now call *unconscious cerebration*. I mean of the fact that a very large number of our thoughts, motives for action, inferences are quite unconscious.' I know that your question started Hicks reading and thinking, and I have no doubt that he has answered it fully. I am not in a position to do so: but I may as well put down what occurs to me. I fancy that Carpenter invented, or at least popularized, the term *unconscious cerebration* to describe 'a doctrine which has been current among the metaphysicians of Germany, from the time of Leibnitz to the present date, and which was systematically expounded by Sir W. Hamilton—that the mind may undergo modifications, sometimes of very considerable importance, without being itself conscious of the process, until its *results* present themselves to the consciousness, in the new ideas, or new combinations of ideas, which the process has evolved.' Carpenter's *Principles of Mental Physiology*, p. 515. 1874. The stock instance is the process by which we all recover some fact or name which we do not remember. Note that this is a process of *discursive* thought. Now it seems to me that you include with this process of discursive thought what used to be called 'Innate Ideas,' intuitions or fundamental principles which are apprehended without process or 'discourse of reason,' e.g. the principle that the whole is greater than its part. Having made this distinction, I may go on to say what I believe to have been Plato's position. I know of nothing which shows that he had observed the unconscious

[156]

GREEK PHILOSOPHY

process by which we recover a missing fact or name, or put two facts unconsciously together: but in his middle period his theory of ἀνάμνησις—for which see *Meno, Phaedo* and compare the *republic*—distinctly and definitely assumes that we bring with us into the world certain innate apprehensions of the eternally existent ideas: in other words, that we already possess, and do not acquire by experience, certain fundamental notions. There is, I think, in the later dialogues no evidence to show whether he did or did not continue to make ἀνάμνησις a plank in his platform. Is this clear?

I was much interested by what you wrote both to me and to Hicks about your boy. It occurs to me to ask whether you have taught him the game of whist. In early days, when my youngest brother was a complete invalid, my father and my brothers got much out of it. In case you read novels, let me recommend Mason's books, and in particular *Miranda of the Balcony.* It is a fine book for young and old. I have read it to my girls and my younger boy.

Aldourie, Bournemouth

13 *July* 1901

I think I have owed you a letter for some time....I write at once in reply to your letter received this morning. In this 5ᵗʰ chapter of the *categories* Aristotle, from the point of view of logic, calls the *particular thing* πρώτη οὐσία, and he marks this in the words which you quote ὁ τὶς ἄνθρωπος ἢ ὁ τὶς ἵππος. The particular man, Joe Chamberlain, or the particular horse, Gladiateur, cannot be predicated of anything; unless you call 'This is Joe Chamberlain,' 'this is Gladiateur' predication. I think that A. would call it 'naming.'

You say 'If οὐσία is the substance of which things are made, it seems to me as if it could be predicated of those things.' Aristotle would agree, if, as I think, by substance you mean *matter*. Flesh and blood can be predicated of Joe Chamberlain and of Gladiateur. But, let me warn you, it is not often that either οὐσία or 'substance' means matter. If however by οὐσία or substance you mean the specific form, Aristotle in this very chapter affirms what you desire when he says that ὁ ἄνθρωπος (i.e. the universal man) καθ' ὑποκειμένου λέγεται τοῦ τινὸς ἀνθρώ- που: e.g. 'Joe Chamberlain is a man.' In short, unless I mistake, you understand Aristotle to say that οὐσία, either in the

[157]

rare sense of *matter* or in the usual sense of *form*, cannot be predicated of the particular. What he says is that the particular cannot be predicated of anything—except, by a strained use of the term, of itself. The phrase ὁ τὶς makes A.'s meaning clear.

But you may fairly say, and I think Wallace calls attention to this, it is odd that, whereas in *metaph.* 2 the specific form is πρώτως ὄν, in the *categories* πρώτη οὐσία should be the particular. The nomenclature is confusing, as is the use of πρώτη and ἐσχάτη ὕλη to mean matter in its most abstract conception. But there is *no* confusion of thought. For, the particular is *known* only in so far as it represents the species to which it belongs, and the species, the object of knowledge, does not occur except in the particular. The logician starts from the particular and calls it πρώτη οὐσία in *categ.* 5: the metaphysician from the specific form and calls it πρώτως ὄν in *metaph.* 2. Is this clear?

21 *August* 1901

Grote on the Sophists—indeed Grote always—is amazingly interesting and helpful. But, though the Sophists, as he says, had no creed, they agreed in rejecting philosophy, the search for truth: and though people had not given them credit for the good work which they did in making Greek prose grammatical and effective, I doubt whether *any one* had ever made of sophistry the bugbear which Grote belabours....

I do *not* recommend the scrappy reading of Aristotle. Read the *ethics*—Grant's edition is the best introduction: Susemihl's the most useful text: Stewart's is the fullest commentary, and I think the best. You will find the *ethics* exceedingly interesting: but there is not a great deal of philosophy in the narrower sense in it. Still it is one of the great books, and I think that you had better attack it at once. It is an *aperient* book, if I may use the phrase. I have never forgotten the effect which it produced on me when I was an undergraduate.

I fancy that your letter which I never answered was one of June 29....In it you spoke of your interest in Plato and the way in which he interested you. I was very glad to have it, for it made me wish more than ever to do anything I can to help you, but it did not contain any definite question. I must go to bed.

18 *March* 1902

...I always think people get most out of the studies which attract them: I mean, get most education. As for later life, it seems to me that everyone wants a hobby in addition to the routine of his profession: but I doubt whether it is possible to tell in advance what the hobby should be.

I agree that Aristotle's μεγαλόψυχος is very like Carlyle's 'hero.' Don't think that I don't admire the μεγαλόψυχος. I do admire him. But don't you think he is too egotistical to be an agreeable companion? Do you want to have him for your friend? Now for your remark about ἔνδοξα. I think that you have not quite taken Aristotle's point. In order to make a scientific system—in other words, to establish a science—premisses are wanted. How are they to be got? Plainly not from the science which is to rest on them. Now to make Zoology the science maker will examine animals, and to make Botany he will examine vegetables. But for ethics and politics, what is to be done? The modern will say, collect statistics, read blue books, study history. The Greek race had had a very short history, and not much of what they had, had been written. So it was not unnatural that Aristotle should collect the proverbs of the many and the aphorisms of the few, that is to say, the results of their experience, should criticize and compare their conclusions, and should in this way fix the premisses from which his scientific demonstration should start. If you like, you can call this heckling of experience philosophical: it is *not* in Aristotle's sense of the word scientific, because it is outside other particular sciences, and outside the particular science which is to spring from it. Probably you have got Grote's Aristotle with you. Grote seems to me very good about this dialectical, non-demonstrative, procedure. You will observe that even preliminary inductions will be dialectical, in as much as they are not demonstrative, and are always subject to revision. Whatever risk may be run in settling the premisses, the subsequent demonstration, if rightly carried out, is scientific.

13 *July* 1902

I fear that I must not think of attacking Nietzsche for some time to come. Just now I am reading in a leisurely way Eckermann's *Gespräche mit Goethe*. Eckermann is indeed a Boswell 'made in Germany'; stupid, commonplace, well-informed: and I don't like to think of the great man as the recipient of the little man's unctuous adoration. But now and then the little man records exceedingly interesting dicta. Still I hardly think that

[159]

OBITER SCRIPTA

I shall ever like it as well as I do my old favourite—*The Table Talk of S. T. Coleridge.*

I wonder how you have been getting on with the *politics*. It is out of my professional line: but I have a profound respect for it. It seems to me one of the most sagacious books—if not the most sagacious—ever written. But you have to keep in mind the differences between the Greek πόλις and the modern nation: such as, that Athens, a complete selfcontained unit, never numbered more than 31,000 full citizens of years of discretion: that representative government was unknown (there is only one allusion to it in the *politics*, I think): that all the drudgery was done by slaves: that Aristotle himself had at Athens no status in the πόλις which enabled him to take part in politics: that appointments were made to a good many offices at Athens by lot.

Compare 28 December, 1918 to G. A. H.

Have you ever read Aristotle's *politics*? I am going to lecture on parts of it next term. It is a great book, and seems to me to have a Shakespearean appreciation of human nature.

24 July 1902

...relation of politics and ethics. A. puts this in different ways at different times. At the beginning of the *nicom. ethics*, ethic for the individual stands side by side with politic for the state, the larger man. At the end of the *ethics*, politic is invoked to help ethic by training the individual so that he may attain his greatest happiness.

In the *politics* it is assumed that the well-being of the individual depends upon the well-being of the state, and indeed that it is only as a member of the state that the individual can even hope for his best ἐνέργεια: and accordingly we seek politic first, and ethic as a means to it.

These are three distinct relations: but I think that ethic and politic stand to one another in all three, and that Aristotle is not exactly inconsistent in thought.

The *Meno* is, as Mill says, 'a gem.' For *Homo Mensura* you must read the *Theaetetus*, not the *Protagoras*. Don't misunderstand me about Eckermann. I respect his enthusiasm and his knowledge and his simplicity. But he is tiresome, and his servility draws out Goethe's egotism. I suppose that, in truth, I much prefer the way in which the *Table Talk of S. T. Coler-*

idge is done: fragments of his talk, without the intrusion of the reporter. But, believe me, I am sincerely grateful to Ecker-mann. The 'table talk' of a great writer, if well done, may be better than his writings.

15 August 1902

Most certainly Heraclitus exercised upon Plato a very im-portant influence. He began his philosophical studies under the Heraclitean Cratylus: so that his starting point was Heracli-teanism. But I think he must early have drawn the sceptical inference to which (see the *Theaetetus*) Heracliteanism pointed. (You will remember the place in the *Theaetetus* where he points out that the Heraclitean doctrine is suicidal.) When he left Cratylus, he was, then, a sceptic, ready to receive Socrates' non-philosophical or agnostic teaching. Later, when he re-turned to philosophy, he accepted the scepticism of Heraclitus as far as the world of sense is concerned, and *therefore* looked elsewhere for knowledge. Thus, though Heracliteanism gave him an impulse, it contributed nothing *positive* to Plato's teaching, and consequently I do not draw a connecting line. In the same way, Heraclitus influenced Parmenides: but Heraclitus did not contribute positively to Eleaticism, and therefore I refrain from drawing a connecting line, though I deliberately place Parmenides in the same column with Heraclitus.

In the nature of things *all* the predecessors influence, directly or indirectly, the successor. My lines are intended to mark the direct connections of the positive teaching. My stemma is in fact a pedigree.

I connect Plato with Parmenides, because while Zeno on the one hand and Empedocles etc. on the other have abandoned the recognition of ὄν and μὴ ὄν which seems to me of the essence of Parmenides' teaching, Plato reverts to it. He is a better Par-menidean than any of the one-sided people who have intervened. Let me put it in another way. Plato learns from Heraclitus that he must not look to the sensible world for knowledge. Parmenides tells him that there is an ὄν as well as a μὴ ὄν. Socrates tells him to seek λόγοι. Plato then proceeds to seek λόγοι of ὄντα. Thus Parmenides and Socrates contribute something positive: Heraclitus' contribution is negative: i.e. he has warned Plato off the world of sense. Is this clear?

OBITER SCRIPTA

I am glad that you have taken to Coleridge's *Table Talk*. Of course we want very often to quarrel with him. If the book had been read to him, he would have very often quarrelled with himself. For is it not table talk? It gives one side of a question, and does not necessarily pronounce final judgment. But it is wise, eloquent, and stimulating.

. . . . . .

It seems to me that in the later Platonism *all* the previous systems are represented—with the exception of atomism: and even atomism influences him, because he is always protesting against its materialism.

30 *March* 1903

I am heartily glad to hear that your Greek studies continue to flourish. By this time you have got through the drudgery.... I rather think that the great point both in Plato and in Aristotle is that they are imbued with the Socratic spirit, and instead of doing your thinking for you, invite you to join them in their investigation....By the way, you will find that it pays you well to read and re-read and re-read again Plato and Aristotle. These old folks pack a great deal of thought into a small compass, and stand re-perusal far better than most of our modern books.

2 *September* 1903

Tell me some time how you find Augustine. I once read a small part of the *de civitate dei*: but I know nothing about Augustine except Kingsley's lively picture of him in *Hypatia*. If you do not know that great book, read it. C. Kingsley was a real genius, and in *Hypatia* he is at his best. I always rejoice that I knew him personally as well as in his books: and it was a pleasure to me once, when I looked up *all* the ancient authorities about Hypatia, to find how skilfully he had used them in constructing his story....Did you see Rostand's address on his admission to the Academy? I think that I have never seen anything more characteristically French. They make literature which is literature and nothing else.

To PROFESSOR J. A. PLATT
27 *September* 1911

Do you know that S. Andrews is upsetting the history of Greek philosophy, and asking us to believe that Socrates was a Pythagorean philosopher, who kept a school of philosophers who dined together, that Socrates received from the Pythagoreans the theory of ideas as presented in the *Phaedo*, and the *republic*, and that that theory was always numerical? So says A. E. Taylor on the authority of Burnet. A large mouthful.

To G. A. HIGHT
6 June 1912

There is a new fashion in Greek philosophy. The new people —A. E. Taylor, John Burnet and perhaps (I am not sure) Cornford, say that Xenophon and Aristotle knew nothing about Socrates and Plato, that Plato was a mere reporter of what Socrates said, that Socrates kept a sort of School or College, and taught what I call Platonism, and that he got it from the Pythagorean school, of which he was a member. You will see that this means the rejection of the evidence of Xenophon and Aristotle. Of course I scoff.

HARCOURT, SIR WILLIAM VERNON
To PROFESSOR J. A. PLATT
3 October 1904

I am grieved to see in today's paper the news of Harcourt's death. I have been reading in the *Standard* a very ill-natured obituary: but people should always say what they think. What was Randolph Churchill's 'even more forcible retort' when Harcourt said 'You little ass'? He was a man whom I heartily liked, and I am inclined to think him one of the honestest of politicians. His edition of Lucan has never appeared: but he died at Nuneham not at Trinity.

HORT—LIGHTFOOT—WESTCOTT
To A. O. PRITCHARD
1 June 1916

Hort was a wonder of versatility: in my opinion a greater man than either Lightfoot or Westcott.

27 May 1916

Tell it not in Gath, but I thought * * * highly respectable, but a dull dog, vastly inferior to Lightfoot, a man of learning, and Hort, a man of insight. A French theologian once asked me to characterize Hort, Lightfoot, and Westcott. I said offhand

[163]   11-2

that Westcott was *will*, Lightfoot *learning*, and Hort *esprit*. I think this really expressed my estimate.

The fellows of this College in the fifties were commonly Alpine Clubmen. As late as 1876 I met Lightfoot at the Aeggischhorn, and took mild walks with him. I think that at that time Hort still went to Saas Fée. R. Burn was still king of the Aeggischhorn, and Hardy of Sidney of the Riffel. You tempt me to tell you two stories. Hardy once said to a Cambridge lady that he was too old for Alpine work, of which he had been bragging. She said 'In fact you are now in your *table dotage*.' The same lady said of Hardy that 'When he had been in Switzerland, the flies suffered from D.T.' You will say that I am in my anecdotage, and you will be right.

PROF. HOUSMAN'S INAUGURAL LECTURE

To PROFESSOR J. A. PLATT

10 *May* 1911

Housman's discourse was excellent. He smote with all his might two tendencies of modern scholarship—on the one hand, aesthetic criticism; on the other hand, the slavish, mechanical, methods of the Germans. The V.C. was absent, and asked . . . . to speak at the end. I fear that . . . . was shocked that Housman washed his hands of aesthetic criticism: he hoped that what Housman had said was all ironical. So in effect his neat speech was at once stupid and rude. For myself, I rejoiced exceedingly in the texts of Housman's preachment. And the manner was perfect. He trounced Swinburne most effectively in respect of a reading in Shelley. His denunciation of the 'slave labour' of the big German-Latin Dictionary rejoiced me especially. And, personally, I was much pleased with what he said about Munro and Mayor. He was kind, just and truthful.

IDLE READING

To BERNARD JACKSON

9 *January* 1909

I have been very idle. I have been reading Robertson Smith's *Religion of the Semites*—an interesting book, but he writes so easily and fluently that he is apt to be longwinded, and it is a little difficult to master his results. I have also done some preparation for my lectures on Aristotle's *de anima*, and am feeling more than ever the difficulty of the subject.

We finished *Guy Mannering* last night. It is a comfort to find that I like it at least as much as I did the last time I read it. It seems to me, as a whole, far better than *Rob Roy*—better in construction and better in composition.

Did you ever read Henry Kingsley's *Geoffry Hamlyn*? I began turning it over last night once more, and enjoyed it as always, in spite of its extravagances. Did you ever read any Balzac? When I come to France I generally read a volume. This time my venture has not been very successful: but it is 'all in the day's work,' for I intend in course of time to get through the forty solid volumes of the *Comédie Humaine*. At present I have not disposed of more than a quarter of it. I suppose that when I have got to the end of it, joy at the achievement of the feat will prejudice me in Balzac's favour. He was certainly a great student of manners and character, but is not *light* reading.

LITERATURE, MISCELLANEOUS

To BERNARD JACKSON
6 *October* 1918

Somehow the Sheffield people of 60 years ago hardly knew that father was the most literary man in Sheffield, and spotted the good things in literature in a very wonderful way. J. F. McLennan's *Primitive Marriage*—an epoch-making book—came out in 1865: but father had it, and I annexed his copy, and preached McLennan versus Maine (with modifications) to the Apostolic Society. And I think that father's *Professor at the Breakfast Table* was an American edition. That too I took to Cambridge before people there knew it, and I planned a local, Cambridge, imitation, as likely to be better than a University novel.

By the way, do you know *Wheat and Tares*? A short story by (Sir) Henry Cunningham—a forgotten Indian official. I have always backed it as the best of short stories, and I think that I must have advertised it to you. I have been reading it again. I think that it must have come out in the later sixties, for I have no recollection of mentioning it to father or hearing of it from him. People did not like Sir H. Cunningham. A lady once said to me 'If you like his novels, I can have no confidence in your judgment: but you shall come to stay with me, that I may introduce you to him.' My friend was a Lawrence and Cunningham married a Lawrence and the family thought her too good for him. But whatever Cunningham may have been, *Wheat and Tares* is a very good book. Once C. was at my rooms, but he was overcrowed by a bigger man, Goschen.

MACAULAY—KIDD (SIR C. DALTON)—TRUTH

To J. M. IMAGE

3 *July* 1911

I think that Sir Corny completely makes out his case. It is a sickening story, which may rank with that of Byng.

As to Macaulay, the confident, epigrammatic, sentences are quite like those with which he damns Warren Hastings and Impey. You will remember Fitzjames Stephen about them.

It is very difficult to get at truth. Small differences in the telling of a story completely alter the effect. I once wrote a paper on 'Ought we to believe half what we hear,' and I worked out three instances.

(1) The notion that Rousseau cared for the beauties of nature; (2) the story that Byron erased ἄθεος after Shelley's name in the Montauvert album, whereas what he erased was Jane Clairmont's name; (3) Thompson's 'infallibility of the youngest' which is always misconceived as a brutality, for want of knowledge of the circumstances. No one felt it so at the time.

I am afraid that Macaulay's eye for the effective in exposition disqualified him for the discovery of the truth. I am sorry: for when I was young, nothing stimulated me more than Macaulay's *Essays*, and I am therefore eternally grateful to him.

MACAULAY

11 *July* 1911

I think that Macaulay's style influenced most of us for good, by teaching us to aim at simplicity and clearness. (We have not as many 'relative' sentences as the pre-Victorians.)

For example, contrast the styles of Fitzjames and Leslie Stephen with that of their father Sir James. They all wrote well: but Sir James is before Macaulay, and the sons are after him. I think that some of the deliberate imitators took no harm, because it was not in them to be more than workmanlike:

[166]

e.g. John Morley. But I quite agree with you that with G. O. T. imitation is so servile that it reads like parody. He has somewhere a sentence about North or some other xviiith century minister to the effect that 'he called for troops as often and as urgently as he called for trumps.' The jingle would be bad anyhow: but the minister could not call for trumps, because Porchapelles did not invent the signal till 50 or 60 years later. G. O. T.'s allusions often seem to have been crammed for the occasion and to encumber the exposition, whereas T. B. M.'s are the outpourings of a full memory and are genuinely illustrative.

MACAULAY—DAME ALICE LISLE

To J. M. IMAGE
8 *July* 1911

I too had classed C. B. Ward with Jeffreys. Three or four years ago I was at a child's birthday picnic in the New Forest within a quarter of a mile of Moyle Court where Dame Alice Lisle lived and did a good work. Ours was a very merry party: but for me the tragedy was in the background all the day. I think that the love of justice is one of the most prominent traits of English character: so when ministers of justice misbehave, we are infinitely shocked. It is strange that Macaulay did not get hold of the truth: for he had written eagerly about Alice Lisle and the Bloody Assize as early as *Knight's Quarterly*.

I cannot help thinking that Macaulay's prodigious memory spoilt him as a historian. He read some highly flavoured narrative, and it fixed itself. When the time came for writing, he drew upon his retentive memory, instead of investigating his facts *ab initio*. Probably in this case he never read up the trial. And without doubt he had an eye for a picturesque incident or a telling phrase. Did you ever read Eachard's *Causes of the Contempt of the Clergy?* Many of Macaulay's best phrases are taken straight from it. It is excellent stuff.

MAHAFFY AND TRINITY COLLEGE, DUBLIN

To A. J. BUTLER
28 *March* 1904

I always regret that I have never seen T.C.D. Twice I have had to decline an invitation to go there—once when they were celebrating Berkeley, the other time when they were keeping a centenary. And I am heretical: I like and believe in Mahaffy. At Cambridge I dare not say so: for, as Mahaffy once wrote on a postcard to S. H. B., 'The God of the Cantabs, like the God of the Hebrews, is a jealous God.'

MATHEMATICIANS' ALPHABETS

To PROFESSOR J. A. PLATT

8 September 1911

Your remark about the mathematician's greed for alphabets reminds me of a fellowship election story. A mathematician of even exceptional ignorance—perhaps * * * —was a candidate. Thompson said that there was no evidence that he knew the Greek letters. 'Indeed Master,' said a mathematical elector, 'we use all of them.'

METAPHYSICS

To SIR G. GREENWOOD

21 September 1904

I have read Balfour's address once and mean to read it again. One man described it to me as the Diversions of a Politician. I should think that Whetham's book will have a run: for when physicists become metaphysical and revive the speculations of Democritus and other such ancient folk, the man in the street can more or less follow their arguments. Metaphysics is a great leveller: for no one *knows*.

You criticize the phrase—'the assumption that a certain process *is not going on* anywhere throughout the depths of time and space.' I suppose that he means *does not go on*: for though *is not going on* refers to the present moment only, *does not go on* = cannot occur in past, present, or future. In a word, this is another illustration of my theory that in modern English the simple present ('I write' as opposed to 'I am writing') is an aorist, and not a present. Of course W. D. W. is wrong.

As to time, Spencer, and Kant, I am an ignoramus. But I am quite clear that time and space are not things, but two *sorts* of relation in which things stand to one another. In fact, I imagine them as two planes of relation at right angles to one another, the plane of sequence and the plane of coexistence. In so far as a thing is related to another thing at the same moment, they

[168]

are in space. In so far as a thing is related to another thing successively, they are in time. This being so, I cannot call time and space entities, unless I give the same name to coexistence and sequence. (I think Plato would regard time and space as sorts of difference, and it takes difference and sameness in combination to make existence.) But, as Plato makes Socrates say somewhere, 'you must not look for clearness from me.'

When we were discussing Balfour's address, one man thought my 'planes at right angles to one another' helpful, whilst another considered it quite the other thing.... The moral of the difference of opinion between my two friends is that metaphysics is what Plato would call 'mythical,' and that each man must make his own myths.

NIGHTINGALE, FLORENCE
To MRS SIDGWICK
20 July 1902

I have seen it stated that the new Order of Merit is open to women as well as to men: and it occurs to me that there could be no more proper recipient than Miss Nightingale.

There are perhaps few people who realise that she is still alive: but I think that there are many who remember how she stirred the country by putting her knowledge of nursing at the disposal of the Government in 1854. Surely the nomination would be popular. I have always thought that it was her action at that time which prepared the way for the movement for the education of women: and when we were hoping for degrees for women, it was my earnest wish that she might be one of the first to receive honorary degrees under the new system. Could you and would you do anything? I hope you will not think me indiscreet for writing this letter.

NOVELS
To PROFESSOR J. A. PLATT
7 January 1916

Tell me what you think of *The Caxtons* after this new reading. It belongs I think to one of my by-gone periods. Do you know *My Novel*? With me that also is, I imagine, by-gone.

I tried a collection of short pieces by Masefield, but I did not catch on.

[169]

OBITER SCRIPTA

I have finished another reading of *Esmond*, and still think it the best of all novels. I rather think that I put *Barry Lyndon* second: but it is a question with me whether the history of a scoundrel is admissible. I am glad to think that I caught on with *Esmond* when I was thirteen, and that I have not changed my mind as to its greatness: and I laugh when I remember that I tried to tell the story in my bedroom at school after lights were out. My attempt was a failure: they went to sleep. But my failure made me appreciate Thackeray more. About 1865 some of us at my rooms drew up lists of five favourite English novels. H. Sidgwick named the five George Eliot novels then published. I took my five from different authors: *Esmond, Rob Roy, Roxana,* the *Initials,* and (perhaps: I forget) *Persuasion,* or *Pride and Prejudice* or the *Mill on the Floss.* Nowadays I think I should say *Esmond, Rob Roy, Pride and Prejudice,* and stop at the three. Or add *Guy Mannering* and *Barry Lyndon* or *Persuasion,* abandoning my limitation of one author one book. Anyhow George Eliot drops. Must the *Vicar of Wakefield* and *Cranford* come in? But damn triposes, the curse of the xix[th] century—anyhow, they need not invade the xx[th]. But I am a foolish product of the xix[th], and do not appreciate the greatness of Rupert Brooke. Anyhow I am not, thank goodness, a peace-crank. I only wish I were not an old foguey—or is it fogey?—and could go and kill a German or two. I used to have a dread of the shedding of blood. It now seems to me a sacred duty, just like the slaying of mosquitoes, and I should like to say this to our U.D.C.: but as I am too gouty to volunteer, I feel that I am silenced.

What can Simon mean? His speech was rotten to the core: for it never touched his principle.

[Earlier in the same letter.]

The deaths are grievous: but it is better to think of the deaths than of the shirks.

JANE AUSTEN

To BERNARD JACKSON

25 *January* 1885

I have been reading *Pride and Prejudice* again—I stick to it that the characters are *not* ordinary, though they are natural. Elizabeth's prejudice is, I think, thoroughly natural: a very little prejudice, not kept at all in check, + a very little mis-

[170]

NOVELS

representation + faults in Darcy of a very obvious sort, lead to
a thoroughly natural dislike, which in due course disappears.
As to Darcy, he clearly 'has not been at a public school,' and
consequently has to get his kicking from Elizabeth: but it is
to be remembered that his original impertinence is *overheard*.
What wants explanation is the mixture of good taste and bad
taste in the same society and even in the same family. But,
query, was not this so in country places at the beginning of the
century?

To PROFESSOR J. A. PLATT
19 *April* 1901

I thank you for calling my attention to *Emma*, vol. iii, ch. iv. It
is a good instance of J. A.'s care of detail. Emma remembers
about Knightly: Harriet remembers about Elton. What Harriet
says is 'Ah! I do not know: I cannot recollect.' In reality, she
is surprised to hear what Emma tells her: but instinctively she
expresses a polite surprise that she has *forgotten* what Emma
confidently asserts. This seems to me quite sound.

.   .   .   .   .   .

I have read nothing lately worth mentioning to you except
some superb Greek compositions of Archer-Hind's. They are
amazing, and, when they appear, ought to make a stir, if anyone
still cares about such things.

3 *January* 1911

I have not read *Emma* lately: but you cannot overpraise it
to me. I don't remember the points which you note: but they
are very characteristic. Please do not imagine that I put
Dickens in the same class with Jane Austen. I look respectfully
at the house in which she died every time I pass it, and that is
not seldom. I am glad to think that Sir Walter appreciated her.
I must look up the conversation between Frank and Emma.
I think that Frank is excellent. Miss Austen damned him with
faint merits, and has not damned him too much. But good as
Emma is I think *Persuasion* more perfect, and I delight in *Pride
and Prejudice* most.

27 *September* 1911

I rank *Mansfield Park* very high as literature: but I should
not much care to associate with the people: they would bore

[171]

me. I could more easily be in love with (1) Elizabeth, (2) Anne, or (3) Emma, and *therefore* I put *P. and P.*, *P.*, and *E.*, before *M. P.*

To PROFESSOR J. A. PLATT

15 *August* 1913

I am rather glad that you are a little in love with Fanny Price: but I fear that I think her a well-meaning worm constitutionally incapable of turning....I too am in a state of dissatisfaction. For example, life and character in Miss Austen seem to me to want pepper, salt, and mustard. Whence is your phrase 'The fashion of this world passeth away' etc.? In 'the eternal' also I desiderate those three condiments. But I suspect that Miss Austen's time, locality, and mode of life, were exceptionally stagnant, just as English politics were stagnant in the early and middle sixties. And it must be admitted that dissatisfaction may be due to other things besides stagnation. At the present time one source of dissatisfaction is, I fear, vulgarity, as seen in Lloyd George and the suffragettes. But do not think that I am a traitor to Jane Austen. She may have had a dull time, but she has made it live, and the triumph is all the greater, because she does not draw the long bow. The most exciting thing in the stories is the elopement in *P. and P.*, and for an exact parallel see *The Francis Letters*. I wondered whether their story was the foundation of *P. and P.* But *P. and P.* was written before Eliza Johnson and her Captain bolted to Gretna Green, with a brother officer in attendance and Bow Street runners in pursuit. If you do not know that story, you should look it up. The family letters are worthy of J. A.

24 *April* 1905

It is amazing how exactly Jane Austen conceives her situations, but in my opinion it is still more amazing how she brings in the little details.

If you were to make a collection of Jane Austen's *bores* and *sticks*, *Emma* would provide a huge number of specimens but how wonderfully they combine! How many of the characters would you care to know?

[172]

NOVELS

WILKIE COLLINS
To PROFESSOR J. A. PLATT
15 *September* 1909

I am glad that you are an enthusiast about the *Moonstone*, sorry that you do not share my delight in Gaboriau. By the way, Miss Clark's diary may be poor stuff, but it amuses me. I am sorry that you do not like Rachel: surely she is better than that Harrow monosyllable, Franklin Blake. One of the cleverest things in the book is Betteredge's account of the monosyllable's 'dragging up': it prepares us for his monosyllability and enables us to excuse him. I have read the book twice this summer, and I have also read *Bleak House*. *Moonstone* must have α + +: *Bleak House* at most β +; for the sake of Miss Flyte the β may have the +. I do not know how often I have read *Le crime d'Orcival*, and *Le dossier* 113, and I hope to live to read these and *L'argent des autres*, and *L'affaire Lerouge*, and others, again.

CONRAD
27 *August* 1906

Do you read the stories of one Conrad? I have been reading, or rather skimming *Youth and other Stories*. They have merit, and in particular, force. But they are nautical and they are diffuse. One of them, about the demoralizing effect of African savagery on Europeans, is grisly; but to my mind, because so long-winded, not as grisly as a similar story of A. E. W. Mason's, or as Grant Allen's *Mr Creedy*.

DE MORGAN
2 *November* 1910

I read *It never can happen again*, and I am heartily glad that it cannot. The chief man is too much of a bounder.

DICKENS, *Edwin Drood*
26 *September* 1908

I suppose that the true Dickensian likes in *E.D.*, Sapsea, Durdles, Deputy, the Billickin, and the early Grewgious. I don't: I should like the book better if all this grotesque tomfoolery [were cut out].
28 *August* 1909

I have a great respect for Lang's serious work: but I think that the little book about *Drood* is sad rubbish. His facts are often

[173]

hopelessly wrong, and his suggestions are often silly. I agree
to what you say, that I am the last man in the world who should
take *Drood* seriously. Just now, fresh from *Bleak House*, I
can only wonder that the man who turned out *E. D.* could
'*under* any *circs.*'—may the V.M. forgive me—have perpetrated
the other. It is almost a justification of the hypothesis that
Bazzard = Datchery.

To R. ST J. PARRY
13 *July* 1909

I went to Dublin on the 30th, and we did our business on the
1st. On the night of the 2nd I went to London, and so to
Rochester, to meet Shipley, James, and other Dickensians,
my object being to study the topography of *Edwin Drood*. I
came home on the 7th and on Saturday I was at Winchester.
I am certainly very much stronger than I was when I left
Cambridge.

To PROFESSOR J. A. PLATT
15 *September* 1909

As to J. J., remember that he imagines himself, under opium,
doing something which, out of opium, 'he had in his mind,'
but 'had not quite determined to do.' I agree with you, that if
he did not remember, he must have *suspected* himself: and I
admit that, without opium, he must have known tolerably well
where the body had been placed. But I will not inflict more of
this stuff upon you.

3 *January* 1911

I think that it is sufficient to read *town* for *tower* in the second
sentence: but I am sorry to say that last Saturday I did not look
particularly at the first sentence in the manuscript. Afterwards
I noticed that error was possible in the first sentence also....

I hope that I have read my tract about *Edwin Drood* for the
last time. I used to think that I would dedicate it 'to the sole
begetter of these ensuing pages, H. O.,' i.e. Herpes Ophthal-
micus: but I have not done so. I hope at any rate to draw something amusing from Andrew Lang, and some rubbish from the
Dickensian. Anyhow the amateurs ought to be grateful to me
for a serviceable map of Rochester. I sometimes wonder
whether it is a good thing that *Edwin Drood* remained a

[174]

fragment, *not* because it thus became a conundrum, *but* because C. D. could not have finished it as well as he began it. Anyhow I wish we knew something about the opium woman's animosity.

As to what you call your old heresy, you do not explain 'the unaccountable expedition.' I am convinced that E. D. was thrown from the staircase *inside* the tower. You forget that on your theory there would be a horrid mess in the church yard. But here I trench upon what I have written in my pamphlet, and it is a case of *manus de tabula*. I expect that it is only old stagers like myself who can care for Grewgious; and that, even if you are not Chestertonian, you will be shocked by my likings. Amen.

19 November 1911

Of course I am a very bad Dickensian. All good Dickensians are sure that that duffer Edwin Drood survived. If he did, it is a good thing (from my point of view) that Dickens did not. If Edwin was murdered I can pity him: but if he lived, I have no patience with him, and I think Jasper not only a criminal, but also a blundering fool.

To G. P. BIDDER
28 May 1912

Best thanks for the loan of your books (*sic*) [*Edwin Drood* in the original covers].

p. 28[1]. I had not overlooked the proof that Jasper supposed himself to know exactly what jewellery Edwin carried about with him.

p. 32, ll. 7, 8. Omit the words 'has taken a room there,' and add 'there' after 'watch.'

p. 34. Yes: I had expressed myself too strongly. But on the other hand I think that you make Grewgious' thoughts about Jasper unduly definite.

p. 50. May not Datchery *affect* ignorance of Mrs Tope's lodgings just as at pp. 216, 217[2] he affects ignorance of the Drood mystery? And is not 'the second look of some interest' quite natural? See my p. 51.

pp. 47, 48. My argument, that, if Helena had been in London, she would have visited Rosa, drops. It was not safe for Helena to visit Rosa, as she might thereby betray to Jasper Rosa's hiding place. See E. D. p. 254.

---

[1] Of H. J.'s book.   [2] *Edwin Drood*, 1st ed.

[175]

p. 89. My reference to 'F. C. B.' is wrong. I do not remember who fathers this identification: perhaps some wild ass in the *Dickensian*.

On second thoughts I am not so sure that I retract my phrase at p. 34[1]. Grewgious noticed Jasper's white lips and 'put it down to the chilling account of the Cathedral.' In his 'somewhat sharp' answer he 'knew' Jasper's affection 'for his nephew' etc. At the bottom of p. 104 he carefully associates himself with Jasper. At p. 105, though he notes Jasper's odd phrase, there is nothing to show that he resents it. In a word, there are oddities in Jasper's behaviour which might later give Grewgious matter for thought: but I fancy that when they 'shook hands to part' Grewgious betrays neither coldness nor suspicion.

p. 49. You do not say what you think of Cuming Walters' identification of Datchery with Helena. I think that Dickens had great faith in the possibilities of theatrical disguise. I have seen him in a short hour impersonate a lawyer's clerk, a grave digger, an old woman, and other characters, and he seemed at home in all of them. Your remark that the shriek suggests murder rather than suicide seems to me sound and important. I thought of murder first: but I shrank from putting too much villainy upon Jasper, and therefore minimized the previous misdoing. I understand—am I right?—that you suppose Jasper to have taken quicklime from the Cathedral (and not from his yard) to the Sapsea monument to dispose of the remains of the girl. If so, how had he been able to deposit them there? That he did not bring quicklime from Maidstone Road is, I think, quite certain. I hope that you were as grateful as I am to the man who made the map[2]. I got a great deal of amusement out of this pamphlet, and I am callously indifferent to the fact that my publication of it shocks some donkeys.

To THE SAME
31 *May* 1912

Best thanks for your letter and for the sight of the MS. [on *Edwin Drood*] which I return herewith.

(1) Your dates agree with my vaguer chronological scheme, and my statement, which you criticize at your p. 3, last four lines,

[1] *Edwin Drood*, 1st ed. p. 64.   [2] In H. J.'s *Edwin Drood*.

covers yours. The difference between us is that you give exact
but conjectural dates, while I do not go beyond C. D.'s quite
clear assertions. For my purpose this is sufficient, but I am glad
to note that when you assign exact times and seasons, you still
find C. D. consistent.

(2) The Sapsea monument. You suppose that Mrs Sapsea
died Dec. 17 or 18 and was buried in an unfinished monument
on Dec. 24, and that on the same day Jasper hid the body of a
murdered girl in the unfinished monument. (Do you suppose
that Durdles actually heard the shriek which the girl gave?) It
seems to me that an unfinished monument was a very bad
hiding place. Durdles or his men must have infallibly found the
corpse: for you confess yourself that the monument could not
have been completed.

My hypothesis is that the girl died—whether by murder or
suicide—on Christmas Eve but not at Cloisterham: that
Durdles had a dream on Christmas Eve: that Durdles' mention
of a mysterious death on the previous Christmas Eve pricks
Jasper's guilty memory and frightens him. I had originally
thought of murder, and when I substituted suicide, I did so
from a desire not to assume more than was absolutely necessary
to fill the gap. I recognize the force of your argument in favour
of murder: for Jasper could hardly have been so much alarmed,
if he had not remembered the shriek. I am glad that you take
pp. 144, 145 seriously.

(3) The identification of Datchery with Helena binds the
story together as nothing else would do. Helena is marked out
for a great part, and plainly Datchery is henceforward very
important. Helena herself suggests setting a watch upon Jasper.
Datchery has not the air of a professional detective. But I must
not begin writing about Datchery = Helena. Try the other
hypothesis—that Grewgious set Datchery to watch Jasper. Did
he take the step before the Conference? The interview in the
garden, and the Conference lose all their importance. Did he
take it after the Conference? Helena's suggestion becomes in-
significant.

By the way, I have sometimes thought that C. D. meant to
leave the identity of Helena and Datchery unacknowledged, i.e.
that Datchery would disappear, without any explanation.

OBITER SCRIPTA

I believe that I have never thanked you for your letter of May 28ᵗʰ 'about Edwin Drood.'

I think that your hypothetical paragraphs are quite good. As to the previous victim I had not supposed the death to be at Cloisterham. I suggested suicide (not murder) with a view to economy of crime. In fact, I supposed Durdles' vision to have been pure imagination on his part, and to have no relation whatever to anything which happened. So I do not suppose the victim to have screamed or the dog to have howled. My notion was that, when Durdles talked about a weird experience on the last Christmas Eve, Jasper was reminded of a horror which happened on that day, and exploded, as he does with Deputy at the end of ch. xii. I think that Jasper is meant to be 'jumpy,' if I may use the word.

By the way, I think that the phantom Edwin has his hand on his breast because *we* know that that pocket contained the all-important ring. Of course I do not accept your theory that the girl's remains are in the Sapsea monument: and I think that Jasper would have blundered badly, if he had afterwards put Drood's body in a place where Durdles would poke about. You will see that I cannot accept the view that Jasper hid two victims in the same place—one without quicklime, the other with it.

I think that you are hypercritical about Jasper's two rooms. Remember that in 'Daggers Drawn' they drink their wine in the outer room and that we know of the inner room as dining room only.

I grant that *at present* we know of nothing which can explain the 'wistful' look, unless either D = Helena thinking of Crisparkle, or D = Tartar thinking of Rosa: and, with xviii in its present position, guaranteed by the corrected proofs, these identifications seem impossible. Is it after all conceivable that Datchery is tracking Jasper independently of the Cloisterham mystery? We know that Jasper has a past; and I can imagine that Dickens finds an interest in making a number of people *concentrate* their suspicions on J. J. So far as we know, Datchery is working single-handed; but it is clear that he will get help

[178]

from Durdles, Deputy, and Puffer, and it is possible that, sooner or later, he will join hands with Grewgious. It may be that at the end Datchery, and not Grewgious, was to take the lead. It is important to remember that Dickens did not complete the half of the story.

To SIR G. GREENWOOD
12 *January* 1917

Is Tartar Datchery? Datchery settles in Cloisterham, ch. xviii, about June 30 or July 1. Tartar comes upon the scene in ch. xxi, July 4, knowing nothing about the Cloisterham tragedy. Can you get over this? See also pp. 41, 42.

When I identified Datchery and Helena, I thought that C. D. would have placed xviii between xxii and xxiii. I now know that he corrected the proofs without doing so and have to acknowledge that the identification falls to the ground. In a word Datchery is a new character.

DUMAS

To PROFESSOR J. A. PLATT
3 *October* 1904

I don't suppose I shall ever read *Le Vicomte de Bragelonne* again. I read the whole series one autumn here, and joyed in it. But life is too short for two readings of *Le Vicomte*. Besides, that incomparable young man bores me. Porthos is delightful, and so is D'Artagnan, and so is Athos, but I am not sure that Aramis is not the real hero. He is quite one of the most detestable people in fiction.

HARDY, *Tess*
24 *April* 1905

Tess does not add to the gaiety of nations. It is an agglomeration of horrors. There are some people whose palates require pepper of this sort; indulgence in such things has blunted their sensibility to less violent impressions, for, as saith the wise man, *Excellens sensibile corrumpit sensum*.

19 *April* 1908

I have never caught on with Thos. Hardy. Did I ever show you the picture of him which Rothenstein gave me? *Life's Little Ironies* made me sick. *Tess* made me sorry. I am told that Mrs T. H. devised the plot of *Tess*. A few pages of *Jude the Obscure* put me off.

OBITER SCRIPTA

HENRY JAMES—R. L. S.—MASON

To PROFESSOR J. A. PLATT

16 *September* 1900

I am glad that you abuse Henry James. Still I think that he has merits. I forget whether I commended to your notice *The Author of Beltraffio* and *The Path of Duty*. These seem to me to have real subtlety, and in the former he does the business of the aesthetes, in my opinion, better than Pater could do it. Even 'the portrait of a lady' must have merits: for when I got to the end, and found that the heroine at the last page repented of having behaved as a lady, and proposed to offer herself to ὁ τυχών, I felt very angry. Seriously, *The Author of Beltraffio*, though unpleasant, is well worth reading. I am not sure that James has ever done anything else as good.

I am now reading the volume of Stevenson which contains *Olalla*. Do you know that? How good Stevenson would have been, if he had *not* had such an infernally good opinion of himself. I think Mason is the coming man.

KIPLING, *Stalky and Co.*

10 *July* 1910

I have been refreshing myself with another reading of *Stalky and Co.* It is an amazing book, and ever new.

27 *September* 1911

I do not agree with your condemnation of Stalky. It seems to me to exhibit as nothing else does the devilish ingenuity of the normal boy, who, having no intellectual interests and acquiescing in the lower of the two school moralities, puts his masters under the microscope as you might do a tadpole. The boys and the masters and Kipling himself are of course bounders: but even of bounders there is a natural history, and *Stalky and Co.* provides it.

GEORGE MEREDITH

From COMMONPLACE BOOK

8 *May* 1909

George Meredith died. The Dean of Westminster's refusal to allow burial in the abbey is not, I think, wrong from the point of view of posterity: but it is a shock for the moment. G. M.

wrote things good, bad, and indifferent: and I cannot think him one of the greatest. One newspaper thinks him the greatest novelist of the century. If he means the xix[th], as he ought to do, how about Scott, Thackeray and Jane Austen?

GILBERT PARKER, *Valmond*

To PROFESSOR J. A. PLATT
1 *January* 1902

I never said that *Valmond* was either a great book or an attractive one. What I said was that Parker had hit upon an original idea, and that there was cleverness in the presentation of the Napoleonic type. Since I read *Valmond*, I have read *The Pomp of the Lavilettes*, in which he tries to work the same motive without the Napoleonic idea, and the book is comparatively weak. I am glad that you have some enthusiasm to spare for *Miranda* and for *Clementina*. Yes, I think that your comparison is a good one. But which is the perfectly abominable episode? I should have liked to cut out part of ch. xiii and ch. xxii.

As yet, I have not read more of *La Chartreuse de Parme* than the Waterloo episode. I had assumed that you would be intimately acquainted with this famous book. To tell the truth I am not a great admirer of Beyle, whom I know chiefly from *Le Rouge et Noir*.

THACKERAY

26 *September* 1908

Did you not know that Thackeray had a small fortune which he lost immediately after he came of age in the company of Deuce-ace and Co.?

I don't at all believe in Dizzy's caricature of him. I heard him lecture, twice, when I was a schoolboy: but I never shook hands with him. When he lectured at Sheffield, he stayed with my father, who was delighted with him. And I think that he and Thompson were genuinely fond of one another. To a man whose wife is in a madhouse much may be forgiven: but, for myself, I cannot think that the man who wrote *Esmond* was noxiously cynical. My father in his short last illness got one of my brothers to read *Esmond* to him, and I think that anyone who was fond of human beings might well do the same. Under such circumstances it would be waste of time to read Dickens.

Esmond text

From SIR F. DARWIN
21 November 1917

In *Esmond*, Book iii, chap. 5 the duel in which Duke Hamilton was killed is described as happening 'three days after Nov. 15, 1712' whereas in the diary of Thomas Hearne it is said to be on Nov. 15. Thackeray's is a very odd way of mentioning a date....

To SIR F. DARWIN
22 November 1917

Best thanks for your letter. Put comma after 'after' and another after '1712,' and all will be well. I see that I had noted the correction in my copy. The duel was at 7 A.M.—not as in *Esmond*—on 15 Nov. 1712. This is proved by an extract from Swift's journal to Mᵣˢ Dinsley, of which Charles John Smith gives a facsimile in his very interesting *Historical and Literary Curiosities*, Bohn 1841. Smith says the Journal is Sloane MSS. 4804, Fol. 80.

THACKERAY—DICKENS

To PROFESSOR J. A. PLATT
16 September 1900

I have never read *Catherine*. *Denis Duval*, when it came out, seemed to me to promise something big. *Lovel* disappointed me, and I have never returned to it. But of course I should never dream of putting these anywhere near *Esmond* and *Barry Lyndon*. And of course I don't dream of comparing Dickens with Thackeray, any more than I should compare Laviche with Shakespeare or Molière. Dickens missed his vocation, which was to be a great actor. I always think that I saw Dickens at his best, when I was 13 or 14 years old, when he acted in Bulwer's *Not so bad as we seem*, and when—before his readings were familiar—he read *The Christmas Carol* to an audience which had never heard of dramatic reading. We went to look at the man: and his change of voice and feature and gesture took us

NOVELS

all by surprise. The very coarseness of his work fits it for the
stage: the cheap pathos and the large points. Also his reading
of *Boots at the Holly Tree Inn* was a thing to remember. But
I should not have cared to meet Dickens and his waistcoat in
private life, whilst I always regret that I was at school when
Thackeray was at Sheffield, so that, although I heard two of his
lectures at Cheltenham, I missed the opportunity of seeing him
face to face. This is anecdotage with a vengeance, a clear proof
that I am too old to live. There is one man still alive who acted
with Dickens in those old days, Alfred Ainger.

MRS WOOD—TROLLOPE

To PROFESSOR J. A. PLATT

13 *August* 1904

I have read the *Channings*, but not recently. I thought it
good of its sort; and there are several of Mrs Wood's books which
I have read with interest. But she wrote *down* instead of *up*:
and some of her books seemed to me to be written for domestic
servants of the less educated sort. I once read a series of stories
called *Johnny Ludlow*, which made me heartily ashamed of
the time which I wasted on them. If she had had a classical
education, it would have checked her flow of words and done her
a lot of good. But in her line, surely Antony Trollope is un-
approachable, and will be for the historian of society in the
Victorian age a treasury of information. I have been reading
again certain Merrimans, such as *The Isle of Unrest* and *In
Kedar's Tents*. Do you despise them? They please me.

Have you learnt the game of Bridge? I am learning. It is not
the real thing; but it is entertaining, and perhaps the more
recreative because it is not the real thing. Even so Trollope and
Seton Merriman are good to lounge over.

The Secret Orchard

3 *October* 1904

...I don't remember what you mean by the 'gaping rents and
faults' in the *Secret Orchard*. I had no wish to put the book
on a pinnacle and of course the people behave idiotically in
worshipping the cub; but it was a happy thought to make him
a member of that hateful family which always was faithfully
served and eagerly supported and never deserved it. This

[183]

reminds me of Merriman's *Last Hope*; but I think I told you about it, comparing it with Parker's *Valmond*. Stuarts, Bourbons, and Bonapartes, were all of them beasts, and the Bonapartes were cads into the bargain: and yet how loyal their besotted followers were to them. By the way I gathered from Mad. de Rémusat that the Marshals and the people about the Court backed the great man from fear rather than from liking.

OXFORD

To PROFESSOR J. A. PLATT
16 *August* 1905

I am glad that you have been making acquaintance with Oxford; I always like it immensely. I love the streets, the Colleges, and the houses; and the domesticity of their tiny foundations has on me a novel effect. I always feel that New College exists for Spooner, Matheson, George, H. H. Turner, etc., whereas we, at Trinity, Cambridge, exist for the College....My knowledge of All Souls is small. I used to like the notion that it might be attached to the Bodleian, each fellow earning his dividend by doing a little library work of the higher sort.

To MRS DICEY (*after an* Ad Eundem *dinner*)
20 *May* 1912

I am very grateful to you and Dr Dicey for your great kindness in putting up, not only myself but also two other ad Eundems, at a time when you were ill and suffering. I had the longest and best night that I have had this term in the very comfortable room which you call small: and I returned from Oxford as always refreshed and renewed. In the Lent Term it was 50 years since I first saw Oxford, and 43 since the ad Eundem began to give me occasions for returning there periodically. I think that Cambridge was the right place for me: though there was a time when I had doubts of this. But I am quite sure that my election into the ad Eundem was one of the best things which ever happened to me. My life would have been a different thing if I had not been, in this way, in touch with Oxford friends: and the sight of Oxford is always a joy to me.

To PROFESSOR J. A. PLATT
15 *August* 1913

Yes: Murray is a 'very attractive person.' Indeed I think that Oxford is very successful in breeding 'attractive' scholars: more

OXFORD

so than Cambridge. And this is not surprizing. For *we* dare
not talk our shop in a mixed company, and even in a scholars'
party we are very conscious of our limitations as specialists. It is
curious to think how few scholars there will be in Cambridge
in thirty years' time. Unless the system is altered, the fellowships
will be held by bursars, tutors, deans, and pass teachers of
history, engineering and law.

To A. O. PRITCHARD
11 June 1916

Have you at Oxford any one who has recorded the traditions of
the Oxford which I had the happiness of beginning to know in
the late sixties? Who are left who knew it at that time? William
Sidgwick is alive, but he is hopelessly flighty. Dicey is vigorous:
but I can hardly fancy him as a chronicler. Tommy Case? But
he too is not cut out to be a sympathetic recorder of what is
past and gone and of the change. It has been my great good
luck to have known Oxford since 1862, and from 1869 to have
been there frequently, and there is nothing in life for which I
am more grateful than the hospitality of New College. When
I became a nominal fellow of Winchester, the welcome which I
had from New College delighted me. Forgive all this egotism.

To C. E. SAYLE
11 December 1917

To me he [John Morley] seems journalist, rather than man of
letters, and administrator rather than statesman. The object
of the book is, I think, to connect the literary period with the
political, and incidentally to show that his literary hand has
not lost its practised cunning. Also to explain politics.

He is a typical product of 'Greats' in 1860: and I wish that
he had had more to tell of the Oxonians of that time. It was not
till Feb. 1869 that I began to know something about Oxford,
but from that time it has been an important part of my life. Of
all non-Oxonians I claim to be Oxford's truest lover. I have
been so extraordinarily fortunate in my Oxford friends, from
Henry Smith onwards to Henry Pelham and the rest. People
talk about the differences between the two places. They are
superficial: as when the Oxonian parted his hair in the middle,
and the Cantab at the side. By the way, there is one difference:
and it is significant. You can talk classical shop in a mixed

[185]

OBITER SCRIPTA

company at Oxford and people will understand. At Cambridge to do so would be an offence.

Of my old Oxford friends one remains, a very great man, Albert Dicey: a survival of the fifties, who has still his old fire. I don't know whether the Oxonians of the present day appreciate him. The men of the present day are taken up with politics and administration, and have no time to be Academic. Mind, I do *not* blame: I only regret. But I am always thankful for my Oxford attachments: and I like to think of its spacious streets, and of Oxford as I see it on my way to Didcot on Sunday, midday, and of Magdalen Ditch, and Cowley Meadows, and the Cherwell on the way to Islip, and of a host of other beautiful things. They refresh me whenever I see them. You will excuse this outburst.

From COMMONPLACE BOOK
Note on *The Romance of the Oxford Colleges* by F. Gribble

This is in no way a remarkable book: but I am glad I have read it. The man is a fairly clever *litterateur*. But I think that he misses all that is best in Oxford. It surprizes me that he nowhere mentions Roger Bacon. Once more, I feel amazed that, whereas Oxford seems to do everything, and Cambridge nothing to stimulate poetry, enthusiasm, and imagination, their list of great men, and especially of great poets, lags far behind ours. It is once more a warning against looking to the environment for the production of real genius.

PHILOSOPHY: KNOWLEDGE AND SENSATION
To C. E. SAYLE
13 *August* 1901

As to 'the philosopher' Aristotle writes to the effect of your sentence in *posterior analytics* II, xix, 99^b 32 ff. See especially 100^a 10, 11: but I cannot quote the exact equivalent of *omnis nostra cognitio oritur ex sensu*, and I hardly think that there is one. Doctrines were epigrammatically formulated in course of time, and then came epigrammatic modifications. Hamilton, *Logic* ii 27 and Reid 772^a quote from Patricius *Nova de universis Philosophia*, p. 1, '*cognitio omnis a mente primam originem, a sensibus exordium habet primum.*' This is plainly a correction of your phrase. I have never been able to assign to any particular person, either '*nihil est in intellectu quod non prius in*

[186]

sensu,' or the antagonistic supplement '*praeter intellectum ipsum.*' You will see that these phrases are exactly parallel. In short, I think that you may fairly refer to *posterior analytics* II, xix for the substance of what would be called, I suppose, your *brocard*—a learned word which bothered me much when I first came across it.

PLATO

To R. ST J. PARRY

4 August 1909

Horace is reading English History. People find their subject after the Tripos. I did myself. As an undergraduate I steadily neglected Plato.

Dialogues

To R. D. ARCHER-HIND

21 July 1881

I have been reading Zeller very carefully. As far as I can make out none of the authorities have dreamt of the possibility that the *sophist* and the *politicus* belong to the period of which we read in Aristotle, and I am glad to find that Zeller commits himself to the definite statement that the later Platonism is not represented in the writings.

The Socratic dialogues worry me because they contain so little positive doctrine: e.g. the *Laches* which I have just read. I think the *Hippias major* Plato's, but written towards the end of the Socratic period, when Plato was just beginning to say Socratic things in a Platonic way. On the other hand I have concluded to reject the *Anterastae* and the *Menexenus*.

At present my list stands thus:

Apology	Gorgias	Parmenides
Crito	—	Philebus
Euthyphro	Theaetetus	sophist
Laches	Phaedrus	politicus
—	Symposium	Timaeus and Critias
Charmides	Cratylus?	Laws
Hippias	Meno	
—	Euthydemus	
Lysis	republic	
Protagoras	Phaedo	
—	—	

[187]

OBITER SCRIPTA

The notion that the *republic*, because a great work, must belong to the last period, seems to me to have led to a good deal of confusion.

27 July 1881

As to the *Euthydemus* which I have just re-read—the solitary reference to the theory of ideas seems to me to show that it belongs to the period in which things are what they are by participation in ideas, not to the period in which things approximate to the idea or type in proportion as they are more or less perfectly informed by the number.

Further, the aim of the dialogue is to bring into contrast

1 eristic
2 dialectic
3 rhetorico-politic.

Now the quarrel with Socrates and the rhetorico-politicians rages in the *Gorgias*, the *Phaedrus*, and the *republic*, and is glanced at in the *Theaetetus*. It is perhaps glanced at in the *sophist* and the *politicus*, but it is there treated only incidentally.

There are no doubt passages which recall the *sophist* and the *politicus*, but they seem to me to recall only the subordinate topics of those dialogues, whilst I doubt whether when Plato had begun to criticize his own earlier doctrine he would have turned aside to fix, once more, his relations to his contemporaries. The resemblance in the minor topics seems to me a reason for placing the *Euthydemus* late in the second period, but not for putting it in the third, when the metaphysical theory had become more than ever important. As to the *sophist* I have not yet re-read it. What I go upon is that the *Philebus* emphasises the divergence from the earlier theory of ideas, whilst the *sophist* in the passage about the higher abstractions ταὐτόν, θἄτερον, οὐσία, etc. reminds me of the *Timaeus*.

11 August 1881

As to the *Euthydemus* and the *sophist*—(I have not yet re-read the *sophist*, so as to know how far the resemblance between the two dialogues goes) your remark about the reference to the earlier Ideal theory seems to me to show that that reference is not (as I had thought it) decisive. But I am inclined still to think that the controversial aspect of the dialogue belongs rather to my second period than to my third. There are no doubt references to eristic in the *Philebus* and the *sophist*, but they

[188]

PLATO

occur in the parts of the two dialogues which are *not* characteristic of the third period: in the *Philebus* the logical episode about the One and the Many is a mere repetition of what has been said in the *Phaedrus*, confessedly introductory to the new matter of the metaphysical episode; in the *sophist* the definitions go back to the 5th century sophists, the term being (if I remember rightly) defined in the sense in which it is applied to (1) Gorgias, (2) Evenus, (3) Socrates as well as in the sense in which it is used in the 4th century. But you will say, have we any evidence that the eristic sophistry existed before the time of the *sophist*? I am writing offhand, but I fancy that the word occurs in the *Theaetetus*, whilst that dialogue shows pretty well that the thing existed.

I believe that you are right in placing the *sophist* before the *Philebus*. I had always taken the same view till this summer, and I suspect that, when (without re-reading the *sophist*) I took up the other view, this was only another instance to show that αἱ δεύτεραι φροντίδες are not as wise as the first and the third. In fact last term when I was writing about the date of the *Philebus*, I thought I had found a reference to the *sophist*—cf. *Phileb.* 14 C 15 DE with *soph.* 251 B....

Very many thanks for your suggestion that the later theory should be treated as a development of the earlier, rather than as a reconstitution. This is certainly right, though as a matter of fact the alterations are considerable, including (1) the introduction of a *matter*, (2) the abandonment of the assumption that every καθόλου implies the existence of an idea, (3) the conception of the ἰδέα as a type from which particulars diverge, (4) the notion that ἰδέαι are knowable, not because they are external to nature, but because they are fixities in nature, as opposed to the varieties of divergences.

To BERNARD JACKSON
25 January 1885

I shall not write you much of a letter tonight, as I have had to give my time to a bit of extra work. Robertson Smith told me on Friday that he wanted short articles on Prodicus and Protagoras (preparatory to my future article on *Sophists*), and further on Saturday that he wanted them posted to Edinburgh on Tuesday next. Each article will be not more than an octavo page, but I have had to spend a good deal of time in looking up the authorities and in packing my information. If I had to do it on a large scale and had plenty of time, I think I should like making articles for an Encyclopaedia. There is a certain satisfaction in sweeping away unnecessary details and stating dogmatically one's results. Perhaps I fancy it because it is so unlike my Plato work, in which every step has to be carefully explained and justified.

To F. J. H. JENKINSON
27 July 1890

My work has gone partly ill, partly well: *ill*, for I had hoped to complete the revision of my Plato papers, and I found that there were still places where the argument seemed to drag; *well*, for I discovered that my old paper on the *Philebus* was weak just because I wrote it *before* my paper on the *Parmenides*, and that, reversing the order, I could now get a heap of new things out of the *Philebus*. So I have been reading and annotating the *Philebus* from the new point of view, and am getting some very pretty results. I can now weld the *Parmenides*, the *Philebus*, and the *Timaeus* into a compacter whole, and show that the ethical argument makes important contributions to the settlement of the metaphysical problem. All this has been really interesting; but before I began to see light the work was dreary and discouraging in the extreme.

To H. O. D. DAVIDSON (*draft*)
30 December 1894

Ever since you were at Cambridge I have been intending to write to you. I am afraid that you thought I wanted to shirk talking Platonism, and I want to explain that this was not so. In the early part of the evening I feared to embark in a serious talk as I had to hold myself free to look after the various smokers and others: and later, when people began to go away, I was disappointed to find that you were going with them and that I had lost my opportunity.

It occurs to me that I might possibly put down in a rough and ready way the chief points of my system. But you will easily understand that what I am going to write is a mere sketch: if I were to attempt more, I sh^d have to do at a burst the book wh. I have been lingering over for years. I must begin by emphasizing a few preliminaries.

PLATO

The early Ionians asked themselves What is Being? and looked for an existent one underlying the various and varying plurality of things. Assuming change to be perpetual, Heraclitus perceived that of what is in flux there can be no knowledge, and so the question What is Knowledge? came to the front. Zeno, as Plato plainly states in the *Parmenides*, though the modern historians mostly neglect this important fact, rested one of his disproofs of plurality upon the premiss that like cannot be unlike, nor unlike be like: and amongst Socrates' hearers one or more maintained that no predication wh. is not identical is legitimate. Thus the question What is Predication? arose.

When Plato tired of Socratic limitations and attempted anew to get at philosophic truth, it was necessary that he sh^d provide an answer to the three questions which I have enumerated: What is Being, What is Knowledge, What is Predication.

The theory of ideas, as it appears in the *republic* and the *Phaedo*, is intended to be an answer to these questions. It consists of a fundamental proposition—'apart from sensibles, there are eternal, immutable, supra-sensual, unities, called ideas,' together with two supplementary propositions, 'sensibles are what they are by reason of the presence or immanence of the corresponding idea' (*Phaedo*), 'wherever two or more particulars are called by the same name, there is a corresponding idea' (*republic* 596 A). These supplementary propositions were necessary in order to make the fundamental proposition available as an answer to the question What is Predication? (That Plato looked to this theory of ideas for the explanation of predication, he says plainly in the *Phaedo*, the *republic* VII, and again in the *Parmenides*.) And the answer is that the particular (*e.g.* this piece of blotting paper) is *red* because it has the idea of *red* in it, *dirty* because it has the idea of *dirt* in it, that it is *like* another piece because it contains the idea of *like*, and *unlike* because it contains the idea of *unlike*. Plainly, if predication is to be explained in this way, there must be an idea wherever there is a predicate, and, as we are told in *republic* 596 A, so it is. But, granting for the moment that this explanation of predication will serve, how are we to know the ideas? In *republic* VI *ad finem* it is suggested that we are to mount through provisional def^{ns} of ideas, got by the study of particulars, to the idea of the good, and to take the attainment of the idea of the good as the proof that the provisional def^{ns} are correct. But this

[191]

mounting through provisional def^{ns} to the idea of the good is just what cannot be done: and accordingly in the *Phaedo*, Socrates plainly despairs of attaining to the αὐτὸ ἀγαθόν, and is content to accept such def^{ns} as are not disputed by the opponent in argument. In a word, the *republic* provides an educational scheme wh. has philosophy for its nucleus, but the philosophy is only sketchy, and in the *Phaedo* is admitted to be defective.

There are however other defects wh. must now be mentioned. It is plainly stated at the beginning of the *Parmenides* that Plato had looked to the theory of the immanent idea to explain how it is that the same thing can be at once like and unlike, namely, by the simultaneous inherence of likeness and unlikeness. But Plato makes Socrates immediately confess 129 E that this explanation is not available when an idea is the subject of the proposition, because by assumption it is a unity, not as the particular is now supposed to be, a bundle of ideas. Further Parmenides asks how it is that the idea, without sacrifice of its unity, can be inherent, by multiplication or division, in a plurality of particulars, and this same difficulty reappears in the *Philebus*. Finally in the last sentence of the *Parmenides* it is emphatically remarked that likeness, unlikeness, etc. are *relations*. Now when once it is realized that likeness and unlikeness are relations, it is easy to see that the same thing may be at once like and unlike, and Zeno's puzzle falls to the ground.

ἡ κοινωνία τῶν εἰδῶν

To J. ADAM
26 *August* 1897

In the *republic* and the *Phaedo* Plato explains the three propositions

(1) this act is good
(2) this person is good
(3) this (idea of) just is good,

in the same sense: i.e. the idea of good is immanent in each of the three subjects. It has not occurred to him that there is any difference between the immanence of the idea of good in a man and the immanence of the idea of good in an idea. Nor has it occurred to him that the simultaneous immanence of the idea of good in two persons implies a *pluralisation* of the idea of good. In fact, he inconsistently assumes that all ideas are (1) units, (2) capable of immanence in particulars. In the *Parmenides* he

[192]

shows that if an idea is a unit, it cannot be immanent in particulars, and he goes on to argue that μέγα βαρύ etc. are relative notions. Then in the *Philebus* he finds that the relative notions (μέγα βαρύ etc.) and the qualities (θερμόν ὑγρόν etc. and presumably δίκαιον ἀγαθόν) are not unities. Then in the *sophist* he shows that the relative notions, not being unities, may participate in one another. In fact, the ideas most prominent in Bk. v (*rep.*) (1) δίκαιον, ἀγαθόν etc., (2) μέγα βαρύ etc., have ceased to be ideas. But Bk. x recognises also ideas of substances; and though the *sophist* has disposed of ideas of artificial substances, ideas of natural substances remain—man, horse, etc. These are still unities, and therefore cannot be immanent either in particulars or in one another. Thus if we start from the list of the *republic* and the *Phaedo*, we have

	republic and *Phaedo*	Later dialogues
(1) δίκαιον, ἀγαθόν	Unities and immanent	Not unities
(2) μέγα, βαρύ	Unities and immanent	Not unities
(3) ἄδικον, κακόν	Unities and immanent	Not unities
(4) κλίνη, τράπεζα	Unities and immanent	Not unities
(5) ἄνθρωπος, ἵππος	Unities and immanent	{ *unities* { *Not immanent*

In the *sophist* etc. any general notion is called an εἶδος, but it is only the αὐτὸ καθ' αὑτό or substantial εἶδος such as ἄνθρωπος, ἵππος, which is a unity. They are not immanent in the homonymous particulars but imitated by them: whilst plainly there is no κοινωνία between the idea of horse and the idea of man.

The permanent element of the theory of ideas is then—'apart from particulars, there are unities, eternal and immutable, which are (1) existent, (2) knowable.'

But (*a*) according to the *republic* and the *Phaedo* there is such a unity wherever a plurality of particulars is called by the same name, and the unity is immanent in the several particulars. So, and so only, the attribution of the common name to the particulars is explicable. There are therefore ideas of (1) qualities, (2) relations, (3) things evil, (4) artificials, (5) naturals. But so far Plato is thinking *mainly* of (1), (2), (3).

(*b*) according to the later dialogues, it is not necessary to have ideas to explain common names in the case of (1), (2), (3), (4), and accordingly there are no such ideal unities. In particular the notion of relation is carefully studied, and the *sophist* shows that there may be relations, and that these relations may be related to one another, without the intervention of any ideal unity. As for the members of a natural kind (man, horse) they have a corresponding idea: but the idea is not immanent in the particular; it is reflected or imitated by it.

Thus ideas of natural substances alone are left, and these are true unities, not (inconsistently) unities and yet plural.

Now set the *republic* and the *sophist* side by side. In *republic* v πρᾶξις and σῶμα participate in δίκαιον and ἀγαθόν, which are ideal unities and participate in one another. In the *sophist* δίκαιον and ἀγαθόν participate in one another, but are not ideal unities. In the *republic* the intercommunion of ideas is taken for granted and in the *sophist* it is matter for investigation. Thus the ἀλλήλων κοινωνία of the *republic* is not the κοινωνία of the γένη of the *sophist*.

What puzzles people about the earlier theory is that it contains a grave inconsistency, which Plato discovered afterwards. What puzzles people about the later theory is that it recognises ideas of natural substances only, whereas in the earlier theory these were in the background.

Please say whether this screed is fairly intelligible.

Phaedo

To PROFESSOR J. A. PLATT
2 *April* 1898

I thought it a good sign when I found you darting away from Bacchylides to Plato, seemingly with the intention of carrying war into my country. But, you mistake, I have no desire to fight. I see that I spoke of the chapter in question as a description of the Platonic Socrates. By this I meant only that the Socrates of the *Phaedo* fathers the failures and aspirations. I quite agree that the passage describes the general course of Greek thought, that τὰ ὄντα are the physical principles of the Ionians, as opposed to τὴν ἀλήθειαν τῶν ὄντων, and that the logical difficulties about great and small are difficulties raised by the Eleatics. Plainly the historical Socrates did not go through all the phases described; he had no sympathies with the Ionian conception, and never reached the standpoint of the *Phaedo*. But I think that Plato *might* speak of himself as beginning in Ionian Monism, as influenced by Eleaticism, and as arriving by means of Socratic conceptualism at the theory of immanent ideas. For surely he resumes in himself all previous Greek thought.

Hence I do not care to affirm that this development is *not* Plato's. That it represents the general course of Greek thought I am quite clear.

Textual

To R. D. ARCHER-HIND
5 *January* 1901

I have hit upon a plausible explanation of an old puzzle in *Philebus* 18 B. Since πρῶτος = a, for ὃς πρῶτος write ὅσα, and punctuate ἐπειδὴ φωνὴν ἄπειρον κατενόησεν εἴτε θεὸς εἴτε καὶ θεῖος ἄνθρωπος—ὡς λόγος ἐν Αἰγύπτῳ Θεύθ τινα τοῦτον γενέσθαι—λέγων ὅσα τὰ φωνήεντα ἐν τῷ ἀπείρῳ, κατενόησεν οὐχ ἕν, κ.τ.λ., λέγων ὅσα κ.τ.λ. = 'proceeding to count among the infinitely numerous sounds which were vocal.'

28 *September* 1901

By the way in correcting a proof the other day I hit upon an escape from an ancient difficulty. *Metaph.* Λ. 1072 a 24 ἐπεὶ δὲ τὸ κινούμενον καὶ κινοῦν καὶ μέσον τοίνυν ἔστι τι ὃ οὐ κινούμενον κινεῖ. See Bonitz' reconstruction. Read ἐπεὶ δὲ τὸ κινούμενον καὶ κινοῦν καὶ μή, ὂν τοίνυν ἔστι τι ὃ οὐ κινούμενον κινεῖ: 'since there is a κινούμενον which is κινοῦν and a κινούμενον which is μὴ κινοῦν, there is an ὄν which οὐ κινούμενον κινεῖ.' Split ⊢C into ⊢ C and you have EC. But the blunder is as old as the Pseudo-Alexander. I have an old grudge against this passage: so that I am much pleased with a plausible λύσις.

From SIR G. O. TREVELYAN *to the Editor*

In December 1903 I wrote to Henry Jackson, specifying my favourite and familiar dialogues of Plato—The *Protagoras*, (may be), the *Gorgias*, the *Symposium*, the *Euthydemus*; and the Death dialogues, such as the *Apologia*, the *Crito*, and the *Phaedo*. Appealing to him as to one who knew my tastes, I asked him to recommend me other Dialogues which I should be sure of liking. He replied in a letter (now pasted into the fly-leaf of my Bekker's *Plato*) for which I was, and am, deeply grateful to him. For indeed I have read the *Meno* thrice, and the *Euthyphro* five times, during the last fifteen years,—and the *Laches* more times than I can say. In the terrible years of the Great War one was never tired of hearing what was to be

said about the quality of courage by such a philosopher, and so
valiant a soldier of the Athenian Territorial Army, as Socrates.

To SIR G. O. TREVELYAN (*with a note taken from the draft*)
1 *December* 1903

Dear Trevelyan,

'ἱππέας εἰς πεδίον προκαλεῖ,' when you invite me to
recommend parts of Plato which are not technically philosophical.

Charmides, Laches, Euthyphro, Ion, Lysis, are short 'Socratic
Dialogues': that is to say, they seek definitions of moral
terms such as Socrates used to define; and the tricks of his conversation are carefully introduced—so far as written discourse
can imitate conversation. They are more like the *Crito* than any
other dialogue on your list. Billy Johnson's lines apply to
them;

> Still live the soft and intimate discourse,
> The wit that makes us tolerant perforce,
> The mystic legend, and the verse that drops
> As snow-flakes shower on wintry forest tops,
> The questions working wedge-like to the proof,
> The threads of prayer from old religion's woof,
> The courteous skill of keen rebukes that chide
> The learner's folly, and the sophist's pride.

I am convinced that you will like them, though in comparison with the *Phaedo* they may be slight.

You may find the latter part of the *Phaedrus* rather dry; but
you will thoroughly like the first half.

You will enjoy the *Meno.* Extracts which would interest you
are—*republic* I and VII[1].

The episode about the philosopher, and the man of the world,
Theaetetus 172–177 C.

The myth in the *politicus,* 268 E–274 E.

The chief omission in your list is perhaps the *Meno*: but I

---

[1] On this point Henry Jackson was in agreement with a famous
Cambridge scholar of a generation before his own. At the end of the
First Book of the Republic Macaulay writes in pencil: 'Very interesting
and curious. The characters are, as usual, admirably supported': and
on the margin of the earlier pages (514–518) of the Seventh Book:
'This is one of the very finest passages in all philosophy' G. O. T.

[196]

am inclined to think that you would not repent reading the *whole* of the *republic*. The philosophical element in it is not more than five per cent. and it abounds in wise sayings about life, society, and education.

Please write some time, and tell me your experiences.

Yours ever,   Henry Jackson.

[*In the draft* of the above letter, Jackson gives a list in order of the dialogues with notes, which is sufficiently interesting to be preserved here:]

It interests me to compare your list and my supplements with my scheme of Plato's writings, which is as follows:

I	Apology Crito Euthyphro Charmides Laches Lysis	purely Socratic exercises in clearer thinking about matters of conduct.
II	Protagoras Euthydemus Gorgias Phaedrus Symposium Meno	criticisms of educational theories, past and present: 'ideas' appear vaguely in *Phaedrus* and *Symposium*.
III	republic Phaedo Cratylus	*republic* propounds Plato's theory of education, resting it upon the 'earlier' theory of 'ideas': 'the earlier theory' is completed in the other two dialogues, and of these *Cratylus* is the more 'professional.'
IV	Parmenides Philebus Theaetetus sophist politicus Timaeus	Strictly 'philosophical' dialogues, which criticize sharply 'the earlier theory,' and expound 'the later theory.'
V	the Laws	a sober, serious, treatise on legislation, as conceived from the later standpoint.

OBITER SCRIPTA

To T. W. DUNN
22 *August* 1906

On Jan. 27 you wrote me a very kind letter for which I have never thanked you. Commenting on my praelection, you noted that I had not made clear how I conceive Plato's idea. I was obliged to scamp this part of my discourse, because I was anxious to put before the Senate something which I had not previously published. My notion of Platonism is, in brief, something of this sort: what exists is universal mind, and its thoughts and the thoughts of its thoughts. Its thoughts, as thoughts, are the ideas. Some of its thoughts are thought by it in space and in time: these are the stars. We are the thoughts of the stars, thought by them in space and time. The universe is the sum of all these thoughts as apprehended by us in space and time. This contracted statement is however hardly intelligible. I will try to explain myself when we next meet.

What I doubt in your statement is whether you secure to the ideas the objectivity which they must have.

To R. ST J. PARRY
26 *September* 1909

I think that the *Gorgias* is the Apologia Platonis—the explanation why he, who had thought of a political life, must be a looker on. Thompson is very good about it. But somehow I have always had an uncomfortable feeling that I had not disengaged the ethical doctrine from the dialectic, and that I should not be able to see my way in this part of the *Gorgias* till I had disentangled the maze of the *Protagoras*—an undertaking which makes me shiver.

To PROFESSOR J. A. PLATT
10 *August* 1911

The Platonic letters are absurd. The man who wrote them makes Plato a bounder, and I am sure that he was not of that sort. And, as you say, they are dull, drearily dull, poisonously dull, so that in consequence of them I am good for nothing.

I am glad that you recognise—at last—the greatness of 'our father Parmenides.' The man who saw that physic and metaphysic must not be confounded was no fool: he seems to me far greater than the much overpraised Heraclitus. It is a pity that he made his ent spherical: but it is not easy to think of form without matter, or of matter without extension. Aristotle would have saved the situation by calling in an 'underpaid, faithful' δυνάμει ἐνεργείᾳ δ' οὔ.

To SIR G. O. TREVELYAN

12 *March* 1916

Best thanks for your letter and for the cutting from *The Times Supplement*. I have had the cutting pasted into the volume of Macaulay's 'marginal notes' which you gave me nine years ago. Of course I read the 'marginal notes' again with renewed pleasure. It seems to me that he got the real pleasure of classical literature, and that you get it, whilst we professionals are no better than 'damned scholiasts' too much occupied with unimportant difficulties to be able to enjoy the real thing.

I will read the *Laches* again and Ast's criticism of it. It is so long since I read it that I shrink from giving an opinion: but I do not recollect that I have ever doubted about it. I see that I read it 1 Septr 1902, and noted 'purely Socratic.' This means 'written when Plato was attempting nothing more than to do by his writings what Socrates did by his talk,' i.e. make men think exactly and be accurate in their use of general terms. But it certainly implies that I had no suspicion whatever. But I will take Ast's highly sceptical book home with me. (I think that he recognizes only nine dialogues. In Acton's phrase—'a mountainous jackass.') Did you hear, and do you remember, what your uncle had to say against the *Laches*? People are apt to forget that Plato was (to use his own word) πολυχορδότατος, and that he kept till near the end of his life his power of writing in different styles. Read the opening pages of the *Parmenides*. The myth in the *politicus* and the myth in the *Timaeus* are written in a weightier style than that of the *Symposium* and the *Protagoras*, but they are great literature. Somewhere in the 'Anthology' there is an epigram addressed to some one who denied the genuineness of the *Phaedo*. Says the Epigrammatist: εἴ με Πλάτων οὐ 'γραψε, δύω ἐγένοντο Πλάτωνες. If the *Parmenides* and the *sophist* were not written by our Plato, the other man, though not as attractive, was a magnificent stylist, and in philosophy beat our Plato into fits. His contemporaries, and he himself, had lost themselves in the mazes of logic. The author of those two masterly dialogues clears up all Plato's puzzles

[199]

I don't believe that anything more truly epoch-making was ever written. But to appreciate them, it is necessary to realize how completely he and his contemporaries were befogged. I gather that Lord Macaulay was interested in the ethical and socio-logical side of Plato's thought: and that he did not care about his logical, metaphysical, physical, teaching. My belief is that Plato took all philosophy for his province, and that he 'grew' philo-sophically more than any other man from scepticism, through metaphysic, to science.

Once or twice I have dared to read a translation of the last pages of the *Phaedo* to a lecture room full of beginners. In general I am content to read a few lines from Maine's un-successful prize poem.

I hope that you have good news from George. I have no doubt that he is doing excellent work somewhere.

To SIR G. O. TREVELYAN

3 *March* 1918

I was very glad to receive your letter of Feb. 26 and to hear that you liked the *Meno*. It is, as I think J. S. Mill calls it— 'a gem.' But do you ever read the *republic*? I think that it is the most modern of all ancient writings. He saw that over-population is the cause of crime, disease, and war, as no one else saw it till the Rev. T. R. Malthus, fellow of Jesus, 120 years ago. (Surely Malthus was one of the greatest of Cambridge men: yet no one remembers him, just as Oxford men do not realize their greatest man, Roger Bacon.) Plato's metaphysic greatly in-terests me but there is plenty in him besides metaphysic; and in the *republic* the metaphysical element is small, perhaps about 5 %. I always feel that Plato was a real gentleman—καλὸς καὶ ἀγαθός. I have no sympathy with Burnet and A. E. Taylor who try to make out that Plato only repeated Socrates' talk, and that Socrates was a Pythagorean. According to me they were *two* of the world's very greatest men: they were poles apart, but there was room for both.

I am not surprized that you would like to have Livy's account of the Caesar and Cicero period. He realized the stories which he told, as Charles Kingsley did. (For this reason he is quite the right author to set for translation in an examination of the Cambridge type.)

PLATO

By the way, have you read John Morley's recollections? It
a little surprized me by its egotism. And it pained me to read
of the time when Mr G. was losing his grip of affairs....

20 April 1918

I am glad that you praise Grote. His strong common sense,
and his appreciation of situations and events, delight me: and
I like his exposition, which is broad and masculine and never
evasive. But he has a certain credulity which is especially
obvious in his acceptance of suspicious documents. Not long
ago, perhaps in 1911, I spent the best part of a long vacation in
reading again the Platonic Epistles, and books about them: and
again I concluded that they are all spurious. They have no
'guts.' I have no patience with the people who admit that some
of them are inane, but put up a fight for the rest. It is important
to remember that the forging of such things was a fashion, and
that a collection of so-called Platonic epistles was inevitable.
I am afraid that I made very few notes: for I lost patience with
the rubbish and with its advocates. But I think that it would
amuse you to read them in a sceptical spirit. It seemed to me
that in the absence of better testimony about Sicilian affairs,
Grote caught at anything which he could find in these letters.
But to me the stuff seemed unreal, the twaddle of an un-
imaginative man who made Plato in his maturity imitate his
earlier style. In short, I thought the forger a 'barren rascal.'
But I am rusty about these things, and must not try to say a
last word about them.

'Did I ever hear any thing of Sam Butler at Cambridge?' Very
little. I think that James Robertson had known him: but he did
not tell me much. Possibly John Venn may have known him:
but we seldom see that excellent man. The truth is that, except
to go to hall, I seldom leave my rooms. Gout and rheumatism
greatly hamper me. Indeed the journey to Bournemouth is a
more serious undertaking than the journey to the south of
France used to be in my Cannes period 1889–1898.

Did you ever read Plato's *politicus*? If you do not know it,
read at any rate the myth, beginning (say) at 268 D.

To T. W. DUNN
7 May 1918

Do you ever read the socalled Epistles of Plato? If you have
not done so, read them and tell me your views. To me they

seem absolute rubbish: but it shocks me that we professionals in Greek take opposite views. Indeed I think the forger was 'a barren rascal.' I am very sorry that Grote swallowed the rubbish without thinking.

5 June 1915

Sincerest thanks for your letter. You hit off exactly my sentiment about the Platonic Epistles. But the fashionable school swallows them whole, and even appeals to them as authorities. I don't wonder that you reproach me, but you have done me a kindness by fastening on some of the marks of forgery and debility which I had noticed myself. I think that I shall read the letters again: but argument from style is a ticklish thing, and in controversy useless. You should read Bentley on *Phalaris*: for it is a joy to see Bentley's mastery. But I shall not be shocked if you say that you do not care to waste time upon the exposure of imposters.

See also p. 240.

PLAUTUS

To BERNARD JACKSON
9 *January* 1903

I have just now been reading a play of Plautus with Horace. It is very entertaining foolery of a rough and ready sort, and must have been very amusing on the stage. But I never cease to wonder at Lessing's dictum—which he solemnly defended— that the *Captivi* is the best play ever put upon any stage.

PLUTARCH

To A. O. PRITCHARD
17 *March* 1918

I am very grateful to you for sending me your Plutarch: all the more so because you have chosen a series of essays which specially interest me. I had hoped before this to read at any rate part: but I have not found time for it. I am however looking forward to reading the whole in the vacation.

I was glad to read what you say about Bywater. To me too his death was a great blow.

By the way, our late Master, W. H. Thompson, told me that Bentley used *forte* in the sense of *fortasse*, and I satisfied myself that it was so. But sometimes he contracted *fortasse* into *fort*.

POLITICS

POLITICS

To F. W. MAITLAND

3 *January* 1906

You give the new Ministry a very honourable title. I had thought of them as the ministry of mediocrities. What tramps (with a small initial) politicians are! In this morning's newspaper there is a manifesto from A. J. B. to his constituents, which, from a fishwife, I should have thought a disgrace to Billingsgate. Scratch Arthur, and you will find—Joe. And I don't think it any defence to say that this is part of the political business. Pat Currey used to say that the gentleman was the man who behaved himself as such when he was drunk: I think that the gentleman ought to behave as such when he is in politics.

Which remarks will show you that even if I were not a radical and a republican I should not do for the House of Commons. If I had had money, and had not cared for books and academic studies, I should have liked the parliamentary life; but I don't see how anyone who respects his academic studies can go into parliament.

4 *April* 1906

I wonder what you think about politics. I am in a state of complete funk; because we liberals have so big a majority and so many of us want educating. Moreover, the ministers, most of them, are without experience. Just think how much depends upon Birrell! I am horribly afraid that in this parliament there are too few of those country gentlemen, who, whether tories or liberals, have made it their business through life to help their neighbours, and who, in helping their neighbours, have educated themselves in matters political.

To SIR GEORGE GREENWOOD

19 *September* 1906

It was good of you to bear with me, and to write again. I think that I was an ass to write my first letter, and that I ought to apologize for it; because every man must settle for himself at what point he will protest against the doings of his political friends. That this must be done, no one knows better than I. Very often in supporting a measure, a man must say openly that he regards it as no more than 'half a loaf,' and sometimes

[203]

when a Government is slack, it must be necessary to take up a *hostile* attitude. My letter—a blunder, I now acknowledge—was prompted, not by what you wrote to *The Times*, but by your comments in your letter to me. Let me explain. I always like to see in the house men of your sort: thorough going, chivalrous, radicals. Sir W. Lawson was one. But your letter to me made me think that you were in danger of damaging your influence as a practical politician by taking up what people call an 'Academic' or 'Platonic' line: and I sh^d very much regret this. Moreover, I have some sympathy with governmental people who are trying to get all they can for liberalism when people come kicking their heels from behind because they don't try to get more than they can. Finally, it seemed to me rather early in the life of this parliament, which promises to be an active one, to begin abusing the government.

The Education Bill seems to me unsatisfactory on the grounds which you mention: but I think that just now there is a great deal to be said for the line of least resistance. It seems to me that there is a great deal of pigheadedness all round.

I can put you up in College on Octr 10 to 13 or 14, and it would be a great pleasure to me to do so. But I shall not arrive till midday on the 10th from Oxford, and on Sunday the 14th I shall have to go to Dublin.

To PROFESSOR J. A. PLATT

10 *August* 1911

If you should vouchsafe me a reply, you might as well tell me how you voted in last Thursday's division.

  i Government, from conviction
     (α) without misgiving (β) with misgiving.
  ii Opposition (a) voting with Government
          (b) abstaining
          (c) voting against Government.

Poor things! What a comfort it is, not to be a professional politician, drawing parallelograms of forces, with principle pulling one way and expediency another. I suppose that the parliamentarian becomes callous: if he does not, the wear and tear of his conscience must be prodigious.

RESEARCH

To G. A. HIGHT
6 *June* 1912

You ask me what I think about home rule. I have been a confirmed home ruler since 1882. So I am glad to find that people have got sick of the question and are prepared to accept the bill. I expect that more money will be wanted to float the scheme: but that both Commons and Lords will pass it.

RESEARCH

To PROFESSOR J. A. PLATT
26 *October* 1910

The time will come when fellowship dissertations will be denounced as the sources of rotten and rubbishy generalizations, some of them truisms, others lies. A rock ahead is bogus research, research for reputation's sake. I don't believe in research which is artificially stimulated: the man should plod along with his studies, and humbly say a grace, if something new turns up to amuse and encourage him.

27 *September* 1913

I think that what you say is sound. Those modest sciences which interrogate nature have an objectivity of a humble sort: those immodest sciences which call themselves philosophies are aggressively subjective. But the misfortune is that so many of the people who work the physical sciences are pigs[1]. So it is better to be Socrates dissatisfied than a pig pleased. The truth is that it is the merit of the physical sciences that they can be worked by '——'s journeymen,' and it is also their demerit. I think that it will be a loss to the strength of the College if the immodest philosophies drop out, and we elect only people whom Auguste Comte would have approved as useful workers.

But hang it all! I am again relapsing into a loathly pessimism —which be damned. Pessimism is damnable. Vade retro Satanas!

ROMAN CATHOLICISM

To A FRIEND *on his joining the Roman Catholic Church*
14 *August* 1903

I ought before this to have thanked you for your letter: but it reached me just as I left Cambridge for Brighton, and when I was there, I spent all my time talking with my two brothers.

[1] See Plato, *republic*, ii, 367 D, 372 D.

[205]

I was heartily glad to hear from you, and hope that you will find time to write again.

Your news came to me as a surprise. I am of course sorry that you should have found yourself obliged to take this step: for it must have caused you anxiety beforehand, and it must have been a wrench at the last. Moreover it may well be a trouble to your friends. But it does not dismay me, if my friends find in formularies other than those of the Church of England the best expression of their religious convictions and aspirations. I hope—or rather I pray—that you may have all the help that Christianity can give us. Is your news public? Might I mention it, for example, to * * *? I had not heard of * * *: but I find my people know of him as a remarkable preacher.

I shall hope to hear some time about your studies in Thomas Aquinas. It is a huge subject and an important one. I have an idea that of late very few people have studied him from the Aristotelian point of view: and I am inclined to think that, whilst he is a sound Aristotelian, his modern interpreters do not understand Aristotelian principles. If so, confusion must be the inevitable result.

ROUSSEAU, ETC.

To DR F. MELLAND
19 *July* 1907

What you say about the encyclopaedists makes me ask you whether you have read Diderot's *Letters to Mlle Volland*? Also I note that you do not mention Rousseau in your list. Now in a certain sense I have a contempt for Rousseau: I think him mean, egotistical, and vain. But the *Confessions* is to me one of the most interesting books ever written; and if you have not read it, I should most strongly recommend it to you. The man could not speak the truth: but he displays himself both in his strength and in his weakness.

Like you, I am interested in the 18th century French people. They were none of them serious students. But Voltaire, Rousseau, and Diderot, entertain me exceedingly, and so do the memoirs of Madame d'Épinay.

To PROFESSOR J. A. PLATT
6 *December* 1906

I am reading a Mrs F. Macdonald's big book about Rousseau. She has got at the history of Mme d'Épinay's memoirs, and in spite of her frantic and illogical comments, her facts are to me very interesting. I suppose that my curiosity about such things is what people call 'degrading' or 'morbid,' but I admit that I am 'amused.' Indeed if I had not so many 'things that are nearest' to do I should like to write a *Quarterly* article on this book. As far as I have got Mrs M. shows that Madame d'Épinay dictated a novel of real life with real persons under sham names, that Grimm and Diderot suggested changes and additions, that Madame d'Épinay made the changes and additions with her own hand. (That the memoirs were a novel with the real names restored, has always been known.) But Mrs M. infers, from the fact that Grimm and Diderot made suggestions, that (1) the statements made are not true, (2) that there was a plot to prepare an attack upon Rousseau which should not be published until no one was left who could contradict it. But I must not spend time in telling you things which don't interest you when I ought to be writing business letters. The truth is that I am at a garrulous age, as appears in the fact that I not long ago remonstrated with a restless radical M.P., a friend of mine, who seemed to me in danger of quarrelling with his natural leaders. I admit that I, of all men, am the last to preach on this text. But I do know that, when governmental people are trying to get what they can, it is an infernal nuisance for them to be kicked by their friends from behind for not trying to get what they cannot.

To C. E. SAYLE

28 June 1909

Mrs Macdonald has got good material: but she is deficient in judgment. Also instead of printing originals, she translates, paraphrases, and interprets. So there is far too much of herself in her book, and I don't altogether trust her. Le Maistre's book is one of the very best literary studies I have ever seen so far: perhaps the best of all. It is very severe; but not unjust: and it is a joy to find someone who speaks the unvarnished truth by such an one as J. J. What made me put the question to you was the reading of Gribble's book *Rousseau and the Women he Loved*. It is a mere compilation, but it is not ill done: and I have got from it a number of references to authorities, all of them tolerably recent.

[207]

OBITER SCRIPTA

A SCHOLAR'S PROGRESS—SCHOLARSHIP

To SIR G. O. TREVELYAN

26 *October* 1916

I am very grateful to you for your letter dated on St Crispin's day. It greatly interested me: but it carried me out of my depth. I never knew anything either about the life of Cicero or about his speeches. When as an undergraduate I had to translate pieces from them, I took them as mere unseens: and the very excellence of his writing made it possible for me to take this line. My ignorance of the contemporary history is disgraceful. Later I kept clear of Roman history, and especially of Cicero's period. I know of course that I have missed much which would have greatly interested me: but, after plunging about in such authors as Lucan, Martial, Plautus, I drifted into Greek philosophy and found that the pre-Platonics, Plato, and Aristotle, wanted all my time. The truth is that just because I am a professional in a small corner of Greek literature, I have not been able to have the enjoyment of Greek and Roman literature as a whole which you have and your uncle had. I have often envied you and him: for I think that you and he more than other men have enjoyed what Currey called 'these Classic tombs.'

As to Petronius, I wish that we had him entire. He gives the seamiest side of the seamy Roman life, but he gives that life in its actuality, and the idiomatic, unliterary, talk at Trimalchio's banquet hugely interests me. I don't greatly respect the Romans, and therefore the unmitigated vulgarity of the nouveau riche Trimalchio does not *disgust* me: I enjoy the presentation of it. Of course the forged supplements are absolutely without merit of any sort, and are indeed a mere nuisance.

Whatever the history of the *Iliad* may be, it is amazing. The critics condemn some of the latest books: but, whoever wrote them, some of them are prodigious. It is story telling of the best, and stirs in their intensity the emotions of ἔλεος καὶ φόβος.

I have not yet made myself acquainted with Sam Butler's life of his grandfather. But what you say will make me do so. I am not sure that I rank as highly as you do the Shrewsbury influence on English scholarship. It may have made the Cambridge scholarship of the middle of the last century; but I think that just then English scholarship was at its worst. Munro was a great scholar just because he was not of the sort which Ben Kennedy bred. But I must not develop this criticism.

[208]

SCHOLARSHIP

After the war how much English scholarship will be left? Not the scholarship of Porson, Thompson, and Munro. Scholarship will be dead; and I think that it ought to die. But whilst it has lived, it has, I think, encouraged much intellectual endeavour of which the world need not be ashamed.

SHAKSPERE AND SHAKESPEARE

To A. J. BUTLER
28 July 1902

The real Baconians keep quite clear of Mrs Gallup and Co. They argue:

(1) Shakspere the actor came to London knowing nothing—a butcher, a groom, and then an inferior actor. Yet before he had been long in town Shakespeare's poems or plays began to come out, full of culture, classicism, and learning.

(2) Shakspere the actor retired early to Stratford, and took no trouble about his supposed writings: but the plays of Shakespeare the author came out in a revised form with others not yet published some years after Shakspere the player died.

(3) There is no evidence that Shakspere the player was supposed to possess any special gifts, or that he had any access to polite society or the society of wits.

(4) Ben Jonson disliked and abused Shakspere, and lauded Shakespeare to the skies in terms resembling those which elsewhere he used of Bacon.

(5) Bacon possessed the culture, classicism, and learning, which Shakespeare also possessed, and Shakspere did not.

These are I think the main points. It seems to me that they forget how completely the literature of the time was steeped in classicism. What I don't make out is how they would meet this dilemma: 'By assumption Bacon elaborately concealed his authorship of the plays. Hence contemporaries attributed the plays either to Shakspere or to an unknown. If they attributed them to Shakspere, then, they who knew him, did not think him, as you assume, incapable of writing them. If they attributed them to an unknown, how is it that no indications of this have come down to us? and how is it that they made no attempt to penetrate the mystery?'

There are of course other points which they have tried to make and heaps of retorts. George Greenwood is a little sick

about some of the parallels. But he does not realize that innumerable classicisms which are unfamiliar now were familiar
then: e.g. Wright blunders over

> Sense, sure, you have, else could you not have motion[1].

Greenwood points out that this comes from the *de anima*
and shows by a quotation that it was familiar to Bacon. Of
course it was familiar to parsons and all moderately educated
people.

Both Shakespeare and Bacon talk of 'discourse of reason,'
and (think these Baconians) no one else does. Greenwood
now tells me that some one has shown, what we all assume,
that the phrase is common to many authors.

Your passage is one of the favourite parallelisms, but Reed
shows his incompetence to touch this question by writing

'The common source was undoubtedly Cardan or Galen,
one of whom had previously published a Latin translation of the
original Greek work, *Prognostica*, containing the passage, and
the other a commentary upon it.

'Cardan and Galen, almost alone among their contemporaries and successors, however, take the right view.

'Here is very nearly absolute proof that the author of the
play had studied Cardan's translation of the *Prognostica*, or
Galen's commentary upon it.'

Surely I am not uncharitable in thinking that Reed supposes
Galen and Cardan to be contemporaries. The strength of their
position is the fact that the collected editions did not come out
till after Shakspere's death. If Shakspere revised before his
death, why did not he publish? But they are able to make a
plausible use of the rubbish which people have written to prove
Shakespeare's omniscience, e.g. Lord Campbell on his law.
But I have written enough and more than enough about this
stuff.

To BERNARD JACKSON
9 January 1903

I have had a huge correspondence with George Greenwood—
do you remember him?—about 'Shakspere' *v.* 'Shakespeare.'
But I think that we have reached the point at which it had better
cease. It seems to me that the case in favour of the Stratford
player has suffered a good deal from the advocacy of Sidney

---

[1] *Hamlet.*

[210]

SHAKESPEARE

Lee, who, having edited the *Dictionary of National Biography*, has somehow come to be regarded as an authority about English literature. I notice that over and over again, Greenwood is in reality attacking not the identity of 'Shakspere' (the player) and 'Shakespeare' (the author), but some statement loosely made by Sidney Lee. The literature of this controversy is already enormous, and it is constantly growing. Of course the people who engage in it ought to read a lot of Elizabethan literature besides 'Shaker' (as H. calls him) and Bacon. The real issue is—'Could a man who notoriously had had small literary and social advantages so soon have contracted (what seems to us) a very ornate, elegant, and learned style? Could he in particular have written the sonnets?' Another point is now again emphasised. It is argued that he must have been a learned lawyer, and I hear that Lord Penzance has just now brought out a book to prove it.

SHAKESPEARE—BACON

To MR JUSTICE MADDEN

19 *November* 1906

Whilst I regard the 'Shaconian' theory as an absurdity, I recognise that the 'Shaconians' have a line of argument which it is not easy to refute in detail. They point out that something which is not familiar to us is familiar at once to Bacon and to Shakespeare. For example, Hamlet says to his mother 'Sense, sure, you have, else could you not have motion.' The commentators don't understand this and say that 'motion' = 'emotion.' My anti-Shakespearian friend points out that this is the Aristotelian doctrine that plants have φυτικὴ καὶ θρεπτική— that the lowest animals have φυτικὴ καὶ θρεπτική, and also αἰσθητική, and animals of the next grade φ. καὶ θ. and αἰσθητική, and also κινητική: so that the possession of κινητική implies the possession of αἰσθητική. The queen is moving about the stage, and therefore must have αἰσθητική. Bacon has the same notion, says my friend: is it not remarkable that both should have the same bit of out of the way learning? My answer is that, what is out of the way learning now was often familiar then, and that this Aristotelian science may have been familiar in sermons and otherwise: but though this conjecture is plausible, it is not easy to demonstrate its truth. Perhaps old Farmer might have known how to prove it, but Sidney Lee has not a tithe of Farmer's learning.

To SIR G. GREENWOOD
19 *June* 1900

It is strange that the commentators on Shakespeare have been blind to the explanation of 'Sense, sure, you have, else could you not have motion.' I imagine that this Aristotelian philosopheme would be quite familiar. You will find it, for example, set out at length in Sir John Davies' philosophical poem *Nosce teipsum*, published 1599. W. S. might have got it from him, or from a sermon.

To F. W. MAITLAND
7 *February* 1904

I have been looking in *Notes and Queries* for something, and I have stumbled upon the statement that the motto of Laharpe's *Cours de Littérature* is 'indocti discunt, et ament meminisse periti.' Plainly it should be 'discant.' I don't know the origin of this line, which seems familiar enough: but I will try to locate it. Is it possible that 'discas et ames meminisse[1]' became proverbial, *without* the distinction between the 'indocti' and the 'periti'? As if we were to say 'Mark, learn, and inwardly digest.' The knowledge of the old folk is quite as wonderful as their ignorance, or more so. W. W. Greg sent me a year or two ago a wretched eclogue by Fairfax in which two 'Shepherds' (?) discussed 'ancients v. moderns,' the feats of the Greeks and Romans v. the discoverers of America etc. I had to work hard to run down the farfetcht references to the Classics, and it wanted Oldham to fix some of the geographical allusions. This is *one* of the things which the 'Shaconians' do not realize. But I must not launch out upon that theme, upon which George Greenwood tackles me.

To C. E. SAYLE
28 *June* 1909

The strength of his [Greenwood's] position is also a weakness. Whilst he maintains that the Stratford actor did not write the

[1] Maitland had asked him about this.

plays and the poems, he refrains from attributing them to any
one else. This saves him from the responsibility of a definite
theory: but at the cost of assuming that the writer was some one
unknown to his contemporaries. Greenwood's favourite argument that the writer of the plays and poems knew things which
the Stratford actor could not have known, seems to me feeble.
Lubbock, in his pleasant books, tells (1) how Pepys, when he
began to be important at the Admiralty, went to a mathematician
to be coached in the multiplication table, and (2) how shocked
he was to find that his nephew at Christ's did not know how
Aristotle connected 'the four qualities' with 'the four elements.' Nowadays we all know the multiplication table;
whereas I am quite certain that a few years ago there were at
Cambridge no professed classical men, except the very few who
took Part II § B., who could have answered the question which
Pepys put to his nephew. Again, the Girondins, who probably
knew no Greek, were familiar with anecdotes in Plutarch
which I do not know or do not remember, though I have been
reading Greek for sixty years. But I must not write a pamphlet.

To PROFESSOR J. A. PLATT
1 January 1902

I read Mallock's article hastily, and did not suppose him to
commit himself. In Mrs Gallup's book there must be a great
deal of work and a great deal of fudging, or else a great deal of
deliberate falsehood. What I want to know is whether the
fudging is wholesale or retail. Lutoslowski fudges wholesale,
and lies wholesale on the top of everything.

To SIR G. GREENWOOD
1 July 1902

I have been spending a dreary afternoon and evening, first,
writing out answers to a circular about school and university
education sent out by a committee of the British Association,
secondly, writing business letters. So instead of settling down
to work I am moved to write my thanks for your letter received
this morning.

Last night I began Judge Webb. This morning your letter
came. At present I have not read much more than half the book,
so that I don't know anything like the whole of Judge Webb's

case. As far as I have got, I find a good deal which seems to me unsatisfactory.

He begins well enough by showing that it is absurd to suppose that Shakspere had had a good education: but is he warranted in supposing that he had none? He shows that of great tracts in Shakspere's life we know nothing: but is he warranted in assuming, as he constantly does, that there was nothing to know? He shows that *Shakspere* was not a learned scholar: he *assumes* that *Shakespeare* was a learned scholar. This I deny. He knew a heap of mythology: but he did not know Latin authors as Ben Jonson did. He does not recognize that Shakspere might perfectly well know the literary allusions of the time—which were principally classical—just as well as many another risen press man knows the literary allusions of our own day. (By the way, the supposed misquotation from the *ethics*, common to Shakespeare and to Bacon, is a mare's nest. Look at the passage, *Nic. Eth.* I, iii, 5, and read the context §§ 1–8, and you will see that Shakespeare and Bacon more truly represent Aristotle's meaning than Webb does, when he lays stress on the words τῆς πολιτικῆς.)

Then again he plays off the players' man who never blots, against Jonson's man who laboriously files: and there is a tacit implication that the former is Shak*spere*, and the latter Shake*speare*. But (1) the players' man is the writer and not the player, and (2) Jonson also has a Shakespeare who does not blot, and, (if Webb is right in his identification), a Shakespeare who elaborately files. Is it not obvious for us who are not Baconians to say that the players' Shakespeare who did not blot was the man who dashed off pieces to be acted, and that the Shakespeare who elaborately filed, was the same man when he was no longer hurriedly turning out pieces (as Molière did) to be acted by the company to which he belonged? Again, I resent the assumption that Shakespeare would make no corrections unless he was thinking either of resultant money or resultant fame. The writer was anyhow a great artist, and was certain, from the artistic point of view, to make changes, irrespective of all ambitions.

But, above all, it seems to me that Webb has not envisaged the consequences of his own argument. He supposes that Shakspere, the player, fathered the plays which Bacon wrote: that Bacon's authorship was a profound secret: that the plays

SHAKESPEARE

'astonished the world': *but* that Shakspere was a mere nobody, that his antecedents were such that it is absurd, and therefore was absurd, to attribute the plays to him, and that he 'never once during the five and twenty years that he lived in London claimed to be the author.' Surely if the world was astonished, the world must have asked who wrote these plays and these poems: and if the people of the time were content with the answer that it was Shakspere the player, Webb's argument— Shakspere was a poacher, a butcher, a groom, a servant, and an unknown, inferior actor, and therefore it is absurd to attribute literature to him—drops. If Bacon got his work fathered by some one, he must have chosen some one to whom the attribution was not impossible. Webb tries to show that the attribution was impossible.

But I must not go on scribbling, as it is almost 3 a.m.

Probably Webb is right in rejecting Sidney Lee's views: but if so, why does he darken counsel by dragging in Lee's statements? This sort of argument tells against Lee only.

To THE SAME
5 *July* 1902

I write a few more lines in continuation of my former letter.

At p. 220 Webb speaks of 'discourse of reason' as 'a peculiar' phrase, and in the index he goes so far as to call it 'peculiar to Bacon.' But surely 'discourse of reason,' 'discursus rationis,' is a recognized philosophical phrase in common use, and if the critics altered it in *Hamlet* for the reason which Webb suggests, in the first place they did not know their Shakespeare, and in the second, they did not know the literature of the time. And when I call it a philosophical phrase, I do not mean a phrase peculiar to philosophers, but a phrase which would be used in sermons, etc. I don't remember whether it occurs in Sir John Davies' *Nosce teipsum*—a little later I suppose: but I should be surprised if he does not use it. Again, you might try Phineas Fletcher's *Purple Isle*.

Again, I demur to the inference from the use by Bacon and Shakespeare of the words 'obsequious,' 'oblation,' p. 163.

Again, at p. 164, it is argued that the player, if he had written the plays, would not have described *Venus and Adonis* 'as the first heirs of his invention.' Why then should Bacon? if, as Webb supposes, in the sonnets 'written about the same time,'

[215]

p. 64, he 'clearly intimated that Shakespeare was not his real name.'

And now look at this Sonnet lxxvi. I deny that the four lines mean what Webb supposes. Look at them with their context. What the writer means is that he is always harping on the same string, so that his inspiration always appears in the same garb, and every line has the sign-manual of the author.

Then again Matthew's letter, p. 253. I understand Matthew to mean that 'the most prodigious wit' etc. is Bacon, though he is now called Ld. Visct. St. Alban.

Then again I am astonished that any one should lay stress upon the difference of spelling of Shakspere and Shakespeare. Some years ago I was looking up the pedigree of some ancestors of mine called Sayle. I found the name only two hundred years ago spelt Sayle, Sayl, Sail and (I think) Sale. Indeed, I had thought that indifference to spelling was a recognised characteristic of the past.

Again, look at the criticism of Jonson's lines about 'The Swan of Avon,' p. 134, 'no poet...wd. be mad enough to talk of a swan as *yet* appearing...some seven or eight years after it was dead' (see the passage). It seems to me clear that the person whom Jonson apostrophizes *is dead*.

What a sight it were,
To see thee in our waters yet appear.

And observe! that if, as Webb supposes, 'Mine . . . . etc.' implies that Jonson 'regarded Shakespeare as living,' he makes Jonson contradict himself, for by confession '*the Swan of Avon*' Shakspere was dead.

The note on p. 136 is surely nonsense. The epithet (? nostra*te*) does not *specialize*, it *describes*: that is to say, in French it would properly stand before the noun, and not after it— *l'anglais Shakespeare*, not *le Shakespeare anglais*.

By the way, his honour ought to know that *nom de plume* is not French; and at p. 2 is 'Scott' a misprint for 'Strutt,' or is Strutt supposed to have got some inspiration from Scott?

There is one very important matter which it is difficult and indeed impossible to handle satisfactorily. Webb assumes that if a man had not been at a great school and a great university he could not be, as the prigs say, 'abreast' of the general knowledge and cultivation of his time and could not use the ordinary literary allusions freely and easily. I demur to this. Look up

Wells' antecedents, in *Who's Who*, and then read his books: and there must be plenty of other press men. And in the Elizabethan age, with a smaller London, a smaller society, a smaller literary coterie, it would be much easier than it is now. Moreover, it is to be remembered—what people, I think, often forget —that, though social grades were very clearly marked,—Kings and Liptons, perhaps, did not fraternize so much,—people of different grades *met* much more than they do now. In Pepys' *Diary*, you find him, on the way to the office, taking his 'morning draught' at a pothouse, one day with Ld. Sandwich, and the next with his barber or his tailor.

Webb puts Shakspere's start in London as late as he can and minimizes his opportunities when he got there. Webb forgets that, in so doing, he proves too much. If it is inconceivable now that the poor player should have written these plays, it was inconceivable then: and yet (1) Bacon, ex hypothesi, ventured to make him *father* them, and (2) people had no suspicion. Note further that the *players*, at any rate, must have detected the fraud.

But you will be wearied to death if I write more. Please keep these two letters, for I have half a mind to write a screed for my 'Dons' Essay Club,' the 'Eranus,' and these notes might help me. I have written for Reed's book.

To THE SAME
7 *July* 1902

Many thanks for your letter, which has crossed one from me. I am ashamed of having bothered you at a time when you have other things to do. So though I write again, you must not think it necessary to answer either this letter or its predecessor.

In your couplet Jove = Jupiter and Satur = Saturnus look like the merest memoria technica:

Compare

ΕΚ ΜΕΤΑΓΕΙΤΝΙ ΒΟΗ ΠΥΑ ΜΑΙΜΑΚΤΗΡΙ ΠΟΣΕΙΔΟΝ
ΓΑΜ ΑΝΘΕΣΤ ΕΛΑΦΗ ΜΟΥΝΥΧΙ ΘΑΡΓ ΣΚΙΡΟΦΟΡ

I got this out of a XIXth century school book.

You must not make me answerable for what Sidney Lee says. But it does not follow because Shakspere had not read Seneca that he knew no mythology. I suspect that many a French boy knows, and that every Frenchman and Frenchwoman from the time of the Gironde to the consulate knew more of the ordinary mythology and anecdotage of the Romans than I do, and, what is more, than I ever did.

I gather that you distinguish so sharply between Shakespeare and Shakspere that you do not believe that, after the publication of poems and plays in the name of Shakespeare, any one supposed them to be attributed to Shakspere. I had not previously realized this, and I suppose that in so thinking you break away altogether from Judge Webb.

What is *Shakspere not Shakespeare?* Who is the author?

There was one point which I forgot to mention in my last letter. Webb is shocked that 'the omniscient Shakespeare' should have 'consistently maintained' 'exploded error,' in

> Doubt thou the stars are fire;
> Doubt thou the sun doth move.

But do these lines prove that Shakespeare 'consistently maintained these errors,' and were they 'exploded' if Bacon maintained them?

There was an old story that some one told Sir Arthur Miller that according to the best authorities the seat of the affections was not the heart but the intestines. Whereupon he asked whether we were to read in future:

> Maid of Athens! ere I cut
> Give me back my upper gut.

The popular physiology would have been good enough for Byron, just as *ridiculous Geography* was good enough for Shakespeare. By the way, I don't feel clear that the ridiculous Geography would have commended itself to Bacon. Again, by the way, though I don't much trust my own or any one's instinct in matters of style, whilst it is small surprise to me that Shakespeare should be able to turn out prose of the Elizabethan sort, of which Bacon's is a specimen, it would surprise me much that Bacon should be able to turn out some of the bits of verse which appear in the plays—Full fathom five—What shall he have—Under the greenwood tree, etc.

By the way, do you hold that when *Jonson talked of Shakespeare*, he did not dream that anyone might confound Shakespeare with Shakspere the player? and that although he knew the great secret, that Shakespeare = Bacon, he used Shakespeare to mean no more than the great unknown and expected to be so understood? Did all the world recognize that, while Shakespeare was certainly not Shakspere the player, it was an unknown personage? By the way, Shakescene suggests that there was not so sharp a distinction as I think you assume between Shakspere and Shakespeare.

Turning over your letter once more I note your definition of 'a scholar in the modern sense[1],' i.e. a man who can write Latin Hexameters and Greek Iambics besides Prose Composition. Neither did I mean by a scholar such a person. What I meant was that Shakespeare's skill in writing Elizabethan English and his familiarity with classical allusions and mythology do not necessarily imply more than, if so much as, a smattering of Latin.

'The fact that Shakespeare had elaborately revised his plays, and revised them not for the stage but for the study, not for the spectator but for the literary man.' I am a bit bewildered in this matter. Had the quartos been thus prepared for the reader? or was it only the folio? How came it that the preparation for the reader was so poorly carried out in the *printing*? But I perceive that I must read Swinburne and make out what he has to say.

Are you solitary in holding that 'nobody thought of Shakspere as Shakespeare'? Anyhow, this is a very different system from Webb's.

Please take no notice whatever of these jottings. I am only thinking on paper.

This question seems to be to the early XXth century what the Junius question was to the early XIXth. Years ago I began to be interested in it, and for the last 25 years or so, I have had some knowledge of Sir P. Francis' descendants. My wife is one of them. In this matter there are two or three *visible* proofs which go a long way: e.g.

(1) Of five seals—i.e. of five distinct devices—which are found on the original Junius letters in the B.M., *four* are found also on letters from Francis;

(2) On the original proofs corrections are sometimes written and then elaborately erased, the equivalent being rewritten: i.e. the writer has written the corrections in a natural hand, has copied them in his second or feigned hand, and has then erased the correction in the natural hand. But in *one* case a date in the

---

[1] I bar the definition.

natural hand has survived, and when compared with dates of the same period (one of them the day before or the day after), in Francis' correspondence, the identity of the writing is obvious.

(3) Young Woodfall was once shown a paper written by Francis as cover to a Valentine in a disguised hand: he at once exclaimed 'Junius!'

But I must not bore you about this old story.

Forgive me for writing all this stuff.

(Postcard)
13 July 1902

Very many thanks for your exceedingly interesting letter. I must read more before I bother you with new questions. In particular, I must look up 'discourse of reason.'

My memoria technica is for the attic months Ἑκατομβαιών Μεταγειτνιών Βοηδρομιών κ.τ.λ.

The chief purpose of this card is, however, to wish you most heartily success at your meeting on Tuesday. Both in politics and in literature and in everything, I am for inquiry: so don't think that I want to *burke* Bacon = Shakespeare.

To THE SAME
13 January 1903

I hope to return to College on Thursday, and I am trying to bring my correspondence up to date before I do so. So I write my thanks for your letter of Jan. 2nd and the postcard which followed it. I have not yet seen either Lord Penzance or Mallock: but I hope to do so when I return to a less unliterary neighbourhood.

I have been reading what H. Morley says in his handbook, and I observe that what Greene says, and Chettle apologizes for, refers to 'Shakespeare' rather than to 'Shakspere,' and it is quite intelligible if *Henry VI*, 1, 2 and 3, were old plays altered and improved. You speak of four or five years—between 1586 and 1591-1592—and call it a very short time. But, after all, don't most men know their business in life in four or five years? What a man has to learn is not the aptitude, but the method and the slang.

Of course you and I differ about the thing. I think that it was in the atmosphere: you think that Bacon, 'Shakespeare,' and perhaps the Court, had the monopoly. You think that

[220]

SHAKESPEARE

Shakespeare was a learned classicist: I think that he was a smattering classicist.

I think that your reference to the Roman plays is an oversight: for I fancied that confessedly Shakespeare derived his learning for them from one book (or two books), and that he knew no more of Roman history than (say) G. P. R. James knew of French history, probably less. 'To be or not to be,' as you say, has nothing to do with Eleaticism: neither has the 'That that is, is' of the Clown in *Twelfth Night*. Plato quotes from Euripides τίς οἶδεν εἰ τὸ ζῆν μέν ἐστι κατθανεῖν τὸ κατθανεῖν δὲ ζῆν: but this is a quite different sentiment from 'To be or not to be.' But plainly mistaken identifications of this sort are to be put aside. They do not prove anything for the Baconians, nor anything against their theory. When I return to Cambridge, I intend to look up *M. for M.* in the Cambridge Shakespeare. At present I think that the epithet in this clause, like the epithet in the preceding clause, should contrast with the future life: and I am not dissatisfied with 'delighted.'

I have been reading again—after nearly 35 years—*Childe Harold* and think still that it is sadly overrated. When Byron is content to be witty and worldly, he seems to me excellent: when he pretends to be poetical and sentimental, he seems to me an imposter and a twaddler: when he is purely rhetorical, he seems to me *occasionally* effective. But I have to acknowledge that Canto 3 is vastly better in workmanship than Cantos 1, 2.

To THE SAME
15 *January* 1903

It is not easy to avoid misunderstandings.

Perhaps I mistake: but I thought that some anti-Shaksperians understood Greene to say that 'Shakspere' the actor was swaggering on the strength of another man's writings. I pointed out that he accuses the *writer* of using the work of other people. Chettle seemed to me—but I had not got before me more than Morley's quotation—to assume the identity of the writer and the actor.

I have been reading one Willis on the side of Shakspere. The form of his book is unhappy; for fiction, though it may enable a man to state his convictions, muddles argument. But he has some quotations from sermons which seem to show (1) that a non-legal person, such as a parson, might have a good many legal technicalities at his fingers' ends, (2) that he might count upon a very popular audience to understand those technicalities.

I have not yet seen Mallock's article. Confound 'the literature'! It grows too fast for people who have other things to do.

I think I should be bold enough to maintain that there is nothing *beautiful* in the whole of *Childe Harold*.

I think that Bournemouth was almost as cold this morning as Cambridge is tonight at 2.20 a.m. tomorrow, if you will pardon the bull.

I must go to bed: for I have to attend three meetings tomorrow, and the first is at 10 o'clock, less than 8 hours hence.

To THE SAME

20 January 1903

I have now read the first part, but not the second, of Mallock's *New Facts*.

(1) I am sorry that (p. 78) he has not printed the verses of which he speaks.

(2) Are the explanations on p. 82 serious? or is he making game of the Baconians?

(3) p. 82^b line 6 the words 'that of a poet' seem to me wholly unwarranted.

(4) If this title page prove anything about Bacon, it proves that Bacon wrote Montaigne, or at least translated him.

(5) If the title page of Spenser's *Faerie Queene* means 'Francis Bacon son of Q. Elizabeth and Dudley,' does it not also prove that Bacon wrote Spenser's works? Otherwise, why was the cryptogram put into this book?

(6) p. 86^b line 8 Fr...Jacobus. Query 'Primus Jacobus,' 'Francis' is a syllable too long. F = P.

(7) pp. 88, 89. How about 'Breakspeare'? What does it all mean?

Surely Mallock is making game of the Baconians!

If not, his article ought, if it proves anything, to prove that Bacon wrote Spenser and Montaigne and Gustavus Selenus.

I have also read letters in the 'Speaker.' The writer of the principal letter seemed to hold that, whereas Shakespeare shows learning, *L'Allegro* and *Il Penseroso* do not. Is he too ironical?

I hope to read Mallock's second part soon. As yet I am not

[222]

SHAKESPEARE

moved to buy it. If it is a joke, it is too elaborate. If it is serious,
it is too much like a bad joke.
Forgive me if I write frivolously.

To THE SAME
30 *January* 1903

I have read your article rapidly. Many thanks for it, and for
your letter. Your account of Lord Penzance's book interests
me much. Your attack upon Willis is quite justified. It seemed
to me that he contributed nothing except some extracts from
sermons which seemed to show that a parson might talk law
with the expectation that his congregation would appreciate
his points. I thought that these quotations had a certain value.

I have not yet seen the second part of Mallock's article. In
the Critic, II: Sneer says, 'No scandal about Queen Elizabeth,
I hope?' I never heard that Sheridan had stolen the phrase.

I am heartily glad to hear of your good prospects at Peter-
borough.

I do not remember the exact title of H. Morley's book: but
I imagine that it was *History of English Literature*, a large
text book, meant for young people reading up literature in a
business-like way.

To THE SAME
3 *April* 1903

I gather that when Farmer wrote people were insisting upon the
traces of learning discoverable in the plays attributed to Shakespeare and that he 'hath frequent allusions to the *facts* and
fables of antiquity.' Farmer endeavours to show 'how they came
to his acquaintance.' He *demonstrates* that in some instances
he was taking his facts, blunders included, from English versions; he shows that things which the writer was supposed to
have got from Latin books and books in foreign languages, were
easily accessible in contemporary English books; he quotes one
or two instances of the familiar use of certain Italian phrases;
etc. It seems to me a very solid performance, although it is on
a small scale. I did not know that Maginn had written about it,
but I shall try to read his essays when I return to the land of
books. I should have thought a priori that Maginn on Farmer
would be something like Boyle on Bentley. As to Baynes, one
has to make some allowance for the clannishness of Scots.

By the way, if I understand Lord Penzance rightly, he assumes

[223]

that the six plays added in the Folio had never been *acted*.
Is this so? I note also that the B[aconians] assume that any
improvements made in the Folio were introduced in the preparation of the Folio, after Shakespeare left the stage. Now I
should have expected those improvements to be made in the
theatre copies while Shakespeare was still an actor. Is there
anything which makes this hypothesis impossible?

To THE SAME
12 *April* 1903

Thanks for yours of the 7th. On the strength of it I looked
up Churton Collins' article, and read it skimmingly. I did not
think much of it: but I must read it again.

My own belief is that a boy in Shakespeare's time at an
ordinary grammar school would learn between 8 or 9 and 13
a vast deal more of Roman history and mythology, and vastly
more Latin words, than a boy learns nowadays in those years.
I imagine that besides writing and a little arithmetic Latin
would be his sole pabulum, and that the teachers would be
people who had a good deal of classical learning at command.
Nowadays, history, geography, French, Greek, mathematics,
and even science, etc., disperse the boy's attention: and the
Latin is learnt in quite a different way, a way which takes the
boy's attention *away* from the things which Shakespeare's contemporaries knew as matters of general knowledge.

This is however old ground. I hear that the book which
Murray announces—'Is it Shakespeare?'—is by the *nova
Solyma* man.

Lawson's success at Camborne is great news. Really it looks
as if the tide were turning. I am heartily glad that Lawson has
got in, for the sake of himself, as well as for the sake of the
Country and the Party. He is in such deadly earnest that it
grieved me to think of him as an exile.

To THE SAME
14 *September* 1903

My point wants perhaps a little explanation. It was a time when
people quoted more than we do, and made commonplace books
to help them: and it seems to me that many quotations would

thus become familiar to people who never saw the originals. Even now the ordinary press man quotes freely, 'The mills of God grind slowly, etc.' without knowing either the Greek original or who anglicized it. I was on the look-out for several years before I stumbled upon the original. Let me, however, further note that, if it is in Erasmus' *Colloquies* and Shakspere was for six months only at a Grammar school, he might perfectly well have had it driven into his head there. The *Colloquies* is a school book, for in those days people used easy Latin in teaching the rudiments. I don't know whether you maintain that Shakspere was *never* at school. I imagine that, if he was ever at school, he learnt *some* Latin, and that, if he learnt any Latin, he would *probably* use the *Colloquies*.

I think that you do not make allowance for the scrappy information, more or less exact, which floats about. Since Trilby, we all know 'La vie est vaine: un peu d'amour, etc.': but how many ever heard of the man who made it? I found in a commonplace book of Wm. Henry Brookfield's (Tennyson's 'Brooks') a story that Plato once said—'Hush! we must be serious: there is a fool coming.' I am quite sure that Brookfield never read it in Greek. I don't know where it is to be found. But it must come from somewhere[1].

To THE SAME
25 September 1903

Thanks for your letter and for the note enclosed in it. It seems to me that you have put your point very well: but I am not sure that it would not be more suitable for the *Classical Review* than for the *Journal of Philology*. So I propose to confer with Aldis Wright, and, if he thinks as I do, to pass it on to Postgate.

I have made one alteration. You say 'growth, desire, sense (or sensibility),' etc.—'desire' should follow 'sense.' See *de anima* B. iii, 1. Your point is one which will be generally interesting, and the *Classical Review* is less technical than the *Journal of Philology*. This is why I modify my suggestion.

Please send me the reference for the *de augmentis*, and say whether I may proceed on these lines.

---

[1] [See Goldsmith's *Life of Nash* (ed. 2, p. 160). Dr Clarke, engaged in a merry conversation with Locke and some other friends, saw Nash's chariot approaching. 'Boys, boys,' he cried, 'let us now be wise, for here is a fool coming.' The story was popularised no doubt by its inclusion in Boswell's *Dedication*. Note by S. C. Roberts.]

I think that the paper might be headed 'Shakespeare, *Hamlet* III, iv, 71.' You are right to sign.

The Greek original of 'The mills of God,' etc. is a proverbial line ὀψὲ θεῶν ἀλέουσι μύλοι ἀλέουσι δὲ λεπτά. I had found something like it in Euripides, when in the life of Archdeacon Allen (the original, it is said, of Thackeray's Dobbin) I found the following in a letter from W. H. Thompson:

'I am thankful that you have sent away Mill on Hamilton. I had a good grind at that Mill last summer. ὀψὲ θεῶν ἀλέουσι μύλοι ἀλέουσι δὲ λεπτά. This line, one would think, must have occurred to the great ghost of Sir William, if posthumous criticism reaches the souls of departed authors. (An excellent criticism on Mill on Hamilton!) Let us hope, as Hare said of Scholefield, that someone will be found to perform the same pious task for the critic after his departure,' p. 315.

I don't know what Latin books Lee and Collins suppose Shakespeare to have studied: and I am not posted up. But I should have thought it more likely that a boy would read Erasmus' *Colloquies* than that he would read *any* classical author. I will, however, try to inform myself.

I hope to return to College on Monday.

I hope that you are preparing to smite Joe Chamberlain. Will they go to the country soon?

SHELLEY

To C. E. SAYLE
28 June 1909

I don't know F. Thompson's 'Shelley,' and I wonder what it is. Does Thompson speak the truth about him? The odd thing is that neither Shelley, nor his friends, nor his biographers, seem to be capable of speaking the truth. By the way H. James in *The Aspern papers* makes a very clever use of the story of Jane Clairmont, though he judiciously keeps the promiscuity out of sight.

Rousseau—Shelley—Byron were a bad lot: but it is amusing to read about them, provided that one recognizes that they were bounders.

21 November 1909

I am very grateful to you for making me read F. Thompson's 'Shelley.' It is a very remarkable article. It has great literary merits, though they are not perhaps literary merits of the highest sort. It is helpful to the understanding of Shelley, inasmuch as it insists that Shelley was never anything but a child. Also I am glad that F. T. frankly recognizes the unloveliness of Shelley's life, see e.g. p. 38. If you had not brought the book to me, I should not have read it.

SHELLEY, ETC.—TRELAWNEY

To PROFESSOR J. A. PLATT

27 *August* 1906

I wonder where Criccieth is. I met some one not long ago who knows Tan-y-ralt, and says that there really was some one who broke into Shelley's house and fired a pistol, and that this story was not, as generally supposed, a delusion. Whence my informant inferred that there really was a mysterious lady who pursued him to Italy. Somehow lies congregate like flies about this cracked and unwholesome personage.

I was shocked myself to find that the portrait reproduced in Trelawney's book is a faked up thing. But confound it! here am I; I have forgotten where I read a clear statement to this effect which satisfied me. It is my conviction that Mary Godwin had a bad time with P. B. S.

26 *September* 1908

Maybe Shelley would be as willing as the others to live up to the creed of the crew. But as you say 'what rational being cares'? It amuses *me* to enquire because I am ἄλογος μετέχων μέντοι πῃ λόγου, and accordingly I entertain myself with fictitious history in the same way in which I entertain myself with historical fiction. The crew was a bad one, and this ought to be plainly said. For a time I supposed that Trelawney was a better sort: but a few years ago there was a letter in the *Athenaeum* telling the story of his life at Usk, 1845–1856. It seems that after bolting with Lady Goring, as related at the beginning of the *Amazing Marriage*, he married her, but presently began to treat her very badly, and at last openly deserted her for another woman.

OBITER SCRIPTA

R. SHILLETO

To F. J. H. JENKINSON
27 *July* 1890

As to the Shilleto *Adversaria*—I was drearily disappointed
with them. The qualities and defects of his scholarship were very
curious. The *Falsa Legatio*, written very rapidly (see the preface), is a remarkable performance with a good deal of stuff in it.
The First Book of Thucydides has some good minute observations and shows how he took difficult passages: but here, as elsewhere, there is no width in his scholarship, and he does *nothing*
for the text. I used to hope that amongst the *adversaria* there
would be good things, detached but not unimportant. But when
I glanced at them after they came into the Library, it seemed to
me that they were only the facts which thirty years ago we used
to learn from him in his pupil room. Nevertheless I have
sometimes thought that some of his points had dropped out,
and that a paper for the *Journal* might be constructed out of
these *adversaria* and the recollections and notes of pupils. For
example, Archer-Hind in his *Phaedo* attributes to me an excellent remark of Shilleto's about χαῖρε, ἵλαθι—*valeat, propitius
esto*, and I had to put a correction in the Journal. I believe this
to have been absolutely novel. I always find that people are
ignorant of Shilleto's observation about the accentuation of
such genitives as παίδων μηνῶν δρύων δμώων. I have a letter
from him giving instances of μέν and δέ sentences where
the μέν clause carries the substantial meaning and the δέ clause
the qualifications. Of course it is possible that the newer
grammars have got this kind of thing. Francis used to talk of
transcribing the *adversaria*, and I used to think that, if he would
do this, Greaves and I and others might contribute something
from our note books, and that Neil and others would be able
to say which notes were no longer novelties. But I have to
admit that most of the things which I saw in the books were
trivial. In fact, he had not much in reserve besides what he
used to teach us, and a great deal of this teaching has been made
familiar by his pupils. I used to hope that Francis would at any
rate collect the *adversaria* and so make a consideration of the
matter possible. As to the books, I should have thought a good
many might be kept in a box in their present ricketty and snuffy
condition.

SCHOLIA

HENRY SIDGWICK

To PROFESSOR J. A. PLATT

2 August 1906

I have not yet done more than dip into the *Memoir of Henry Sidgwick*: but I saw a part of it in MS., so I know that it is very interesting. Until I saw the MS., I had had no notion that he was a real letter-writer, who to a few people, his mother, Graham Dakyns, and J. A. Symonds, wrote at length in a literary way. But I think still that he was a bad judge of men, and I think that the book proves it. And I still wonder that he did not go into parliament, as a supporter of Lord Salisbury. He would have liked the life. (See p. 67.)

SCHOLIA

Hisperica Famina

To F. J. H. JENKINSON

24 December 1898

I have been writing out *Hisperica Famina* and meditating upon it, in the hope of following more or less your work upon it. R. T. Wright has told me that you think of adding to your Index Verborum interpretations. This seems to me an excellent notion: *only it must not delay the publication.*

Textual

6 April 1902

I have been very lazy, sleeping a great deal and meditating in a foolish way about the difficulties of *de bona fortuna*. With the help of the collations I got from Munich, I can reconstruct and interpret most of it: but there are still some grievous *cruces*. I have discovered a curious peculiarity: in several instances where at first sight the Greek and the Latin are *not quite* in agreement, *both* are to be kept:

E.g. 1248^{a} 14 οὐδ' ὅτι οὐδέν ἐστι τύχη αἰτία οὐδενὸς δείκνυσι *neque quod non sit fortuna* causa nullius ostendit, read οὐδ' ὅτι οὐδέν ἐστι τύχη οὐδ' ὅτι οὐκ ἐστι τύχη αἰτία οὐδενὸς δείκνυσι. Comp. 1247^{b} 2. By the way οὐδέν ἐστι τύχη, or, οὐδέν ἐστι τύχη 'chance is nothing' or 'nothing is by chance.' But I must not inflict my ἀπορίαι upon you.

OBITER SCRIPTA

To F. J. H. JENKINSON

2 April 1899

I think that I have got a step further with the passage in the *Eudemian Ethics* H v § 4:

διὸ καὶ φῶναι καὶ αἱ ἕξεις καὶ συνημερεύσεις τοῖς ὁμογενέσιν ἥδισται ἀλλήλοις καὶ τοῖς ἄλλοις ζῴοις· καὶ ταύτῃ ἐνδέχεται καὶ τοὺς φαύλους ἀλλήλους φιλεῖν.

I think this should be

διὸ καὶ ⟨ἐ⟩φ' ὧν δίκαιαι ἕξεις, καὶ συνημερεύσεις τοῖς ὁμογε-νέσιν ἥδισται. ἀλλ' ἡδεῖς καὶ τοῖς ἄλλοις ζῴοις· καὶ ταύτῃ κ.τ.λ.

i.e. 'Therefore in the case of those who have righteous habits, daily associations with kindred spirits are most agreeable. But such associations are agreeable also to other animals, and it is in this way that bad men love one another.' In a word, the friendships of bad men come in under the head of the συνημε-ρεύσεις of τὰ ἄλλα ζῷα, which are ἡδεῖς, in opposition to the συνημερεύσεις of τὰ ἐφ' ὧν δίκαιαι ἕξεις, which συνημερεύσεις are ἥδισται. You will observe that whereas τοῖς ὁμογενέσιν is governed by συν-, τοῖς ἄλλοις ζῴοις is not. For this we were prepared. The changes are

Φῶναι καὶ αἱ = ⟨ʼΕ⟩φ' ὧν Δίκαιαι
Ἀλλήλοις = ʼΑλλ' Ηδεῖς

Tripos Verses

To A. O. PRITCHARD

23 March 1918

I have heard Bywater quote[1] 'Dirus asymptotes etc.' I think that he did not know the author. Mallan (I think) once asked me about it: and I fancied that it might come from a set of Tripos Verses by Hope Edwardes Sen., in which occurred the phrase 'natos nulla (in ad?) convivia rhombos.' But this is not so.

The lines may well come from some copy of 'Tripos verses.' I ought to explain that, till late in the seventies, it was the custom to print on the back of lists of graduating honour men three or

[1]   horrida signis
stat paries magicis, simulacraque foeda minantur
e tabula descripta nigra—dirum polyhedron,
dirus asymptotes, faciesque obscoena trapezi.

SCHOLIA

four copies of Latin (or, latterly, Greek) verses. The familiar specimen is Calverley's set, in which there is the couplet:

> O fumose puer, nimium ne crede Baconi:
> Manillas vocat, hoc praetexit nomine caules.

I cannot think that the lines are Porson's. They would have been preserved by Kidd, or by Barker, or in H. R. Luard's very interesting *Cambridge Essay*, or by tradition.

Noscitur a sociis
To PROFESSOR J. S. BEERE
25 August 1915

[In reply to a letter asking if there is classical authority for the phrase in the sense in which it is used in the Law Courts—'He is known from his companions.']

I am grateful to you for writing. I have taken your point: but I did not think it conclusive. White and Riddell say '*cognoscere ab aliqua re* to know by means of something (different from *ab aliquo* to learn from some one): id se a Gallicis armis atque insignibus cognovisse Caesar.' This seems to show that noscitur a sociis might mean 'he is known *from* his associates.' But you will say, 'it certainly means he is known by his associates,' and the familiar use should preclude the other. The Caesar phrase is not ambiguous: for here the familiar use is not impossible. W. and R. note however elsewhere that *si postulatur a populo* may mean either 'by the people' or 'of the people': where the familiar use does not bar another meaning. I am always afraid of condemning a use which can be legitimately traced to a fundamental meaning: and I think that the following lines (which I made acquaintance with in the Classical Tripos of 1862) made me shy of limiting the use of a, ab;

> Tempus *ab his* vacuum Caesar Germanicus omne
> Auferet: *a* magnis hunc colit ille deis.
> Cum tamen *a* turba rerum requieverit harum
> Ad vos mansuetas porriget ille manus.

Ex Ponto IV. v. 25.

We do not stick at 'he is known by his works': is it impossible that a Roman should use a similar phrase? Do not misunderstand me: I say no more than that 'noscitur a sociis' does not seem to me impossible. I have written to Bensly, who has a large and curious knowledge of such things. By the way,

OBITER SCRIPTA

I have always wondered that Cicero could write 'pater conscriptus' in the singular: how can a pater be a conscriptus, or a conscriptus a pater? and how can there be a sevir? Even Latin was capable of development, and the developments of language are not always logical.

To F. J. H. JENKINSON
5 *October* 1901

παχυγάστηρ or παχυγάστωρ would be quite correct. πλατυγάστωρ occurs in Aristotle, as well as πλατύγλωσσος, παχύθριξ. There can be no doubt whatever that this formation is right. It is impossible to 'prove the negative,' but if I were to come across παχεγάστηρ, I should immediately alter the ε to υ, and defy anyone to produce anything analogous. πλατύπυγος is another instance, βαθύζωνος βαθύρριζος etc. etc. etc. παχυγάστηρ or παχυγάστωρ is not made from παχεῖα and γάστηρ, but from παχυ- and γάστηρ.

1885 (?)

The τε γάρ is to be found in *N.E.* x 7 § 2, θεωρεῖν τε γὰρ δυνάμεθα συνεχῶς μᾶλλον ἢ πράττειν ὁτιοῦν οἰόμεθα τε δεῖν κ.τ.λ. The sentence introduced by τε γάρ justifies the statement ἔτι δὲ συνεχεστάτη—οἰόμεθά τε δεῖν continues the main argument. In consequence of the τε γάρ the editors have put a comma after ὁτιοῦν. On γάρ see Shilleto's *Thucydides*, pp. 33, 140 and Index.

There are in Aristotle various places where two γάρ sentences occur in succession, both γάρ's being attached to the main sentence, not the second γάρ to the first. In other words the two γάρ sentences are *father* and *mother* to the main sentence, not *father* and *grandfather*.

θ. φ. *Johnson*

To J. M. IMAGE
28 *March* 1917

I send on the other side the heads of my notes on θ. φ. and α. φ.

Note. In the *Prayers and Meditations*, Johnson 'commends' (1) 'friends living and dead' (2) 'θφ' (3) 'θ friends.' Plainly 'θ' means 'dead.' Now in a Roman muster-roll 'θ' was affixed to the name of a dead soldier; and Galen says that

[232]

SCHOLIA

in a physician's case book v and θ stood for ὑγίεια and θάνατος respectively. Johnson may have known the use from Casaubon's note on Persius iv, 13[1]. In a word θ is a symbol, used as the cross † is sometimes used in German books. I have chapter and verse for these things. See *Athenaeum* 18 June 1887.

Diary of a Tour into Wales, Boswell, ch. xlvi, 14 Aug. 1774 βρῶσις ὀλίγη—καθ. *a. φ.* 'sic, probably for κάθαρσις ἀφελής' no: καθ. *a. φ.* = κάθαρσις ἄνευ φαρμάκου. Croker ignores the full stop after *a.*

To BERNARD JACKSON
n.d. 1915

Now for $\theta. \phi.$ I have not got here either S. Johnson's *Prayers and Meditations*, or Croker's note, or Macaulay's exaggerated comment. My impression is that Johnson prays (1) for his 'θ friends,' (2) for his '$\theta.\phi,$' (3) for dead friends named. Croker rightly said that '$\theta. \phi$' meant 'dead friends': but he wrongly supposed that θ stood for θνητούς. Macaulay jumped upon Croker for supposing that θ meant θνητούς, for θνητούς can only mean 'mortal.' I expect that I have told you my explanation. θ, the initial of θάνατος, was a *symbol* for 'dead,' e.g. (*a*) 'nigrum praefigere theta,' 'to mark for execution,' Persius; (*b*) it was affixed to dead men's names in lists of soldiers; (*c*) in Hippocrates' case book patients who recovered were marked with a v or γ; query, ὑγίεια or ὑγιής: those who died with θ. I have the detail at Cambridge, noted in my Boswell. I think that Theognis means—'Men are fools who weep for deaths and not for youth that is lost': ἄφρονες ἄνθρωποι καὶ νήπιοι οἵ τε θανόντας κλαίουσ' οὐδ' ἥβης ἄνθος ἀπολλύμενον. I forget whether Macaulay ventures an interpretation of θ. Probably he took it to mean θανόντας: and I suppose that this is possible. But I feel sure that it is a conventional symbol. I thought that Johnson got it from a commentary (qu. Casaubon's?) on Persius. I once wrote about this to the *Athenaeum*.

Your cutting contains two reviews which interest me: R. G. Moulton on Literature and Madden on Shakespeare.

[1] [This edition was in Johnson's library. S. C. R.]

OBITER SCRIPTA

ἐντελέχεια

To PROFESSOR J. A. PLATT

19 *April* 1908

I grieve to say that I cannot answer your question about ἐντελέχεια offhand. Not long ago it occurred to me to wonder what was the stock equivalent in the versions of Moerbeke and Co., but I did not look them up. Presumably it is *actualitas*, but I dare not say so until I have returned to Cambridge and looked up the books. There is, I think, a story that Hermolaus Barbarus raised the devil and asked him for a rendering, and that the devil somehow shirked the job, and that H. B. fell back upon *perfecti-habia*. That D. D. impostor M. Tullius Cicero *Tusc. Disp.* I x 22 translates it *quandam continuatam motionem et perennem*: i.e. he did not distinguish between ἐντελέχεια and ἐνδελέχεια. *Sed haec sunt neque hic neque illic*, as the Trinity man wrote *de suo*, when after putting down a declamation thesis he had copied out two casual pages of Livy. If I do not write to you about this ten days hence, please stir me up. I am vexed with myself that I cannot give you off-hand a cocksure statement.

γεννητική and θρεπτική

To THE SAME

6 *December* 1906

I don't know whether anyone has done anything about the connection of γεννητική and θρεπτική: but it has always seemed to me a great idea which would some day prove to be of first rate importance. When the man has learnt to earn his living, he begins to put money into the bank, and draws upon it for occasional expenses. We don't hear much about γεννητική, just because it is so intimately connected with θρεπτική that it may fairly be regarded as part of it. With A[ristotle] the life of the individual is part of the life of the race.

SOPHISTS

To BERNARD JACKSON

29 *May* 1906

Thanks for your cutting about Emil Reich—the complete humbug. He is an admirable lecturer, and an unmitigated quack. I think that he is Hungarian. He teaches at Wren's.

SOPHISTS

When I talk about the Greek Sophists, I find parallels for them:

Protagoras—Mat. Arnold.
Prodicus—Liddon.
Gorgias—?
Isocrates—Seeley.
Hippias of Elis who taught all subjects—Reich.
Euthydemus and the disputants—The Times Leader Writers.

I see in the papers that Reich draws a lot of Duchesses to hear him about Plato at Claridge's. His form as a lecturer is wonderful, and that although he is talking English: but there is *no* solid matter.

SOPHOCLES, *OEDIPUS TYRANNUS*

To PROFESSOR J. A. PLATT

14 July 1915

I am not posted up about the *poetics* and I have forgotten the details of *O.T.* But if I rightly understand you, or rightly remember, I quite agree with you. It would never occur to me to regard the encounter with Laius as a ἁμαρτία. The ἁμαρτία of Oedipus is surely a blind presumption. He ought to have walked warily: and he did not. The flaw in the plot is that, when he heard of Laius' death, he did not remember his recent adventure. But what a play it is!

To THE SAME

19 March 1911

But I know nothing about Sophocles, except that the *Oedipus Rex* seems to me as good a tragedy as ever was written—whereas Lessing's statement that the *Captivi* was the best play ever put on any stage is to me an astounding statement—and that there are passages in Sophocles which seem to me amazing for their grandeur and distinction.

SPECIALISTS

To THE SAME

27 July 1915

If I were to have to deliver an address on classical learning in the xix^th and xx^th centuries, I think that I should say some things which would scare the Master of Trinity, drive Ridgeway mad, and make R. C. J. turn in his grave. But classics is not the only study which, in our time, has over specialized. Of course it is right that there should be some super-specialists: but it is wrong that there should be a whole classical association of would-be specialists who don't achieve their end. I think that the war will divert the attention of some of them in other directions. After all there was a good deal of sense in Comte's protest against useless research. When I try to make out what P. and A. thought, I am no more than a pitiful antiquary. 'Let the dead—.'

SIR JAMES STEPHEN AND THE CLAPHAM SECT

To L. STEPHEN

19 *October* 1902

I always like to acknowledge debts, or to get as near as I can to the acknowledgment of them. So I write a line to tell you that when I was at school, I was told to read the lectures on French History, and did so with very great interest and profit. I have read the essay on the Clapham sect again and again: and it always seems to me an admirable portraiture of people who, whatever their limitations, deserved to be portrayed. I gathered from my father-in-law, Frank Thornton, who descended from the elder brother of Henry, that the Clapham people did not like the essay. I cannot see that there was any reason for this. If it were not for the essay, the men would now be forgotten, and they were good men, and they did at least one very good thing.

Maitland is always delightful and it rejoices me to see him pouring scorn upon 'Verax' of the *Daily News* and others who, knowing nothing, belittle Acton.

LESLIE STEPHEN—TRINITY HALL—JESUS

To F. W. MAITLAND

15 *March* 1904

I expect that you and I knew Leslie Stephen best from opposite sides. You knew him best domestically. I knew him best with his contemporaries—Fawcett, H. A. Morgan, etc.: and delightful as he was from that point of view, I have always regretted that I knew nothing of his home life. Amongst his Cambridge friends he was rather silent, and rather grim. Having more brains than Fawcett and Co., he relapsed into the rowing man, the athlete, and the Bergsteiger, and, if it had not been for his books, I doubt whether I should have realized him except as the best of companions of the genial, ambitious, philistine, Fawcett. Then he left the Ad Eundem, and when he came back to it he was a broken man. In fact, the accident that I had known him at Jesus, and the Hall, rather stood in the way of my knowledge of the real man: though I had, of course, glimpses, and have, of course, the pleasantest memories of meetings, of correspondence, and of books.

In my freshman's year, I was in the rooms of a friend at Trinity Hall one day when the Hall boat had rowed head. They were making a frightful row in the Court, and Stephen came out to stop the riot. They picked up Stephen, and carried him round the Court, shouting more than ever. He was the life of the place, and meanwhile was establishing himself in journalism and periodical literature. You may be surprised to hear that in the late sixties I knew well the roistering crew which assembled at Jesus. Stephen was quite at home there; but I always knew that there was another Stephen, of whom Fawcett, Morgan, and Co. knew nothing.

There is a traditional story how he broke the ice at the first meeting of the Ad Eundem. It is said that Fawcett sat next Henry Smith at Oxford, and talked, as he would do, in a somewhat affected, unreal manner, until Leslie Stephen called out 'Don't talk like a damned fool, Fawcett' which cleared the air.

STONEHENGE

To PROFESSOR J. A. PLATT
28 *August* 1909

As to Stonehenge, I had wholly misunderstood in one respect. I had supposed that the area was considerable: but the fact is that the diameter of the outer circle is about 100 feet—a cricket pitch and a half. The tallest stones are about 28 feet high. Some people speak of the first sight of it as disappointing. To me this was not so. Coming over a little hill you see in an expanse of grass these huge barbaric stones. It was as if one had gone out in a motor and come upon a herd of mastodons feeding; and the tents of the territorial army in the distance strengthened the contrast between new and old. It is a pity that it has to be protected by a wire-fence, a turnstile, a ticket-giver and a policeman: and it is sad that stones have been removed for building bridges, etc.

SUNDRIES

To PROFESSOR J. A. PLATT

17 *April* 1899

There is a difference between private letters and public controversy. There are many things which are all right for safe ears and all wrong for periodicals and their readers....

'Mr Pepys wrote a very good style, didn't he'? Of course he did. But as Mrs Pryme said to old Pryme when on their wedding day he talked to her about the importance of Political Economy, 'Mr Pryme, there is a time for all things.' Pepys also wrote in his diary 'of Moll and Meg and strange experiences' unmeet for the *Classical Review* or the *Journal of Philology*....The phrase which reminded me of Pepys was 'But dear me, all this is very speculative.' These confessions of human weakness amuse me: but they are stones of stumbling and rocks of offence to the many. What would Bevan think of an Orientalist who gave himself away in this manner? I don't say in my heart that all men are fools—very far from it: but I do think that there is a great deal more pedantry in the world than people allow for.

I note that you sandwich FitzGerald between Browning and Tennyson. Do you mean that that is *your* estimate of 'Fitz' or that it is the general estimate of him?

SURTEES

To THE SAME

27 *August* 1901

As to Surtees—I should have thought that the better sort of hunting man would say—'This fellow Surtees is a hunting man who can put things on paper: he thinks that we are a pack of cads and snobs, or at any rate he represents us as such: my neighbours accept and applaud this description: either I must accept the condemnation or I must quarrel with Surtees and all his works.' But there are lots of people who are deeply interested. My boy Hal was shooting in Cashmere in the summer for three months, without any European companion. His books were *Pendennis*, Shakespeare, *Jorrocks*, and two sets of military regulations.

SWINBURNE

To THE SAME
14 *August* 1915

After what you say about Swinburne, I think that I shall have to try him again. Your word 'intoxicates' exactly expresses my feeling about *Atalanta*, and, unluckily, I don't like getting drunk. I suppose that I never caught on: for I think that I did not read *Poems and Ballads* a second time. Just then I was bitten by Browning who in 1862 or 1863 had been described to me as 'Mrs Browning's husband who has also written poetry.'

THEOPHRASTUS

To A. F. SIEVEKING
1 *January* 1907

I think that Theophrastus' characters are humorous, especially if they are read as I (by exception) read them, not as descriptions of types, but as descriptions of particular people. The title and the first sentence very often are not justified by what follows. What follows is often a mixed personality. So I am inclined to regard the title and the first sentence as later attempts to convert into a type what was originally the description of a man.

To PROFESSOR J. A. PLATT
15 *September* 1909

As to Theophrastus, I believe that I agree with you very well. But I have long thought that the initial definitions are later additamenta, and I have even fancied that the body of each character represented, not a *type*, but a *person*, and that there is therefore no reason why an extraneous characteristic should not come in now and then. For example, in a characterization of the inattentive man (ἀναίσθητος), he is the sort of man to put down under recreation in *Who's Who*—'saved the life of a schoolfellow,' which would be absurd. But if he were describing Jex Blake, who is both inattentive and egotistical, this might appear alongside of—'When you tell him that De Wette was followed to the grave by a host of pupils, he expresses great

[239]

interest and then says—"by the way has he got anything new upon the stocks?"' I think that it is the rotten definitions only which suggest a comparison with the *ethics*. Years ago, when Jebb's book came out, I suggested to someone that the characters might be compared to *Happy Thoughts*, and not long afterwards I found this remark and some others in a review in the *Spectator*. My friend was surprised when I afterwards told him that I had observed his authorship of the review.

THOMPSON, WILLIAM HEPWORTH (MASTER OF TRINITY 1866–1886, SOMETIME REGIUS PROFESSOR OF GREEK)

To J. W. CLARK
2 October 1886

A word or two more about the subject of our conversation.

The modern study of Plato assumes that, whereas his writings are at first sight obscure, loosely connected, inconclusive, these characteristics do not imply either vagueness of thought or unskilful statement: that, on the contrary, Plato had a doctrine to teach, but, conceiving didactic exposition to be mischievous, carefully avoided dogmatic expression of his views, and deliberately left it to his reader to combine into a whole the hints and suggestions which he afforded: that we are therefore justified in narrowly scrutinizing the dialogues with a view to their coordination, and that in so doing we are only imitating Plato's disciples, though for us the work is more difficult, because we have no oral hints to help us, we do not fully understand the contemporary references, and above all we do not know in what order the dialogues should be read. In a word, not knowing exactly the phases of Plato's speculative development, nor yet the order of the writings in which his views are adumbrated rather than embodied, scholars have tried to ascertain the mutual relations of his dialogues, and to trace in them the progress of his philosophies.

Schleiermacher's translations and introductions (1804–1810) started this inquiry, and the impulse has not yet exhausted itself. I believe that Thirlwall and Hare first directed English scholars to his writings: and I have always imagined that Thirlwall turned Thompson's attention to this line of study. In pursuing it he showed great learning and a firm grip. The paper on the *sophist*, which was for years buried in the *Transactions of the*

THOMPSON

Philosophical Society, is a masterpiece: and the editions of the *Phaedrus* and the *Gorgias* are, both in matter and in style, my ideals.

As to the statute meetings of 1871–72, I think that, whilst fully aware of the difficulty of the task, Thompson was convinced that reform was necessary. In my opinion it was only his firmness which at one important crisis prevented the Committee from going to pieces.

The statute meetings of 1877–78 were plainly a severe tax upon his strength: he was older: but the points upon which he was not in complete harmony with the majority were few, and not, I think, of great importance.

In the ordinary business of the College I note especially that he never shirked responsibility. It seemed to me that he rose to an occasion, and was far better about great things than about trifles.

By the way, he was an excellent examiner, appreciating good work of all sorts.

Amongst his sayings one of the most characteristic is, in my opinion, his remark about his own portrait—'One would think that that man had a sovereign contempt for all the world.' I believe him to have been a very modest man.

THUCYDIDES

To SIR G. O. TREVELYAN.

19 *March* 1916

Thanks for yours of the 14th. It is wonderful how Thucydides holds one in spite of his lack of grammar. Do you know the old Cambridge parody, which I have always attributed to Augustus Vansittart? 'Awkward animals to drive is a pig, one man many of them very.' I have always been especially interested in the viiith book. When I was taking pupils, 1862–1868, I used to read it with them. I used to think that it was unfinished. But, for all that, the story of the 'moderates'—the Girondins of the time—with Theramenes for leader, attracted me. I think that, after the restoration by Thrasybulus and Thrasyllus, the 'moderate oligarchs' were still a danger. Under the amnesty they could not be attacked directly. Hence the accusation on a charge of heresy against Socrates, who was a typical member of the party. I have long thought this, and Bryce encourages me

OBITER SCRIPTA

to print my stuff. Also the intrigues of Alcibiades interest me. What a clever scoundrel! I think that I can prove from the *memorabilia* of Xenophon that Socrates held the opinions of what I call 'the moderates,' i.e. the people who disliked both the ἄκρατος δημοκρατία and 'The Thirty.' But it is rather a long story. [See pp. 249 ff.]

By the way, have you read the *memorabilia* lately? I like it much, and I believe it to be a truthful account of Socrates' talk.

THUCYDIDES—XENOPHON—PLATO

To THE SAME
22 *March* 1916

You tempt me to write again. I never read the *Hellenica* continuously. Unimportant troubles (say) at Thebes did not greatly interest me. But the beginning of the first book, about the 'moderate oligarchs,' the philosophical radicals who wanted to reform the 'unmixed democracy,' and were crushed by the 'complete oligarchs,' interests me very much. Theramenes is, I think, a very remarkable personage, and is, I think, unfairly treated by historians. By the way, there is a tradition that Socrates tried to rescue him. The *beginning* of the *Hellenica* connects quite closely with the eighth book [of Thucydides], and I think that you would do well to read it.

I think that people depreciate Book viii, because there are in it no speeches—or, as the Trinity freshman said, 'no choruses.' What is the reason? Is it, that there was no adequate opportunity? Or did Thucydides leave the speeches to be filled in later? I wish that he had lived to write the speeches of Critias and Theramenes when Theramenes was condemned. Theramenes' speech would have been a masterly exposition of the views of those whom I call 'moderates': for Thucydides in viii plainly declares his approval. Indeed the philosophers in general were 'moderates.' At a later time Plato and Aristotle devised ideal states on lines which the 'moderates' would have accepted.

You say that 'the duty of taking a patriot's part in public affairs is not of a piece with Plato.' Are you sure of this? Read again 'The Cave' at the beginning of *republic* vii and you will find that the man who has seen the glories of the outer air has to return to the cave and to take his place again amongst the

[242]

prisoners, and that this duty is very carefully emphasized Perhaps you are thinking of the *Gorgias*. It seems to me that there Plato is still thinking of the fate of Socrates, and of the anxious position of all 'moderates.' In short, you there have, not his general position, but his momentary view of the philosopher's possibilities at Athens.

TRIPOSES

To R. ST J. PARRY
4 August 1909

I am sorry I am not awarding certificates this year: for I think that before long 'distinctions' will have to be dropped. The examination has done excellent work: but it is a great mistake to keep an institution going when the time for it has passed. Triposes have done excellent work: but it will be a mistake to keep them going when they have become a hindrance.

TUTORS OF T. C. C.

To A. O. PRITCHARD
11 *June* 1916

Lightfoot was, I think, with us, the first of the new school of tutors: and, when I was an undergraduate, I cursed my luck that I was not on his side. There are two stories to show what the old tutors were:

(1) Conversation at a University Club in Pall Mall: A. Is it term-time in Cambridge? B. Yes, I think so: for I have just now seen Whewell at the Athenaeum, Thorp in St James' Street, and Peacock in Pall Mall. The three tutors.

(2) Whewell, Peacock, and Thorp, the three tutors, were seniors and examined for scholarships. It was said that Peacock voted for his pupils, that Thorp (conscientious) voted against his pupils, and that Whewell was impartial because he did not know who his pupils were. By the way, there is a third story. Whewell invited a wine party of his pupils. One of the invitations was returned: the man was dead. Whewell told his gyp that 'he ought to tell him when his pupils died.'

Forgive these traditions of a period which is as dead to men of my time here as the traditions of my own period will be when the war is over.

OBITER SCRIPTA

VEGETARIANISM

To PROFESSOR J. A. PLATT
2 *November* 1910

I fancied that J. E. B. Mayor had *always* regarded eggs as vegetables and tobacco as flesh.

VERRALL AND EURIPIDES

To THE SAME
2 *August* 1906

Does all the world take Verrall's view of Euripides? A man has sent me proofs of a forthcoming work in which he says—'There can be no doubt that Euripides regarded state religion as an unmixed evil. Lengthy discussion is unnecessary, for the main contentions of Dr Verrall are now generally accepted.' Note '(Verrall p. 138). It is not too much to say that on the Euripidean stage whatever is said by a divinity is ipso facto discredited. It is in all cases objectionable from the author's point of view, and almost always a lie.' If so, surely Euripides wrote burlesques, whereas Aristotle thought him τραγικώτατος. To me it seems that, whatever Euripides may have thought, he meant his audience to accept the situation, and not to deride it. But I have not read the new book. To me it seems that, if Euripides' plays are *reductiones ad absurdum*, they are not dramatic. Am I too hopelessly old fashioned? or does any one sympathise with me? I don't think Euripides as good a dramatist as Sophocles, who seems to me masterly; but I think that Euripides achieves in particular scenes masterly effects.

In the same way I think Aristophanes' *Birds* excellent comedy, and I don't believe that it was aimed at a Jewish synagogue established at Athens.

WHEWELL

To BERNARD JACKSON
9 *October* 1918

I never managed to read the works of S. Bailey. I expect that he will live only in virtue of J. S. Mill's respectful mention. Mill has commemorated one or two people. For example, he says that without Whewell's *Inductive Sciences* he could not have written the *Logic*. As Whewell was M.C. when I sat for a fellowship, I read him and got out of him a good deal in my

[244]

scrappy way. He died in 1866, and since then no one knows anything about him except Sydney Smith's *mot* 'Science is his forte, and omniscience his foible.' It would be truer to say of him 'omniscience is his forte, and science his foible,' and I think this a better epigram.

WINCHESTER LIBRARY

To H. RACKHAM

16 July 1915

Nowadays all the *good* books—e.g. the B.M. books which Kenyon gives—go into 'Moberly,' where they are no use, except as 'picture books.' So practically the fellows' library is useful only to those who know something about the learning of the 16th and 17th and 18th centuries. But I accept the situation, and am content that the Fellows' Library should remain a library of the older learning. I wish that there were more who appreciated the old books, and I wish that I had time to come down, and make a selection of old books which are still useful to those who know of their existence. But the truth is that none of the boys, and very few of the masters, have time to use old books. They want those which have a direct bearing on the examinations of the Colleges and the University. This is inevitable, and we must not regret it. Forgive this tirade. I have made considerable use of Viger, Bos, Hoogeveen, and above all, Stephanus: so I resent the neglect of them. They ought at least to be remembered.

WINCHESTER AND ETON

To C. E. SAYLE

29 July 1909

I like going to Eton: but it reminds me of what Beatrice says when Don Pedro asks 'Will you have me, lady?' 'No, my lord, unless I might have another for working days. Your grace is too costly to wear every day.' Eton is all very well for visitors: but Winchester is the place for a boy to live in and for a boy to love.

OBITER SCRIPTA

WORK AND PLAY

To PROFESSOR J. A. PLATT
8 *September* 1911

I thank you for your prompt reply to my drivel. Business letters are duty: gossip *viva voce* is play: gossiping letters are play in duty's clothing. I suppose that this is why I deluge you with irresponsible chatter.

WYKEHAMISTS

To THE SAME
10 *September* 1914

While I write, a spider is crawling over my table. I may not kill it, because, as a member of Winchester governing body, I am a Wykehamist; and spiders are Wykehamists also. I like these traditions.

END OF PART II

PART III
DISCOURSES

PRAELECTION ON THE CAUSES OF THE TRIAL AND DEATH OF SOCRATES, 1889

THE passage which, with your permission, Mr Vice-Chancellor, and Members of the Council, I am now to expound, is contained in the first and second chapters of the First Book of Xenophon's *Memorabilia*. The special purpose which throughout I shall keep steadily in view, is, the more exact determination of the causes which led to the indictment, the condemnation, and the execution of the philosopher Socrates: but incidentally I shall have something to say about the state of political parties at Athens towards the end of the fifth century before Christ. In dealing with these subjects I shall have no more ambitious end in view than the exact statement of my views, and the arguments upon which I rest them.

In the year 399—five years after the conclusion of the great war, four years after the restoration of the democracy—Socrates, son of Sophroniscus, was indicted as an offender against public morality. His accusers were Meletus the poet, Anytus the tanner, and Lycon the orator. All three were members of the democratic party, men who had suffered for the cause. The accusation ran thus: 'Socrates is guilty, firstly, of denying the gods recognised by the State and introducing new divinities, and secondly, of corrupting the young.' In his defence Socrates made no attempt to conciliate his judges, and indeed openly defied them. He was found guilty by 280 votes against 220. Meletus having called for capital punishment, it now rested with the accused to make a counter-proposition; and there can be little doubt, that, had Socrates suggested some smaller but yet substantial penalty, the proposal would have been immediately accepted. But to the amazement of the judges and the distress of his friends, he proudly declared that for his services to the city he deserved, not punishment, but reward—to be maintained as a public benefactor at the cost of the State; and although at the close of his speech he professed himself willing to pay a nominal fine of one mina, and upon the urgent entreaties of his friends raised the amount of his offer to thirty

[249]

minas, he was not careful to disguise his indifference to the result. This attitude exasperated the judges, and the penalty of death was decreed by an increased majority. Then in a short address he declared his contentment with his own conduct and with his sentence. Whether death was a dreamless sleep, or a new life in Hades, where he would have opportunities of testing the wisdom of the heroes and sages of antiquity, he knew not: but in either case he esteemed it a gain to die. In the same spirit he refused to take advantage of a scheme, arranged by his friend Crito, for an escape from the prison. The rule was, that the condemned criminal should drink the cup of hemlock on the day after the trial: but an accidental circumstance prolonged the life of Socrates for thirty days. During this time he remained in imprisonment, receiving his intimates and talking with them in his accustomed manner. How in his last conversation he argued that the wise man will regard approaching death with a cheerful confidence, and how, when the day was drawing to a close, 'without a tremor, without a change of colour or of countenance, he took the cup and drank it with a perfect serenity,' is known to all men.

Now of Socrates' moral character there can be no question whatsoever. 'He was so pious,' says one of his friends, 'that he did nothing without taking counsel of the gods; so just, that he never did any man an injury; so temperate, that he never preferred pleasure to right; so wise, that for the discrimination of good and evil he needed no counsel, and in his independent judgments was never at fault. If his tact in the exact statement of moral truth was remarkable, his skill in gauging the character of others, in convicting them of error, and in encouraging them to the pursuit of honour and virtue, was no less so. In a word, he seemed to me the best and happiest of men.' *That* is the testimony of the soldier and the country gentleman, Xenophon. 'Of all men whom we have known,' says another of Socrates' intimates (the philosopher Plato), 'he was the best, the wisest, and the justest.' And these judgments are affirmed by the unanimous voice of antiquity.

[250]

If such was the man, how came it that the Athenians—forgetting his loyal performance of civic duties, his virtuous life, and his disinterested anxiety for their welfare—condemned him, and put him to death, as an offender against public morality? The question has been asked again and again, and an answer has been found in three considerations which I will now state.

First, the accusations were not wholly unfounded. If Socrates conformed in all respects to the established faith, it was nevertheless notorious that he rejected certain details of the conventional mythology as the scandalous inventions of lying poets. If his personal character was purer than that of his contemporaries, it was obvious that he waged war against authority, and in a certain sense made each man the measure of his own actions. In a word, his teaching *was*, as the accuser said, subversive of the theology and the morality which had hitherto prevailed, and those whose beliefs and principles he criticised or offended were not likely to perceive, that, in so far as his views differed from theirs, the advantage was all on his side.

Secondly, the life led by Socrates was not calculated to win for him either the affection or the esteem of the vulgar. Those who did not know him personally, seeing him with the eyes of the comic poets, conceived him as 'visionary' (μετεωρολόγος) and a 'bore' (ἀδολέσχης). Those who had faced him in argument had smarted under his scathing rebukes, or at any rate had winced under his searching interrogatory, and may well have regarded him with dislike and fear. Now it is plain that the popular distrust of eccentricity, and the irritation felt by individuals and groups of individuals would go for something in determining the result of the trial.

Thirdly, in his demeanour at the trial, there was nothing to mollify opposition, but rather everything to provoke it: and it is clear that many a man, who, if Socrates had been submissive, would have voted for an acquittal, regarded his proud determination, if not as a new crime, at any rate as an aggravation of the original offence, and that such an one gave his voice accordingly.

[251]

PRAELECTION

Now these three things—heterodoxy, unpopularity, conduct during the trial—may be thought to account for the verdict and the sentence—that is to say, to explain why it was that, when Socrates had been brought into court, the decision of the judges was adverse. But will they—or more exactly, will 'heterodoxy' and 'unpopularity'—account for the *accusation*? Will they explain why it was that, having so long escaped, Socrates was now, in 399, put upon his trial? I must confess to a doubt whether 'heterodoxy,' 'unpopularity,' and 'conduct during the trial' are or are not sufficient to explain the adverse votes: but when I come to the question which I have now proposed—why was it that in 399 Socrates was brought to trial?—I feel no hesitation in saying that the two causes alleged—'heterodoxy' and 'unpopularity'—are wholly insufficient.

For more than a quarter of a century Socrates' heterodox opinions and revolutionary teaching, his angularities and eccentricities, had been known to all Athens: yet except in 404, when the city was under the heel of the Thirty, they had carried no consequences more alarming than the ridicule of Aristophanes: and in so far as the situation had changed, there is nothing to make us suppose that old prejudices had widened or deepened, but rather the reverse. The spirit of inquiry had spread, and it is reasonable to suppose that the younger generation was more tolerant, than the last had been, of heterodoxy such as that of Socrates. With the lapse of time his personal peculiarities had doubtless become more familiar, and presumably their innocence more conspicuous. And in view of the pacification of Greece, the restoration of democracy, and the amnesty, one would expect the Athenians to be less excitable and more generous than they had been when war still threatened them without and oligarchy within. Surely there must have been something else than the old prejudices to induce two leading statesmen, with their tool, Meletus, 'a long-haired man with a feeble beard and a hooked nose, new to politics,' to enter upon the prosecution of a man of seventy, who had hitherto been laughed at, rather than feared, and who, after all, had at his back a considerable number of influential friends. Why was it then, I ask, that Socrates was brought to trial? and for an answer to this question I look primarily to our best witness, Xenophon.

Now the work entitled ἀπομνημονεύματα is from first to last a defence of Socrates. But whereas in general the apology is left to be inferred, the first and second chapters of the first book contain a formal answer to the indictment and the arguments by which it was supported.

Of this formal answer I shall now give a very brief outline.

To the first of the two accusations—that of 'denying the gods recognised by the State, and introducing new divinities,' Xenophon replies that Socrates accepted the established faith and performed its offices with exemplary regularity; whilst, if he talked of a δαιμόνιον, the δαιμόνιον was no new divinity, but a mantic sign divinely accorded to him, presumably by the gods of the State.

In reply to the second charge, that of 'corrupting the young,' Xenophon urged that, on the contrary, he set an example of piety, continence, endurance, justice; and that his lessons in morality were not the less effective, if his self-respect would not allow him to become a professional teacher. How could such an one, Xenophon asks, be a corrupter of youth?

Thus far Xenophon's criticism is directed against the formal indictment. But here, at ii. 9, he proceeds to answer certain arguments which occurred in the speech of the accuser. These arguments are four.

First, Socrates derided the use of the lot in official appointments as contrary to common sense, thus, said the accuser, teaching young people to despise the constituted laws, and making revolutionists of them. To this argument Xenophon replies, not by impugning the statement of fact, but by urging that intelligent men such as Socrates are the last people to resort to revolutionary violence: in other words, that the philosophic radical is a harmless creature.

Again, ii. 12, Socrates numbered amongst his associates those mischievous politicians, Critias and Alcibiades. True, replies

[253]

Xenophon, but their sobriety and decency whilst they consorted with him is the best possible testimony to the excellence of his character and influence.

But again, said the accuser, ii. 49, Socrates taught the young to despise their elders, telling his pupils that he would make them wiser than their parents and relations. No, says Xenophon, what Socrates said was that, if you would have the regard of your relations, you must be kind and thoughtful.

Lastly, ii. 56, the accuser urged that Socrates selected from famous poems their most pernicious sentiments, and with these as texts, taught his associates to be dishonest and tyrannical. Of this, two instances were alleged, of which one was trivial. Of the other, which Xenophon discusses at length, admitting that Socrates used certain lines of Homer in a political sense, I shall have to say something hereafter.

Now, for my purpose, that of determining the motive of the accusation, the passage which I have summarised is principally important in so far as it affords indications of Meletus' argument. Studying it from this point of view, I note the following facts:

First, it would seem that the accuser was at no pains to prove the first of the two charges, the charge of denying the gods recognised by the State, and seeking to introduce in their stead strange divinities. For, had Meletus elaborated this part of his argument, Xenophon, whose subsequent citations from the accuser's speech are careful and detailed, would hardly have omitted to quote from it here. Indeed, had Meletus alleged a single instance of supposed impiety, Xenophon must necessarily have discussed it in connection with his own unqualified statement that 'no one ever knew of Socrates doing or saying anything impious or profane': and had Meletus explained the allegation that Socrates sought to introduce strange divinities, Xenophon would not have conjectured, but would have plainly affirmed, that this charge had for its foundation nothing more than Socrates' frequent references to his δαιμόνιον or 'divine sign,' that is to say, the hallucination of the sense of hearing to which,

[254]

as I imagine, he was subject. And the language of ii. 64, where Xenophon, summing up his answer to Meletus, speaks of the charge of impiety as alleged in the *indictment* and of the charge of the corruption of youth as urged by the *accuser*, seems to lend some countenance to my contention. I note, then, that though the accusers framed their indictment in such a way as to provoke the *odium theologicum*, Meletus in his speech dwelt principally, if not exclusively, upon the charge of corrupting the young.

Secondly, it is remarkable that of the four arguments distinctly attributed to Meletus, three manifestly appeal to political feelings and animosities. When he accuses Socrates of teaching his associates to despise the constitution, and in particular of ridiculing the use of the lot in appointments to office, when he attempts to make him answerable for the misdeeds of Critias and Alcibiades, when he cites his quotation from Homer, Meletus plainly attributes to his victim anti-democratic tendencies: and if we reflect that at Athens democracy was the traditional institution, venerable through age and sentiment, the pride of the older men, whilst oligarchy was a struggling and unpopular novelty, the darling of the younger generation, we shall see that the remaining argument also, in which Socrates is accused of seeking to undermine authority, is capable of a political bearing. In short, if Xenophon's testimony is to be trusted, Meletus, in his speech, distinctly accused Socrates of *political* heterodoxy; and there is no evidence to show that other considerations entered into his argument.

Thirdly, it is to be noticed that Xenophon does not deny the charge of political heterodoxy, and is content to plead extenuating circumstances or at most to put in a somewhat feeble qualification. He *admits* that Socrates denounced the traditional method of appointment to office, but urges, lamely, that he was the last man to encourage revolutionary violence. He *admits* that Critias and Alcibiades were friends of Socrates, but faintly argues that he was not responsible for their acts. He *admits* that Socrates' teaching was subversive of authority, but clumsily explains that he sought to subvert only authority which is unintelligent. He *admits* that Socrates quoted Homer's words in a political sense, and pleads, with something very like a subterfuge or a play upon words, that his 'liberality' appeared in his services rather than in his sentiments. In a word, he is unable to resist the accuser's contention that Socrates was unfriendly to the then established democracy of Athens.

There is then, I think, ample proof that, under cover of the charge of corrupting the young, Meletus represented Socrates as one who held and propagated anti-democratic sentiments, and that it was explicitly on this ground that he pressed for a conviction. But further it is notorious that the accusers belonged to the democratic party, and that Anytus and Lycon were leading members of it. Would it not seem that, in bringing against Socrates what was virtually though not nominally a political accusation, these statesmen had a political end to serve?

Now the theory that the accusers were actuated, either entirely or mainly, by party feeling, is not a new one. But, so far as I know, it has not found favour with our best authorities. And the reasons for this are not far to seek. For, firstly, it seems strange that, so soon after their triumph, the democratic leaders should have occasion to assert themselves, and secondly it seems strange that they should have singled out for attack one who had so recently suffered at the hands of their enemies, the Thirty.

Now both these arguments depend upon the tacit assumption —countenanced by that great scholar and historian, George Grote—that in the last years of the fifth century there were at Athens two political parties and only two, namely, oligarchs and democrats. If this was not so, if there was at Athens a third party, the 'moderates,' if I may so call them, and if, further, Socrates was of this way of thinking, it is easy to see that the democrats, having crushed the oligarchs, might seek a quarrel with the 'moderates,' and that the same man who had suffered under the Thirty in 404, might be called upon to suffer under the democracy in 399.

To the proof of these further propositions—that there was such a party, and that Socrates belonged to it, I now address myself.

[256]

In 412–411, thirteen years before the indictment of Socrates, Athens had been the scene of a revolution. Instigated by Alcibiades, then an exile, a party of conspirators started the notion that an alliance with Persia was their only hope of safety, and that the 'chastening' of the constitution—such was the phrase—was an indispensable condition without which Persian help could not be obtained. Presently, they made it known that the 'chastening' which they desired, would imply, first, that no one should receive pay from the State except for military duty, and secondly, that the political power, hitherto enjoyed by all free citizens, should be vested in a body to be called the 'Five Thousand,' which should include those who were most capable of rendering service in money or in person. This programme was recommended by a series of assassinations: 'if any one *did* object,' says the historian grimly, 'he was presently made away with in some convenient manner'—εἴ τις καὶ ἀντείποι, εὐθὺς ἐκ τρόπου τινὸς ἐπιτηδείου ἐτεθνήκει: and the conspirators soon found themselves strong enough to pass the two articles of the programme, together with a supplementary article which provided for the appointment of a board of Four Hundred. This Board was commissioned to nominate the Five Thousand when they should think fit, and in the meantime had full powers to carry on the government. Of course the Four Hundred—in other words, the conspirators and their associates—did *not* think fit to name the Five Thousand, and preferred to retain the government in their own hands. In a word, the sovereign power passed from the free male population of full age, a body of from fifteen to twenty thousand, to a body of four hundred. The democracy was not 'chastened,' but overthrown.

Nevertheless, amongst those who had been principally concerned in this revolution there were some who were dissatisfied with their handiwork, and, as it would seem, honestly desired the nomination of the Five Thousand. Of these the most important was Theramenes. At this juncture news arrived from Samos that Alcibiades, whilst he approved the more moderate scheme which would constitute a body politic of Five Thousand,

PRAELECTION

had declared himself against the close oligarchy of the Four Hundred. This intelligence encouraged the malcontent members of the dominant faction, and they now began to clamour for the nomination of the Five Thousand, and the 'equalisation,' that is to say the popularisation, of the newly established constitution. The more determined members of the party were alarmed, and endeavoured to strengthen their position by negotiations with Sparta: and this unpatriotic proceeding gave a handle to their malcontent associates. A tumult broke out, which Theramenes fomented. The insurgents secretly desired the restoration of the democracy, but they asked openly no more than that the Four Hundred should be superseded by the Five Thousand.

On the following day negotiations took place. The oligarchs declared themselves willing to nominate the Five Thousand, and to leave the appointment of the Four Hundred to be made by them on a principle of rotation. The democrats were not disinclined to a compromise. Accordingly, in the very midst of the panic caused by the revolt of Euboea, a meeting of the assembly was held, and in the course of it the Four Hundred were deposed, a new constitution was voted, and Alcibiades was recalled. The principal articles of the new constitution were three: first, the sovereign power was transferred to the Five Thousand; secondly, this body was to consist of those persons who were able to provide at their own cost a suit of heavy armour, i.e. of the 'classes' as opposed to the 'masses'; thirdly, no one was to receive pay for official duty, εἰ δὲ μή, ἐπάρατον ἐποιήσαντο. Supplementary regulations were passed later, and in this way a constitution was framed of which Thucydides speaks in brief but hearty commendation. 'For the first time within my knowledge,' he says, 'Athens now had a really sound constitution, in which the oligarchical and democratic principles were both of them represented; and to its existence was due the city's escape from the difficulties of this dark period.'

Now for my main purpose it would be sufficient to note, on

[258]

TRIAL AND DEATH OF SOCRATES

the authority of Thucydides, that in 411 Athens had a constitution in which oligarchical and democratic principles were com-
bined, and that there was at any rate one person, Thucydides
himself, who preferred this mixed constitution, both to the
oligarchy of the Four Hundred and to the old 'unmixed'
democracy.

But no one will wonder if I pause for a moment that I may
mention—with all the respect which an admiring disciple feels
towards a great master—certain points in which I venture to
differ from Grote. In commenting upon the narrative which I
have sketched in the foregoing paragraphs, Grote supposes—

That 'the 5000 was a number existing from the commence-
ment only in talk and imagination, neither realised nor intended
to be realised.'

That it was only when the oligarchs learnt the strength of the
opposition at Samos that 'there *began* to arise [even] in the
bosom of the Four Hundred an opposition minority affecting
popular sentiments.'

And that 'it is not true that on the fall of the Four Hundred
the people introduced a new constitution.'

On these points Grote is, I think, at variance with his chief
authority. Thucydides' complicated story of intrigue, conspiracy, and revolution, implies, I think, throughout, that
besides the oligarchs strictly so-called, such as Antiphon,
Phrynichus, and Peisander, there were persons such as Theramenes, who were opposed both to unmixed democracy and to
close oligarchy, and that it was ignorance whether the support
of these persons had or had not been secured, which made the
strength of the conspirators' position: next, the Greek historian
tells us, in so many words, that when the news of Alcibiades'
protest reached Athens, Theramenes and others were already
dissatisfied with the doings of the oligarchs, and would gladly
have washed their hands of the affair: lastly, Thucydides'
eulogy of the government established in 411—'For the first time
within my knowledge Athens now had a really sound constitution, in which the oligarchical and democratic principles were

PRAELECTION

both of them represented'—is a clear proof that he did not regard that government as a mere revival of the old democracy. Let me try to put the issue more precisely. Grote supposes that from first to last there were on the political stage two parties, on the one hand the oligarchs, that is to say, the Four Hundred and their immediate friends, and on the other, the democrats, whom the oligarchs, with their talk about the Five Thousand, alternately terrified and cajoled, and that, when, as he puts it, 'the old democracy was restored, seemingly with only two modifications,' the democratic party would regard the scheme with unalloyed contentment, as a complete satisfaction of all their demands.

Against Grote I maintain, that besides Grote's oligarchs and democrats, there was a third party, whose members I propose to call 'moderates,' and that it was they, and not the democrats, whose views were represented in the constitution of 411. A detailed proof of these propositions would entail an unduly minute examination of Thucydides' story: and I must therefore confine myself to two or three remarks: first, had there been no third party of 'moderates' who desired a 'chastened' democracy, the professed intention of creating the Five Thousand would have been ineffective both as a promise and as a threat: consequently, the struggle would not have been so long protracted, and the result would have been the restoration of the 'unmixed democracy'; secondly, if the constitution of 411 had been the old democracy restored with no more than trifling modifications, Thucydides' description of it as a blending of oligarchy and democracy would have been absurd, and his commendation of it unmeaning; thirdly, a property qualification high enough to disfranchise a half or two-thirds of the free male population of full age, was fatal to the great principle of democratic isonomy, and from the time of Herodotus to that of Aristotle must have been recognised as such.

So much for the oligarchical conspiracy of 412 and the triumph of the 'moderates' in 411. I now resume the history of Athens at the year 404. Again the Athenians were in the depths of despair. The city had surrendered to the Peloponnesians: the fortifications had been demolished: the political exiles, amongst whom were several who had been members of the Four Hundred, had returned. With the connivance of the Spartan Lysander, the oligarchical attempt of 411 was now repeated. The conspirators procured the nomination of a Board of Thirty with power to revise the constitution, and in the interval to carry on the government. First filling the offices of State with creatures of their own, the Thirty next transferred the judicial function from the Courts to the Senate, there to be exercised under their own eyes. In the proscription which followed, the first victims were men of pronounced democratic opinions; but it was not long before the blood-thirsty Critias turned his hand against less conspicuous personages, and even against men who were notoriously καλοὶ κἀγαθοί, that is to say, opponents of the democratic principle. 'The Thirty,' he said, 'are thirty tyrants, and have no choice but to make away with those who have the capacity to hinder their designs.' Theramenes, who again appears as the representative of oligarchical moderation, pointed out the inevitable consequences. Moved by his arguments, the Thirty proceeded to appoint 3000 persons who should enjoy, at any rate in name, political powers and privileges. This concession was not enough for Theramenes. The political power, he said, should be conferred, not upon three thousand persons, neither more nor less, but upon such persons as could prove their competence; and accordingly he proposed to include in the governing body those who were able to serve the State, on horseback or with heavy armour, at their own charge. This declaration brought the quarrel to a head. Critias contrived to disarm all but those whom he had selected to be members of the Three Thousand, and having thus paralysed his enemies, denounced Theramenes to the Senate. Theramenes replied; and his exposition of his political creed received the applause of his hearers. Critias, now desperate, declared Theramenes an outlaw, and appealed to the statute which resigned such persons to the tender mercies of the Thirty. The execution followed.

[261]

PRAELECTION

It is not necessary that I should recount how a party of exiles established themselves at Phyle; how Critias and his colleagues became increasingly odious even to their creatures, the Three Thousand; how the Thirty gave way to the Ten; and how, in 403, the democracy was restored and the amnesty was proclaimed. But there is *one* circumstance of the restoration which it is important to observe. Even in the moment of democratic triumph there were some who desired a compromise between oligarchy and democracy, and from this point of view a certain Phormisius proposed that political power should belong to those only who were possessors of land in Attica—a regulation which, it was calculated, would disfranchise about 5000 citizens. The motion was rejected; but the fact that it was brought forward seems to show, not only that there were many who preferred a moderate oligarchy—in other words, what Aristotle would have called a 'polity'—both to 'unmixed' democracy and to oligarchy proper, but also that the voice of the people distinguished the theory of the 'moderates' from that of the oligarchs strictly so called. For, had it been otherwise, how could Phormisius have asked and obtained a hearing?

Now in the history of the Thirty, as in that of the Four Hundred, it is throughout manifest that there were at Athens persons, who, while they had no sympathy with the aims of Critias, persistently desired a qualification of the democratic principle. That at the outset the Thirty had the support of these 'moderates' appears, if not in the fact that Theramenes was a member of the Board, at any rate in the fact that persons who approved Theramenes' last declaration had seats in the reconstituted Senate. That there was subsequently a complete break between the oligarchs and the 'moderates,' appears in the fact that Phormisius, who, as I have said, even in 403 proposed a revision of the constitution, had served with the patriots by whom the oligarchs were dispossessed.

In short, the policy of the oligarchs of 404 was conceived on the same lines as that of the oligarchs of 412, in so far as, like them, they relied upon the existence of a moderate party, opposed to the democracy. But, whereas in 412–411 there was no *alliance* between the oligarchical conspirators and the 'moderates,' as appears in the fact that the Four Hundred did not proceed to the nomination of the Five Thousand, in 404, the 'moderates,' by their acceptance of places in the Three Thousand, were implicated in the proceedings of the Thirty. And the consequence was that, whereas the fall of the Four Hundred left the moderates, compact and united, in possession of the field, so that the result was what I may venture to call the Constitution of Theramenes, now, in 404, a considerable section of the moderate party was discredited by their subservience to the Thirty, and the remainder had no option but to acquiesce in the restoration of the old democracy.

And here a word must be said about Theramenes. 'He was a selfish, cunning, and faithless man,' says Grote, 'ready to enter into conspiracies, yet never foreseeing their consequences, and breaking faith to the ruin of colleagues whom he had first encouraged, when he found them more consistent and thoroughgoing in crime than himself,' and, on Grote's assumption, that at Athens, during the last years of the fifth century, every man was either democrat or oligarch, Theramenes' actions may seem to warrant the censure. But if there was at Athens a growing opinion that the democratic principle had been carried too far, that the use of the lot was ridiculous, that the payment of magistrates was corrupting, that the franchise had been unduly extended, but that thoroughgoing oligarchy was at least as bad as thoroughgoing democracy, what proof is there that Theramenes was not one of those who honestly took this view? When Peisander and his associates began their intrigues in 412, they appealed to the moderate sentiment, and Theramenes joined them. They neglected to perform their undertakings, and he left them. They were overthrown, and he assisted in setting up just such a constitution as at the outset they had pretended to desire. Again, in 404, so long as the Thirty confined themselves to operations against the unmixed democracy, he supported them: but when Critias admitted that what he desired was

[263]

PRAELECTION

'Tyranny put in Commission,' Theramenes dissented, and his death was the consequence. For my own part I think that history justifies the words which Xenophon puts into his mouth: 'For myself I have always opposed, on the one hand, those who think that you cannot have a satisfactory democracy unless slaves and others who would sell the city for a drachma are admitted to political office, and on the other, those who hold that you cannot have a satisfactory oligarchy unless the city is dominated by a little party of tyrants. My view was, and is, that political power should be with those who are able to render service to the polity as knights or men-at-arms. Can you, Critias, name any instance in which I have joined either democrat or tyrant in an attempt to defraud the respectable citizen of his civic rights? if you can show that I am trying to do this now, or that I have tried to do this in the past, you are welcome to torture me to death: I should deserve it.' Whatever may have been the faults of Theramenes, he was, I venture to think, the consistent representative of the 'philosophical radicalism' of his time, in other words, of what I have called the 'moderate' sentiment.

And it would seem that the political views of Theramenes were shared by some of the most capable men of the day. Unhappily it is impossible to give Alcibiades credit for honesty: but it is to be observed that, at a time when Alcibiades' future was bound up with the future of his country, so that even he could hardly be accused of wishing her ill, he supported the oligarchs just so long as they professed the policy of Theramenes, and broke with them the moment that they abandoned it. Again, Thucydides is emphatic in his praise of the constitution which Theramenes set up: so much so that editors and commentators have denied the significance of his eulogy or apologised for its warmth. If again we look to the political theories of the next century, we find Plato in his manhood entrusting the government of his καλλίπολις to a military aristocracy, and in his old age providing that there shall be no more than 5040 citizens. In a word, I suspect that thinking men for the most part desired a limitation of the democratic principle.

[264]

TRIAL AND DEATH OF SOCRATES

However this may be, it is at any rate clear that the 'moderates' —who, by their defection, had turned the scale against the oligarchs, and who had been in a position to ask, though not to obtain a revised constitution—were already strong and might soon become formidable. Thus the democrats, though for the moment they could do nothing, would have every temptation to rid themselves of their uncongenial allies, so soon as they should find themselves in a position to strike an effective blow. Hence it will be no surprise to me, if I find the democratic leaders attacking some notable representative of the 'moderate' sentiment. In short, I am prepared to find them seeking to achieve, by the ordinary processes of the courts, the same end which in an earlier period would have been accomplished by means of ostracism—namely, the removal of some representative personage, and the temporary suppression of his political associates.

Is it conceivable then that Socrates was a representative personage on the 'moderate' side, and that, through him, the democratic leaders struck a blow against the 'moderate' sentiment?

Now, that Socrates was not a democrat is certain. To the Athenian of this period it was of the essence of democracy, that appointments to political office should be determined by lot. Thus, in the disquisition upon forms of government which Herodotus strangely attributes to Darius and his brother conspirators, it is expressly mentioned that democracy makes its appointments by lot. And when we come to Aristotle, we find him opposing the use of the lot, as a distinctively democratic institution, to election, which he declares to be distinctively oligarchical. Now from Xenophon's report of the accuser's arguments, we know that Socrates reprobated the use of the lot in the appointment of magistrates, declaring the traditional practice to be no better than folly, and citing instances in which, though the interests at stake were smaller, an appeal to chance would be scouted by common sense. He was not, then, a democrat.

Nor was he an oligarch. This appears beyond the possibility of question in the facts, first, that in the matter of Leon the

Thirty made a deliberate attempt to implicate him in a notorious crime, which attempt he foiled by direct disobedience, and secondly, that they thought it worth while to silence him by an ordinance against 'the teaching of the art of argumentation.' In a word, it is clear that the Thirty regarded him, not as a friend, but as a dangerous enemy.

Thus, negatively, Socrates did not belong to *either* of the extreme parties. It remains to inquire whether positively he shared the principles which the 'moderates' entertained and enunciated. These principles were two: first, that the right of taking part in public affairs, hitherto enjoyed by the whole body of citizens, should belong to those only who were able to serve the State as knights or men-at-arms, providing their own accoutrements; secondly, that no one should receive pay for official duty. Both principles were recognised in the manifestos, formal and informal, issued by the conspirators before the establishment of the Four Hundred. Both reappeared in the 'moderate' constitution of 411. The first, and more important, of them was reaffirmed by Theramenes in 404, in the speech which I have already quoted, and it may be fancied that the acceptance of this principle carried with it the acceptance of the other.

Now, that Socrates held the second article of the 'moderates'' creed is, in view of his loudly expressed dislike of paid educational service, a matter of safe inference. If the teacher could not take fees from his pupils without loss of independence and self-respect, the statesman and the judge could hardly receive a stipend without a similar sacrifice.

That Socrates held, in some form or other, the more important article of the 'moderates'' programme, is, I think, implied in a difficult paragraph of my text—ch. ii, §§ 58, 59.

'The accuser alleged'—Xenophon tells us—'that Socrates was in the habit of quoting certain lines[1] in which Homer

[1]   ὅντινα μὲν βασιλῆα καὶ ἔξοχον ἄνδρα κιχείη,
        τὸν δ' ἀγανοῖς ἐπέεσσιν ἐρητύσασκε παραστάς·
        δαιμόνι', οὔ σε ἔοικε κακὸν ὣς δειδίσσεσθαι,
        ἀλλ' αὐτός τε κάθησο καὶ ἄλλους ἵδρυε λαούς.

describes Odysseus' diverse treatment of high and low—how to the king or notable he spoke softly, but when a man of the commons came in his way, smote him with his staff, roughly chiding: "Sirrah! sit thou still, and list to the words of thy betters—Thou art no man of war! no man of might and leading! Naught art thou but a cypher in war and a cypher in council."' 'Whence Socrates made out,' the accuser continued, 'that Homer approved the maltreatment of the poorer sort.'

To this Xenophon replies that Socrates said nothing of the kind: he was one of the poorer sort himself, so that the cudgelling would have fallen upon his own head. What Socrates really said, was that those who could not make themselves of use either in word or in deed, those who were incapable of rendering service to the army, to the city, or to the demus itself, ought—especially if they were unscrupulous as well—to be put down at any cost. As a matter of fact, however, Socrates was conspicuous, not only for his humanity, but also for his love of the demus, of which he gave clear proof when he placed his time and his powers gratuitously at the disposal of his countrymen.

Thus Xenophon, dismissing the accuser's interpretation as an absurdity, allows that the quotation had a bearing upon contemporary politics, but claims that that bearing was innocent, and should be recognised as such. Further, his comment implies that the point of the quotation is to be looked for in the concluding lines:

> δαιμόνι, ἀτρέμας ἧσο, καὶ ἄλλων μῦθον ἄκουε,
> οἳ σέο φέρτεροί εἰσι· σὺ δ' ἀπτόλεμος καὶ ἄναλκις,
> οὔτε ποτ' ἐν πολέμῳ ἐναρίθμιος οὔτ' ἐνὶ βουλῇ.

Now the argument of this paragraph is perplexed and obscure; and this is hardly the place for the discussion of details. So I

> ὃν δ' αὖ δήμου τ' ἄνδρα ἴδοι βοόωντά τ' ἐφεύροι,
> τὸν σκήπτρῳ ἐλάσασκεν ὁμοκλήσασκέ τε μύθῳ·
> δαιμόνι', ἀτρέμας ἧσο, καὶ ἄλλων μῦθον ἄκουε,
> οἳ σέο φέρτεροί εἰσι· σὺ δ' ἀπτόλεμος καὶ ἄναλκις,
> οὔτε ποτ' ἐν πολέμῳ ἐναρίθμιος οὔτ' ἐνὶ βουλῇ.

Iliad II. 188.

PRAELECTION

content myself with a dogmatic statement of what I suppose to be Xenophon's meaning. It is, I think, this: 'Of course Socrates did not mean that the rich were justified in maltreating the poor. Homer's lines, as used by Socrates, meant, no doubt, that those who were incapable of rendering service to the State, were not entitled to a voice in public affairs and must submissively "list to the word of their betters": but by "betters" he did not mean rich men as such, and he was prepared to recognise service in word as well as service in deed, in fact, any service whether to the army or to the city or to the demus itself.' If, as I think, this is Xenophon's meaning, he admits that Socrates was prepared to exclude from political affairs those who were unable to render service to the State, and even if the qualifying phrases imply something more than a reminder that in making wealth the condition of citizenship he was thinking, not of wealth as such, but of wealth as a test of capacity, what is admitted is, for my present purpose, sufficient. It seems to me to justify the belief, that in this matter Socrates was at one with Theramenes, who in his last speech expressed himself in similar terms: 'My principle was and is that political privileges should rest with those who are able to render service on horseback or as men-at-arms, and that it should rest with them in virtue of such service.'

And now I may note a tradition, which Grote mentions only that he may reject it. Diodorus speaks of Theramenes as the friend and disciple of Socrates, and asserts that Socrates with two others attempted a rescue when Theramenes was dragged away to execution. Aelian too has a plain straightforward account of Socrates' politics, and assigns to him precisely that position, intermediate between the extreme parties, to which I am led by the examination of the earlier witnesses. Now I should be sorry to rest my case upon these traditions: nevertheless, I may fairly quote them as in some sort confirmatory of my views. But, wholly apart from these plausible testimonies, there is, I think, ample evidence to show first, that towards the end of the fifth century there was a party of 'moderates,' drawn largely from the intellectual class, who, though in the face of a close oligarchy

[268]

they might side with the democrats, were, under other circumstances and normally, enemies of the democracy, and that at the time of the restoration these 'moderates' were strong enough to cause anxiety to the democratic leaders; secondly, that Socrates was in sympathy with this third party, and that, as appears from the attempt of the Thirty to implicate him in their crimes, his political views were pronounced and notorious.

These are the results which the second part of my inquiry has afforded.

And now, sir, I will briefly recapitulate. In the last decade of the Peloponnesian War it was the prevailing opinion of the καλοὶ κἀγαθοί or 'classes,' that the political power of the 'masses' was too great and ought to be curtailed. The 'ideas' —if I may use the late Mr Buxton's convenient phrase—upon which this opinion rested, or in which it found expression, would seem to have been two:

Firstly, public affairs should be managed by those who are capable of rendering public service, and of such capacity wealth is the best test.

Secondly, democratic government is expensive, inasmuch as the poorer citizens have to be compensated for the time which they bestow upon public business; and we may well believe that the disastrous expedition to Sicily—which not only displayed the military incapacity of the demus, but also made the need for economy greater and more apparent—gave to these notions an increased significance.

It was to those who desired a 'chastening' of the democracy that the oligarchical conspirators appealed when in 412–411 they issued their programme, and when the oligarchy of the Four Hundred fell, the 'chastened' democracy of the Five Thousand was the triumph of the moderate principle.

Similarly, in 404, the Thirty found themselves obliged to conciliate the 'moderate' party by the nomination of the Three Thousand: but the execution of Theramenes and the excesses of the tyrants presently drove the 'moderates' into alliance with the democracy.

[269]

PRAELECTION

On the expulsion of the oligarchs, the 'moderates' were strong enough to assert their views which, however, they based upon a new idea: the government of the country should be with those who have a substantial stake in it. But they were not strong enough to carry them, and the old democracy was restored. A period of tension ensued, which in earlier days would have ended with the ostracism of some political personage. But ostracism had fallen into disuse, and the amnesty sworn to in 403 precluded a direct attack upon political opponents. Singling out Socrates because, though not a professional politician, he was the very type of the obnoxious party, and had done much to make and to foster the more moderate—and therefore more dangerous—form of anti-democratic sentiment, the popular leaders indicted him as an offender against religion and morality, and under cover of these charges represented him as a traitor to the demus and the city. Probably they expected that he would leave the country, in which case their end would be gained. But his obstinacy disappointed their calculation, and they thus had no choice but to press the capital charge. His eccentricity and heterodoxy, as well as the personal animosities which he had provoked, doubtless contributed, as his accusers had foreseen, to bring about the conviction: but, in my judgment, it was the fear of Socrates' 'philosophical radicalism' which prompted the action of Meletus, Anytus and Lycon. The result was what they had hoped it would be. The friends of Socrates abandoned the struggle and went into exile; and when they returned to Athens, the most prominent of them was careful to announce that he had withdrawn from the practical politics of Athens, and regarded himself as a citizen of a city which is not on earth but in heaven.

In conclusion, I should like to state my reasons for offering to you, Mr Vice-Chancellor and Members of the Council, the subject which I have now discussed. My motives were two-fold.

First, I was not sorry to have an opportunity of setting out at length certain views which I had indicated, very briefly, a year or two ago in the *Encyclopaedia Britannica*. But secondly, and this was the weightier consideration, it is to me a pleasure to read or write or teach about Socrates. 'Whoso hears him,' says the intoxicated Alcibiades in Plato's dialogue, 'nay, whoso hears a feeble report of what he has said, is struck with awe and possessed with admiration. Were I not afraid that you would think me more drunk than I am, I would make oath to you how his words have moved me, aye and how they move me still. When I listen to him my heart beats with a more than Corybantic excitement; he has only to speak and my tears flow. Orators such as Pericles never stirred me in this way, rousing my soul to the sense of my servile condition, and making me think that life is not worth living so long as I am what I am.' Something of this fascination I feel and I am not ashamed to confess it.

LECTURE ON SHAKESPEARE[1]

WAS SHAKSPERE OF STRATFORD THE AUTHOR OF SHAKESPEARE'S PLAYS AND POEMS?

THERE is an old story about Lord Beaconsfield, which, if it is not true, ought to be. Once upon a time, an ambitious young man asked the aged statesman to give him from the treasury of his great experience some precept or caution which might be of service to him in life. Lord Beaconsfield took time to consider, and then delivered himself of an oracular answer: 'If you want to get on in the world, never talk about the authorship of the letters of Junius.' Now I am not an unqualified admirer of Lord Beaconsfield: but I think that he understood the fads, the foibles, and the prejudices of the British public, and that, if he gave the advice which is attributed to him, it would be imprudent to disregard it. In other words, I think that, in general, the British public cares very little about literary problems; and that, if I were to try to prove to you that the letters of Junius were written by Sir Philip Francis, or by any other of the score or more of persons to whom they have been ascribed, you would regard me as an unmitigated bore. But to the general rule there is one notable exception. We are all of us interested—we are all of us keenly interested—in the controversy about the authorship of Shakespeare's plays and poems: for, whether we believe, or do not believe, that they were written by the actor who was born and died at Stratford, we all acknowledge their marvellous genius; and the pride which we take in them and in their author is akin to, and even an element in, the pride which we feel in our British nationality.

It is perhaps sixty years since the hypothesis was propounded that the plays and poems which we call by the name of Shakespeare were written, not by William Shăksper or Shăkspere or Shakespeare of Stratford, but by Francis Bacon, Lord Verulam —Pope's 'wisest, highest, meanest, of mankind.' At the time, there were few who took this daring identification more seriously

[1] Delivered to the Sheffield branch of the British Empire Shakespeare Society on 29 February 1912.

than they did the contemporary suggestion that the *Waverley Novels* were written, not by Sir Walter Scott, but by his brother Thomas. Nevertheless, the theory that the author of the plays and poems was not the Stratford actor but Bacon or another, had come to stay: and it soon found influential sponsors. Let me cite two or three. 'Whether Bacon wrote the wonderful plays or not,' says Whittier, the poet, 'I am quite sure [that] the man Shäkspere neither did nor could.' Again, 'other admirable men,' says Emerson, the essayist, 'have lived lives in some sort of keeping with their thought, but this man in wide contrast.' Again, John Bright, the orator, is very bold: 'Any man who believes that William Shäkspere wrote *Hamlet* or *Lear* is a fool.' And of late years what I propose to call the anti-Shäksperean theory—the theory that the plays and poems of Shäkespeare were not written by Shäkspere of Stratford—has grown and flourished exceedingly. In particular, several lawyers of repute, such as Lord Penzance and Mr Justice Holmes, have joined in the controversy from the sceptical side. I will not trouble you with a bibliography of anti-Shäksperean literature: but I am in private duty bound to name *one* of the anti-Shäksperean critics.

It is upon the writings of my learned and acute friend Mr George Greenwood, M.P., and especially upon his valuable work entitled 'The Shäkespeare problem restated,' that I principally rely for my knowledge of the anti-Shäksperean position: and I am further indebted to him for very many important facts. The truth is, that in literary controversy, no less than in practical affairs, it is a great comfort to have an opponent who knows his own mind: and for this reason, I, who fall under John Bright's condemnation, am heartily grateful to Mr Greenwood for his vigorous statement of the anti-Shäksperean case.

And here I may interpose an explanation. In imitation of Mr Greenwood, I shall speak of Shäkespeare whenever I mean the writer of the plays and poems, and of Shäkspere whenever I mean the Stratford man who went to London to seek his fortune.

LECTURE

But it must be clearly understood that Shăkspere and Shāke-speare are not distinct names but two ways of spelling the same name. When Shakspere took to writing himself Shakespeare, it was as if one who had written himself Peter were to write himself Petrie, or one who had written himself Chumley, were to write himself Cholmondeley: for Petrie is pronounced Peter, and Cholmondeley Chumley. In the second place, it must be clearly understood that the Stratford family has at least as great a right as the dramatist to the spelling Shakespeare. For in 1596 when the father, John, had his grant of arms, it was given to him in the name of Shakespeare, and obviously this spelling was preferred, because it suggested, better than the old spelling, to Shakspere the coat of arms which had for its sole charge a spear. Thenceforward the Stratford family spelt their name Shakespeare. This spelling was used in *Venus and Adonis* in 1593 and in *Lucrece* in 1594: but in *Love's Labour's Lost* in 1598 the name is spelt Shakspere and in *Richard III*, also 1598, Shake-speare. I suspect that the spellings of 1593, 1594 are anticipations of the grant of arms; anyhow the various spellings of the name are of no significance. Meanwhile, this being clearly understood, it is convenient for me to use Shăkspere for the young player, Shākespeare for the dramatist, and to propose my question about their identity in the form 'Was Shăkspere of Stratford the author of Shākespeare's plays?'

And now I will try to state briefly, but fairly, what seems to me to be the mainstay of the anti-Shăksperean tale. The bald facts of Shăkspere's life are familiar to all. William Shăkspere was born at Stratford in 1564. His father was an alderman of Stratford: but he seems to have been illiterate, as he made his mark in legal documents instead of signing his name. There was a free grammar school at Stratford; but we have no evidence about the education which it provided, and there is no proof that William Shăkspere attended it. In 1582 at the age of 18 he married Anne Hathaway, a woman eight years his senior. In 1586 or 1587, being then about 22, he left Stratford and went to London, where he found employment in a succession of theatrical companies. Tradition says that he began at the very bottom of the ladder. But he prospered, and became a considerable actor, though perhaps not one of the first rank. Later, he was one of the proprietors of the Globe Theatre and the Blackfriars Theatre. In 1594 he played before the Queen. In 1596 his father received a grant of arms from the heralds' college. In 1597 he contracted to buy New Place, a house at Stratford. About 1610–1611 he retired to Stratford, and in 1616 he died there. Such being the bald facts of Shākspere's life, is it credible that the Shākspere who had had no better opportunities than these, is it credible that the Shākspere who seems to have been laboriously building up the shattered fortunes of his family, should have blossomed into the Shākespeare in whom we find, not only genius, but also learning, and, in particular, a notable familiarity with Latin poets and other writers of antiquity? In short, Shākespeare was learned, Shākspere was unlearned: therefore Shākspere was not Shākespeare. This is, apparently, the argument which has led Whittier, Emerson, John Bright, and many others to declare confidently against the traditional attribution: and it must be admitted that, if we test Shākespeare's attainments by reference to 20th century standards, the anti-Shākspereans can make out a very fair *prima facie* case.

And now for a few moments I leave Shākespeare and Shākspere, that I may submit to you a general proposition which seems to me to have a direct and important bearing upon our controversy. It is obvious that what is common knowledge to all of us *now*, was not always common knowledge to our predecessors. For example, Samuel Pepys—whose diary of his doings between 1660 and 1669 is perhaps the most precious record now extant of life in the 17th century—was thirty years old, and already an important civil servant, when he engaged a Mr Cooper to teach him Mathematiques: 'my first attempt,' says Pepys, 'was to learn the multiplication table.' Thus it would seem that in the year 1662 the multiplication table was not common knowledge. It is not so obvious, but it is nevertheless true, that what to us now is uncommon knowledge and the knowledge of specialists, was sometimes common knowledge, the knowledge of all, or nearly all educated men, two or three centuries ago. A year after Pepys began to learn the multiplication table, he was grievously shocked to discover that Sir George Carteret did not know that the four letters S. P. Q. R. on Roman standards in a tapestry picture stood for *Senatus populusque Romanus*: 'which ignorance,' he says, 'is not to be borne in a privy Councillor, methinks: a schoolboy should be whipt for not knowing it.' And a month later he was gravely distressed because his brother John, then an undergraduate at Cambridge 'gave so bad [answers], or no answers at all,' when he questioned him about Aristotle's physical theories. 'I find him,' writes Pepys, 'not so thorough a philosopher, at least in Aristotle, as I took him for': and thereupon he makes up his mind 'to take' poor John 'to task.' That is to say, Samuel Pepys expected from a Privy Councillor acquaintance with the rudiments of Roman antiquities, and from an undergraduate some knowledge of Aristotle's physics. For myself, I do not expect every Privy Councillor—nor indeed every Chancellor of the Exchequer—to know anything about Roman antiquities: nor do I expect *every* undergraduate to be acquainted with Aristotle's philosophy, or *any* undergraduate to spend time upon Aristotle's physics, the least profitable part of that great man's writings. Nowadays Roman archaeology on the one hand and physics on the other, that is to say, the physics of Kelvin, Maxwell, Rayleigh, and J. J. Thomson, are specialities pursued by the few: in the days of Pepys Roman archaeology, and physics, that is to say, the physics of Aristotle, were parts of the outfit of an educated man.

Let me give you another instance. My friend Mr Greg, one of the most learned of our students of Elizabethan literature, found in the British Museum an unpublished Eclogue by Edward Fairfax, the translator of Tasso. It was a dialogue, in which one of the disputants maintained the greatness of antiquity, the other the greatness of modernity. The one piled up references to the wonders and the splendours of which we hear in the classical writers: the other told of the adventures and the discoveries of Columbus and the great voyagers who were exploring the world. Of course the advocate of modernity won easily, all along the line. Mr Greg asked me to identify for him the references to the classical writers. It was easy to do this. But it surprized me to find that what may be called the anecdotage of antiquity, which the scholar of to-day is apt to neglect, was to Fairfax common knowledge. The truth is that the literatures of Greece and Rome, in the originals and in translations, formed an important part of the light literature of our ancestors. Once more I may cite Pepys, who reads with his wife translations of Ovid's *Metamorphoses* and of Aesop's *Fables*. I am myself a reader of novels: but I should know more than I do, if there were not so many novelists—good and bad— to distract my attention from the older light literature.

I hold then that what are now uncommon studies, the studies of the specialist, were sometimes, three hundred years ago, common studies, the studies of the educated man, though they were pursued in a popular and not in a technical way. Let me apply this general proposition to a particular instance in Shāke-speare. Hamlet, rebuking his mother, asks her 'Have you eyes?' —and, to prove that she has eyes, proceeds 'Sense, sure, you have, else could you not have motion.' My anti-Shāksperean friend, Mr Greenwood, has suggested, and he is unquestionably right, that we have here a distinct reference to Aristotle's doctrine of the gradation of the faculties of the soul. Let me explain. Vegetable kinds, says Aristotle, have the faculty of nutrition and growth, and no other. Then come the lower animal kinds, which have, together with the faculty of nutrition and growth, the faculty of sensation. Then come animal kinds more highly developed, which, together with the faculty of nutrition and growth and the faculty of sensation, have, as well, the faculty of locomotion. Finally, man, together with all the inferior faculties of soul, nutrition and growth, sensation, loco-motion, has also the faculty of discursive reason. Thus the

[277]

LECTURE

possession of a superior psychical faculty necessarily implies
the possession of all the faculties inferior to it: and as sensation
is lower in the scale than locomotion, the queen's possession of
the faculty of locomotion implies that she has also the faculty
of sensation, and therefore has eyes with which to see. (By the
way, I suspect that the queen ought, at the moment, to be
moving restlessly about the stage, that we may have ocular
demonstration of her power of locomotion. I do not know
whether any such tradition has survived upon the stage.)

Thus Shākespeare was familiar with a detail of Greek science,
a detail so remote that i' remained for Mr Greenwood, who had
given attention to Greek philosophy, to explain the allusion.
Now at first sight this looks like a conclusive proof that Shākespeare was a man of very unusual learning: but I venture to
suggest that any such inference would be wholly unwarrantable,
and indeed hazardous in the extreme. The philosophy and the
science of Aristotle, backed by the authority of the Church,
had reigned supreme throughout the miadic age: and although
in 1538 Pierre Ramée or Ramus, taking as the subject of his
degree essay 'That all that Aristotle has said is false,' had raised
the standard of revolt, and at a later time Shākespeare's contemporary, Francis Bacon, was proclaiming and popularizing
Ramist principles in England, Aristotelian philosophy and
Aristotelian science were still the popular philosophy and the
popular science of the time. This being so, the fundamental
principle of Aristotle's psychology must needs have been a
commonplace, familiar to every educated man; and acquaintance with it is therefore no proof whatever of exceptional attainment.

I claim then to have shown that, whereas many things which
are familiar to ourselves were not known, or not generally
known, to our ancestors, *some* things which are not commonly
known to ourselves were familiar to them: and that for this
reason, when we endeavour to appraise the learning of an
Elizabethan, we must not test his acquirements by reference to
our own 20th century standards. Rather we should try to

[278]

ascertain the opinion of his contemporaries and their immediate successors. And fortunately we have excellent witnesses. First, Ben Jonson, in his verses addressed 'To the memory of my beloved, the author, Mr William Shākespeare,' declares that the dramatist, 'the swan of Avon,' had 'small Latin and less Greek,' by which phrase I understand him to mean that Shākespeare was not, what Jonson was himself, a professed scholar. Secondly, fifty years later, Fuller, in his *Worthies of England*, affirms that Shākespeare's learning was very little, and that he was an eminent instance to prove the rule that a poet is born and not made. Thus a contemporary dramatist, who, to use his own words, 'loved the man and did honour his memory, on this side idolatry, as much as any,' and a ripe scholar of the next generation who knew Shākespeare only in his writings and therefore would not be prejudiced by personal knowledge of the actor, agree in noting that he was not a learned man. Surely Jonson and Fuller knew better than we can do what was at the beginning of the 17th century common knowledge, and what was not, and were therefore better able than we are to say whether 'learning' was or was not a conspicuous quality of Shākespeare's plays or poems: and, this being so, when I find Jonson and Fuller going out of their way to remark in Shākespeare a lack of learning, I do not attach much weight to the off-hand pronouncements of 19th century critics, who, judging by their own very different standards, see in the plays and poems knowledge of a wholly exceptional sort.

It is indeed significant that the cry about the 'learning' of Shākespeare did not make itself heard till 1746, when he had been dead 130 years, and that it did not become insistent till another century had elapsed.

I accept then the judgment of Shākespeare's contemporaries, that he was not remarkable for 'learning': that is to say, that his knowledge was not greater than that of the educated men of his time. But at this point my opponents might fairly say (mind, I hardly think that they will concede as much): 'Be it so: we accept the judgment of Jonson and Fuller, that Shāke-

speare was not, in their sense of the term, "learned," that, in
fact, he had "small Latin and less Greek," and we will avoid the
words learned and learning in future. But you, on your part,
must allow us to amend our plea. We will now put our case
thus. We think that we have in Shākespeare's writings clear
evidence, not perhaps of exceptional learning, but, at any rate,
of knowledge which Shākspere of Stratford, with his humble
antecedents, his small opportunities, and his life of struggle and
affairs, could hardly have acquired. For example, we find that
Shākespeare in the poem called *Lucrece* follows the story as
told by Ovid in his *Fasti*, a work which had not been translated,
and introduces from the original details which other imitators
had neglected. We find that he draws upon Ovid's *Metamorphoses*. We find that the *Comedy of Errors* is an adaptation of
Plautus' *Menaechmi*, which had not been translated, and we
think that in many other instances he derives inspiration from
Latin and even from Greek sources.' Such is in brief the argument which Mr Greenwood bases upon Mr Churton Collins'
elaborate proof that Shākespeare had a considerable knowledge
of Latin and perhaps of Greek literature. I say 'perhaps of
Greek' because I am not sure that Mr Churton Collins makes
out this part of his case.

Now I venture to think that, as the anti-Shākspereans have
overrated Shākespeare's attainments, so they have underrated
Shākspere's educational opportunities and possibilities: and
that once more they have been misled by the assumption that
the standards of the 20th century are applicable to Elizabethan
times. At the present day a public school boy of 14 or 15 is in
school some 25 hours each week, and of these 25 hours, probably six are given to Latin, five to Greek, three to French, five
to Mathematics, six to English subjects. Thus something less
than a quarter of his time is given to Latin. If he shows a special
aptitude for classical studies, the amount of time which he gives
to them will increase as he rises in the school: if he shows a
special aptitude in some other direction, the amount of time
which he gives to the dead languages will diminish. Thus for

SHAKESPEARE

the boy who does not become a specialist·in Greek and Latin, the study of Greek and Latin provides mental gymnastics in the earlier years and little more: and, though doubtless he gains very much by the exercise, he does not carry away with him, when he leaves school, any great stock either of Latin or of Greek; and he seldom or never continues these juvenile studies in later life. Even the boy who becomes proficient and a specialist in Greek and Latin, though he becomes familiar with the principal classical authors and the work which scholars have done upon them, seldom makes practical use of his school knowledge. In particular, though he can at a pinch write a Latin letter or a Latin preface, he is not in the regular habit of doing either the one or the other. In a word, facility in the use of Latin is not nowadays a necessity even for the professed scholar, and those who are not professed scholars for the most part forget such Latin as they have learnt in their youth.

This was not so in the Elizabethan age. In those days a working, practical, knowledge of Latin was, for the educated man, a necessary of existence. Mr A. F. Leach tells us that 'The diplomatist, the lawyer, the civil servant, the physician, the naturalist, the philosopher, wrote, read, and, to a large extent, spoke and perhaps thought, in Latin.' 'Nor was Latin,' he continues, 'only the language of the higher professions. A merchant, or the bailiff of a manor wanted it for his accounts; every town clerk or guild clerk wanted it for his minute-book. Columbus had to study in Latin for his voyage; and the general had to study tactics in it. The architect, the musician, every one who was neither a mere soldier nor a mere handicraftsman wanted, not a smattering of grammar, but a living acquaintance with the tongue, as a spoken as well as a written language.' Such is Mr Leach's summary statement, and I cannot think that it is at all exaggerated. Latin was still a living language; the professional man, the man of affairs, and the courtier, made constant use of it, and I may add that Latin might even enter into amusements. In two pages of the first scene of Marlowe's

[281]

LECTURE

Dr Faustus, Faustus quotes seven Latin sentences, and he uses a Greek phrase which puzzled the more modern commentators to such an extent that they amended it, and so produced absolute nonsense. Again, in the third scene, Faustus professes his apostacy in seven solid lines of Latin prose, and in the course of them Marlowe introduces a classical idiom which escaped a recent editor of one of Cicero's philosophical treatises.

Marlowe would neither have interlarded his discourse with superfluous Latin, nor have introduced what seem to us erudite allusions, if he had not known that many of his audience would understand and appreciate. It is not easy to imagine Mr Bernard Shaw putting into the mouth of one of his characters seven solid lines of Latin: but it *is* easy to imagine what, if he were to do such a thing, the feelings of the audience would be. Now a laugh, or a hiss, or a murmur, would have been fatal to Marlowe's terrific scene, and might have been fatal to the play: he must have felt very sure of the sympathy of his audience.

If then Latin was thus familiarly known to the Elizabethans, where did they learn it? They learnt it in the grammar schools, which, says Prof. Foster Watson in his excellent book on *English grammar schools to* 1660, had for their primary object 'to make Latin live again': and I may add that this primary object was never lost sight of; for, in so far as other subjects were included in the curriculum, they were taught through Latin. In particular, Greek was translated, not into English, but into Latin, so that even when he was learning Greek, the boy was exercizing himself in the use of Latin. Prof. Foster Watson has collected notices of the curricula enjoined in a great number of 16th century grammar schools. I take one as an example: In the statute for Friars' School, Bangor, dated 1568, it is provided that 'nothing shall be taught in the said school but only grammar and such authors as concern the Latin and Greek tongues.' This example is, I think, sufficient for my purpose, which is to show that the grammar schools of Elizabeth's time were, in a very strict sense, classical schools: but, for my own satisfaction, I shall mention another instance.

SHAKESPEARE

In 1604, a grammar school, endowed by Thomas Smith of Crowland in Lincolnshire, an attorney at law, was created by King James in the town of Sheffield: and in the letters patent it was provided that the Free Grammar School of James, King of England, shall consist of one pedagogue or master and one subpedagogue or usher and of children and youth therein taught and instructed. There were to be thirteen governors. And now mark! The Master and the usher were to instruct the youth in Latin and Greek letters. So says Joseph Hunter, the learned, exact, acute historian of Hallamshire, whose name I have reverenced ever since the time when I used to see him in the days of my childhood. I mention this instance not merely because I think it will appeal to you, but also because, though I was not a pupil of the grammar school of King James, it was at the Collegiate School now united with it in the Grammar School of King Edward the VIIth that I received the greater part, and the more important part, of my schooling. I am eternally grateful. You will, I am sure, forgive this digression.

In the reign of Elizabeth then the English boy, having learnt to read and to write and perhaps something more at the A.B.C. school, the reading school, the writing school, the song school, proceeded to the grammar school where he learnt the Latin grammar, studied dialogue books, committed to memory vocabularies, wrote Latin, translated Latin, and studied in Latin whatever else he studied, talked Latin in school, at play, and at home, learnt Greek and translated it into Latin, read a fair number of Latin authors. Is it surprizing that the grammar school boy, even if he left school early, acquired a very consider-able familiarity with the language, a familiarity which would stay with him through life? and is it surprizing that if he became a man of letters, he was able to make effective use of his school reading in Ovid, Plautus, and other writers? I maintain that the grammar school education of Elizabeth's time was sufficient to explain the so-called 'learning,' that is to say, the general knowledge—for at that time Latin was general knowledge—which appears in Shākespeare's plays and poems. It will no doubt be objected that Shăkspere is not proved to have attended the grammar school. True: but is it likely that the son of an ambitious alderman, who asked for a grant of arms as early as 1568, was allowed to escape all schooling after he was seven or eight? is it likely that the actor Shăkspere, who left Stratford for London, fought his way up, made a competence, restored the fortunes of his family, had had no education whatsoever? It seems to me that whatever we may think about the question 'Was Shăkspere Shākespeare,' Shăkspere the actor must have attended the Stratford Free Grammar School, and I protest against the tacit assumption that, if Shăkspere is not proved to have attended the Free Grammar School, he must be held not to have attended it. Attendance at the grammar school was a matter of course.

Thus far I have been on the defensive. The anti-Shăkspereans maintain that Shākespeare was a man of unusual learning, Shăkspere a man of no learning at all: whence they infer that Shăkspere was not Shākespeare. In reply I have tried to show that they have overrated the learning of the one, and underrated the learning of the other, and that there is no such discrepancy as they, misled by supposed modern analogies, have imagined. It remains for me to take the offensive, and to state very briefly certain difficulties which stand in the way of the identification of Shākespeare with any one other than Shăkspere, whether that other be Bacon or an unknown.

First, if we, with our small knowledge of the life and the personality of Shăkspere, the Stratford man, are warranted, as the anti-Shăksperean affirms, in concluding that he did not and could not write the plays of Shākespeare, surely those who knew the actor in the flesh must needs have recognized the absurdity of attributing to him work of which, on the showing of the anti-Shăkspereans, he was manifestly incapable. The incapacity of Shăkspere which, we are told, is, or ought to be, obvious to us, must have been all the more obvious to those who had daily opportunities of measuring the literary and intellectual inferiority which the anti-Shăkspereans so freely and

SHAKESPEARE

confidently impute to him, and it will be observed that the
greater the discrepancy is supposed to be between the attainments of Shākespeare and the attainments of Shăkspere, the
more impossible the imposture becomes.

Secondly, it is admitted that Shākespeare revised and added
to old plays and collaborated with other authors in writing new
ones. If Shākespeare the dramatist was no other than Shăkspere
the actor, this is easily intelligible. But if Shākespeare the
dramatist was an unknown, Bacon or another, hiding himself
under the name of Shăkspere the actor, I find it difficult both
to believe that the great man did journeyman's work for a
theatrical company, and to understand how, doing it, he could
have succeeded in maintaining his incognito. You will observe
that it will not do to conjecture that, whereas Shākespeare wrote
whole plays, Shăkspere revised, added, and collaborated: for,
if Shăkspere could write speeches and scenes which, though
they appear in old or composite plays, are recognized as
admirable products of Shākespeare's genius, why should not
Shăkspere, the poacher, have written *Lear*, *Othello*, and the
rest?

Thirdly, I cannot allow that the anti-Shăksperean is warranted
in disregarding the dedications and the commendatory verses
prefixed to the first folio of 1623. Ben Jonson and another
definitely connect Shākespeare with Stratford. Heming,
Condell, and another explicitly, and Ben Jonson and another
implicitly, identify the dramatist and the actor. Are we to
suppose that, though Shăkspere was not Shākespeare, Heming,
Condell, and Jonson imagined them to be identical? If so,
what becomes of the modern theory that their identity is un-
believable and inconceivable? or, are we to suppose that,
though Heming, Condell, and Jonson profess to identify the
dramatist and the player, they were in the secret, and knew that
Shākespeare was not Shăkspere, but another? If so, I fear that
we must accuse the three of gross and deliberate falsehood—
and what is more audacious, impudent falsehood, liable at any
moment to be exposed. For if a nobody poses as a great man,

[285]

the fraud can hardly fail to be detected, especially if, as in this case, the secret is known to a considerable number of persons.

In short, when I leave the defence of the Shăksperean tradition, and proceed to consider the anti-Shăksperean hypothesis, I find it difficult to understand how Heming, Condell, and the rest, could have failed to detect the imposture, especially when so much of Shākespeare's work was done in collaboration with others, and how, if they were aware of the imposture, they could have mustered up the courage to prefix to the collected works a series of deliberate falsehoods.

And now, to tell, very briefly, the story of Shăkspere's life, as I understand it. I have indeed nothing sensational to suggest: I know no more than tradition relates: and I have no thought of·filling up deficiencies by wholesale conjecture. But I hope in this way to draw together and unite the several threads of my somewhat complicated discourse.

I suppose that Shăkspere's childhood resembled that of most of his contemporaries, that he learnt to read and to write at an elementary school or schools; that he proceeded to the Free Grammar School, and there acquired, together with the rudiments of Greek, a real familiarity with Latin, written and spoken: and that he read Latin poets, playwrights and historians, and thus awoke to the delights of literature. And it seems to me that in this way he would receive by no means a bad education: for we are not to imagine, because Latin pervaded the whole of the curriculum, that familiarity with that language was the only end sought and attained. Then came an imprudent marriage: and presently he left Stratford, and went to London. We know little or nothing of the early part of his London life: but it is obvious to suppose that he who was to be the greatest of all dramatists soon sought employment in some theatrical company, soon discovered that he could write, and soon made himself useful in revising and supplementing plays which the company was to act. And manifestly his experience as an actor would give to his literary work an exceptional value. This being so, I imagine that he was a member of his company

[286]

not only in the character of player but also in that of playwright. Then would come the production of whole plays. And here I would suggest that however countrified Shǎkspere of Stratford may have been when he first came to town, as soon as he had established himself in his company as a man who could edit old plays and write new ones, both his knowledge and his culture would develop apace. I surmise too, but I am not sufficiently learned to produce evidence in justification, that success of this sort would bring him into relations with men of distinction in other walks of life: for in those days even London was small; and when coffee and tea had not yet brought in the practice of breakfasting at home, when men broke their fast at a tavern with a crust of bread and a tankard of ale, all sorts and conditions of men met on easy terms over their homely meals. At any rate, so it was in the latter half of the 17th century when Pepys had his morning draught one day with his great patron Lord Sandwich, and another with his tailor: and I imagine that things were not very different in Shǎkspere's time.

Meanwhile, it is clear that Shǎkspere was prospering in a worldly sense. In 1597, some eleven years after Shǎkspere came to town, being then aged 33, he contracted to buy New Place, and in 1602 the contract was completed. It was when his success as a dramatist was assured, that his father in 1596 obtained in the name of Shakespeare a grant of arms appropriate to the name. At any rate the title of *Love's Labour's Lost* in 1598 bears the name of W. Shakspere, whereas the other two plays published in that year, and, I think, all the writings thenceforward, are by W. Shake-speare. As to the evidence by which the heralds justified their grant of arms, it is to be remembered that the heralds' office has never been very scrupulous, and also that the claim was the survival of one made by John Shakspere in 1568, when William was four years old. Plainly the fortunes of the family were looking up. Between 1577 and 1587 John Shǎkspere had been in pecuniary distress. In 1596 he is in a position to purchase from the heralds' office a grant of arms and in 1597 Wm. Shakespeare contracts to buy the house at

LECTURE

Stratford which he did not occupy till 1610–1611. Surely this means that the son had done well in life: better, one would think, than he would have done, if he had been only a subordinate actor. On the other hand it is easily intelligible that, as dramatist, he would contribute greatly to the success of his company, and would be entitled to a proportionate share in the profits. That he should retire from active life in 1610 or 1611 is perhaps surprizing but not, I think, unexampled. Indeed the purchase of New Place seems to indicate that he had looked forward to retirement for at least thirteen years, and in the five or six years which intervened before his death in 1616, I am not surprized that he did not write: for there are some men who cannot work without direct stimulus, and I can well believe that Shakespeare, who had worked under pressure all his life, was such an one.

I submit that my scheme of the life of the man who with his father began as Shăkspere, and with his father ended as Shākespeare, is not one which can be dismissed on grounds of *a priori* improbability.

And now, ladies and gentlemen, I must make my apology to you. When Professor Leahy sent me your kind invitation to address you, giving me considerable latitude in the choice of a theme, I was tempted to propose to you a very different subject. I was born and bred within a few yards of your Parish Church-yard, and once a Sheffielder is always a Sheffielder. This being so I was tempted to write something about Old Sheffield. But on reflection it seemed to me that such a course would be pusillanimous. You are students of Shakespeare and so, in a humble way, am I. Moreover, partly in consequence of my long friendship with Mr Greenwood, I am more or less ac-quainted with anti-Shăksperean arguments and ways of thought. So, though I am not either an Elizabethan or Shake-spearean expert, I determined to try to justify the faith that is in me. That faith is (1) that the belief that Shākespeare was an exceptionally learned man and Shăkspere, if not an ignoramus, at any rate, very imperfectly educated, began only when in the

[288]

course of time the subjects and the standards of common knowledge had completely changed; (2) that contemporaries who
knew both the player and the works, believed Shākespeare to
be identical with Shăkspere; (3) that the learning, that is to say,
the classical knowledge and in particular the knowledge of Latin
possessed by Shakespeare, though different from ours and in
some respects superior, was not out of the common, and (4) that
it might have been acquired by Shăkspere at the Stratford
Grammar School. I hope that I have not been unduly positive,
for I am very conscious of my own ignorance. Further, Strat-
fordians are sometimes accused of acerbity and animosity in
their attitude towards opponents. I trust that I am secure
against any such charge. Most certainly I am not conscious of
any such feeling. Let me add that in stating my case, I hope
thereby to help and encourage you to make up your own minds.
For I hold always that every man should try to make up his
mind for himself.

A COMMEMORATION SERMON PREACHED 9 DECEMBER 1913, IN THE CHAPEL OF TRINITY COLLEGE, CAMBRIDGE, BY HENRY JACKSON, A FELLOW OF THE HOUSE

IN the general epistle of James, the first chapter and the seventeenth verse, it is written:

Every good gift and every perfect gift is from above, and cometh down from the Father of lights, with whom is no variableness, neither shadow of turning.

There is a period in the life of many a man when he is tempted to say that this is the worst of all possible worlds. He sees amongst his fellowmen sorrow and sickness, folly and crime: and, if his thoughts take a wider range, he finds everywhere in nature a cruel and remorseless struggle for existence. What wonder if his heart sinks within him? What wonder if, with Job, he curses the day of his birth? More than forty years ago I was moralising in this strain to a few friends of my own age. As it chanced, we had with us an older man, our senior by thirty years or more, a man well known in the world, and much loved in the College. When I came to the end of my discourse, he said very quietly and very earnestly: 'You are forgetting *one* thing; human nature is very good.' I do not remember how he developed his theme: but the remark remained with me, and I have found in it an antidote to pessimism and a call to God. If there is much that is evil in man, there is in him also much that is good: and in the goodness of imperfect, suffering, erring, man I seem to see a sure witness to the goodness of God the Giver. For 'every good gift and every perfect gift is from above, and cometh down from the Father of lights, with whom is no variableness, neither shadow of turning.' It is a wholesome thing, and a helpful, to remember the good work which men have done, and to thank God for it and for them.

These thoughts are with me to-day when, by ancient custom, we meet together to commemorate the Founder who established this College and the Benefactors who have enlarged it, and to thank God for their forethought and generosity in thus promoting—amongst young and old—to distant generations—religion, learning, education, and research. The Roll of these principal Benefactors will presently be read. It speaks for itself.

But those who have given to the College from their substance are not its only Benefactors. Those are Benefactors also, who by their life and work have rendered service to the House, or by service rendered to the nation have done credit to this their Alma Mater: and your preacher may fitly and properly name to you some of those who, after such achievement, have recently passed away. I shall imitate in my enumeration the brevity of the Roll.

John Westlake and Edward Macnaghten, both of them fellows and honorary fellows, were great lawyers. John Westlake, the third of Whewell's professors, was one of the founders of the Institute of International Law, and, at the time of his death, its permanent honorary President. Throughout his life he strove to awaken the conscience of nations and to bring them together in amity. Edward Macnaghten was during a quarter of a century a Lord of Appeal in Ordinary, and a notable interpreter and maker of English law.

James Stuart, fellow, was in his youth the apostle of the educational movement which has brought into existence the Universities of Liverpool, Birmingham, Leeds, Sheffield, and Bristol, and the Colleges of Nottingham, Girton, and Newnham. It is nearly a quarter of a century since he left Cambridge to bestow his energies in a wider field: but there are still amongst us those who affectionately remember him as a wise counsellor, a merry companion, and a true friend.

Adam Sedgwick, fellow, inherited a name dear to Trinity men of earlier generations. A favourite pupil of Frank Balfour, he took a foremost part in the making of the Cambridge School of Zoology; and when it was decided to endow and equip anew the Department of Zoology in the Royal College of Science, he was urgently invited to give to the nation the benefit of his unique experience. Yielding to pressure, he accepted the task: but it was his cherished hope that he might one day return to this College, which he loved with all his warm heart. The

A COMMEMORATION SERMON

vigorous personality of Adam Sedgwick the younger will not be forgotten.

Alfred Lewis Galabin, fellow, was an honoured and trusted physician.

Robert Sinker was our librarian during thirty-six years. From the time when he and I were freshmen together, I have continually admired his indefatigable industry, his great learning, and his devotion to the College.

In naming John James Pulleine, suffragan Bishop of Richmond, I think not only of his many years of clerical and episcopal work, but also of the time when he was a scholar of the House, 'setting an example of order, diligence, and good conduct,' and by his blameless life, high principle, and personal charm, winning the affectionate regard and the sincere respect of all who knew him.

In our time no Englishman has been better loved than Alfred Lyttelton: and nowhere was he better loved than within these walls. When he came to us, he brought with him in its perfection that straightness, that love of fair play, which is one of the best products of our public schools. His honesty of purpose, his untiring energy, and his sunny disposition, endeared him throughout life to all sorts and conditions of his countrymen. The gifts which make for popularity are sometimes a snare: but popularity never injured our Alfred. Within the last few days we mourn his brother, Spencer Lyttelton.

Walter Francis Hely-Hutchinson held great and responsible office in several British colonies.

Francis William Maclean was Chief Justice of Bengal.

To this list of men who have rendered special service to the College or to the nation, I will add the name of one whose life's work was of a different order. Augustus Vansittart Thornton, a near connection of my own, was a studious, open-minded, straightforward, parish priest. Thoughtful himself, he had a very unusual power of stimulating thought in others. The last four years of his life were spent among us, and he made here many friendships.

IN TRINITY COLLEGE CHAPEL

All these, and many more, in their several ways have done service and honour to the College which bred them.

But my memory ranges over half a century, and I have an old man's desire to commemorate some of those who were leaders amongst us thirty, forty, fifty, years ago. The period of which I am thinking was a critical one. For, whereas in 1858 our institutions were still mediaeval, in 1883 the lines of a new Cambridge and a new Trinity had been laid down. Many were concerned in the work done during that busy quarter of a century. I propose to name, and briefly to characterise, four, and no more.

James Lempriere Hammond, who had been active in the discussions which prepared the way for the statutes of 1859, was, in the late sixties, our champion in the last stage of the hundred years' controversy about religious tests, and our adviser in our projects of domestic reform. Some of us were sorry that he, a fine scholar and an admirable expositor, deserted study and literature for affairs. But 'do the work that's nearest' is no bad rule of life. The College wanted Hammond's help as an administrator: and, as long as he remained with us, he gave us of his best, without stint and without grudging. He was clear-headed, outspoken, and resolute. He was tenacious of his own opinion, but scrupulously fair to opponents. He was a good fighter and a lovable man.

In the years 1865 to 1868 no one was more conspicuous in our College meetings than Henry Sidgwick. In particular, he carried a resolution to establish a praelectorship in natural science: and Michael Foster's appointment to that praelectorship was the beginning of our Cambridge school of biology. Meanwhile, Sidgwick's resignation of his fellowship, together with other resignations, hastened the abolition of tests. At a later time he took an active part in administering the University Statutes of 1882. It was his wisdom and generosity which restored Frederick William Maitland to the University. These are some of Sidgwick's many services to the University and the College. I do not attempt to characterise the brilliant writer, the acute thinker,

A COMMEMORATION SERMON

the unrivalled critic: nor have I words to express what I personally owe to him intellectually and morally.

Coutts Trotter was, perhaps, too tender-hearted for conflict: and, in the controversies of the late sixties, he was not, I think, a protagonist. But in the early seventies, when the College was addressing itself to the reform of the fellowship system, in the late seventies when the University and the Colleges, under the direction of a Parliamentary Commission, were comprehensively revising their institutions, and again in 1883, when the University was bringing into operation the statutes which the Commissioners had made, Coutts Trotter took the lead in all our affairs. He had a genius for legislation: and both the University and the College are greatly and lastingly indebted to him. Perhaps few realised the width and the reality of his scientific attainments. It was said of him that he was second only to Huxley in his comprehensive knowledge of the work which was being done in the various departments of natural science. He was the kindest and best of friends.

Finally, I will name one whom we commonly think of as a great scholar, but who deserves to be remembered also as a reformer of our institutions. Our late master, William Hepworth Thompson, had an unhappy gift of epigrammatic speech; and, in consequence, he has been strangely misunderstood. Those who did not know him, imagined him to be cold, contemptuous, and even arrogant: and the very nobility of his presence somehow encouraged the delusion. In reality, he was one of the kindest hearted of men: he was unaffectedly modest, judging no man so severely as he judged himself: he was appreciative of merit of all kinds. It is true that anything dishonest, mean, or slovenly, roused in him indignation and scorn: but he was compassionate, generous, large-minded. I have known no one to whom I would sooner have gone in time of trouble. He had a strict sense of duty: he never shrank from responsibility: he always rose to a difficult situation, and faced it courageously. Such was the man to whom, personally, I am indebted, not only for example, guidance, and encouragement, but also for forty-seven years of life and work in this place: for it was to Thompson that I owed my appointment to the staff of the College in 1866, and it was he who proposed my retention on it in 1875.

And now I come to what specially concerns me to-day. When Thompson died, one of his old friends in an obituary notice declared his conviction that Thompson could never have approved the reforms which were carried out at Trinity in 1882. I venture to say that the old friend was mistaken. Thompson was not directly concerned in the formulation of the statutes of 1882: they were drafted by Cayley, Trotter, and one who, happily, is still with us. But Thompson took an energetic and helpful part in the discussions out of which those statutes grew. In particular, the statutes which, after many hours of debate, were sanctioned towards midnight on 13 December 1872—which statutes, though, under the direction of Mr Gladstone, they were disallowed by the Privy Council, became later the basis of the legislation of 1882—owed much to Thompson's initiative, tact, and resolution. I am glad to have an opportunity of justifying this statement by the allegation of two or three significant facts.

The agitation which led to the reforms of 1882 began with a paper which was circulated nine years earlier and was known as the Burn-Morgan memorial. Thompson was the only head of a house who signed it.

Again, when the all-important abortive statutes of 1872 were in preparation, there was a moment when the committee seemed to be on the point of abandoning its task. One of its members had persistently opposed and obstructed: another had ceased to attend: others were half-hearted: the reformers were profoundly discouraged. Thompson intervened. He pointed out that the question before us was, not *whether* the statutes should be altered, but *how* they were to be altered. His appeal braced us: we resumed our deliberations: and thenceforward there was no looking back.

Again, later, when some of the Seniors tried to prevent the

[295]

A COMMEMORATION SERMON

calling of the general meeting for the alteration of statutes, Thompson told them that, if they were not prepared to act, he would call the meeting himself.

It seemed to me that Thompson completely understood the situation. He was aware that the new constitution would put an end to the easy-going methods of the past, and would bring with it difficulties and complications. But he recognised that the old order was passing away, and that Trinity must adapt itself to new circumstances and unaccustomed responsibilities: and he did not shrink. For he was always courageous.

In the next quarter of a century there will be many alterations in the University and the College. Let no man fear change! 'Make all things new' is a great principle: for in reform there is no finality. Meanwhile, let us thank God that in the sixties, the seventies, and the eighties we had amongst us those wise men to lead us; and let us pray that we and our successors may follow in their steps.

'The Lord gave, and the Lord hath taken away: blessed be the name of the Lord.'

END OF PART III

INDEX

This Index does not include the headings of Part II (O.S.), which are arranged alphabetically, nor the main events of the Life (Part I), which are arranged chronologically, but only, for the most part, such references to persons and subjects, as could not be found easily by reference to the Table of Contents, or the above-mentioned arrangements.

INDEX

INDEX

For EU product safety concerns, contact us at Calle de José Abascal, 56–1°, 28003 Madrid, Spain or eugpsr@cambridge.org.

www.ingramcontent.com/pod-product-compliance
Ingram Content Group UK Ltd.
Pitfield, Milton Keynes, MK11 3LW, UK
UKHW042154130625
459647UK00011B/1318